Understanding Christian Ethics

UNDERSTANDING CHRISTIAN ETHICS

WILLIAM M. TILLMAN, JR.
Editor

BROADMAN
& HOLMAN
PUBLISHERS

Nashville, Tennessee

4261-29

ISBN: 0-8054-6129-9

Dewey Decimal Classification: 214

Subject Heading: CHRISTIAN ETHICS

Library of Congress Catalog Card Number: 87-36752

Printed in the United States of America

Scripture quotations marked (GNB) are from the *Good News Bible,* the Bible in Today's English Version. Old Testament: Copyright © American Bible Society 1976; New Testament: Copyright © American Bible Society 1966, 1971, 1976. Used by permission. Scripture quotations marked (KJV) are from the King James Version of the Bible. Scripture quotations marked (NASB) are from the *New American Standard Bible.* Copyright © The Lockman Foundation, 1960, 1962, 1963, 1968, 1971, 1972, 1973, 1975, 1977. Used by permission. Scripture quotations marked (NIV) are from the HOLY BIBLE *New International Version,* copyright © 1978, New York Bible Society. Used by permission. Scripture quotations marked (RSV) are from the Revised Standard Version of the Bible, copyrighted 1946, 1952, © 1971, 1973.

Library of Congress Cataloging-in-Publication Data

Understanding Christian ethics.

   1. Christian ethics.   2. Social ethics.   I. Tillman,
William M.
BJ1251.U53 1988   241'.046   87-36752
ISBN 0-8054-6129-9

To Foy Dan Valentine for his contributions
to our understanding of Christian ethics

Preface

For any professional ethicists who happen to look at this addition to the field, the title will appear presumptuous. For the student, church staff person, and layperson, perhaps the title will provide the promise of something for which they have searched. The contributors hope this writing effort will be something the professionals like. If given the choice, however, the contributors would rather receive the applause of the nonprofessionals for the efforts which follow.

These chapters were written from a decidedly functional perspective. Such was our choice in order to attract a wide readership. Also, Christian ethics must perennially be redeemed from the esoteric existence in which some would place it.

Thus, we wanted these materials to be substantive enough for purposes of dialogue and debate in academic settings. Yet, we hope the thinking can take root first and foremost in local church settings.

The "bait" to get many persons to deal seriously with Christian ethics is the raising and examination of issues. Because of that, many ethics books become listings of sociological categories. The reader of this book will find such categories. They must be here. As well, the reader will discover a serious effort to go beyond ethics in a traditional sense as the writers attempt to raise theological and biblical concerns.

For the professional and the lay reader of ethics, gaps will show up in this material. Without apology we could not be exhaustive. Our hope is that our omissions will be warrant for further ethical exploration as readers and critics of this work find it the catalyst to do their own ethical work.

Grateful appreciation is extended to each of the writers who contributed out of his or her expertise. Each consented to participate in this project knowing full well the time and energy such an enterprise would consume. Each still found time above and beyond other considerable responsibilities to research and to write. No one knows the trouble a writer sees until he or she becomes one!

Special thanks is extended to Sherry Lindsey for double checking biblical references and retyping as I worked through the material. In addition, invaluable help came from J. Jeff Tillman who read the manuscripts for style.

WILLIAM M. TILLMAN, JR.
Southwestern Baptist Theological Seminary
Fort Worth, Texas

CONTRIBUTORS

Bob E. Adams
Professor of Christian ethics
Seminario Internacional Teologico Bautista
Buenos Aires, Argentina

W. H. Bellinger, Jr.
Associate Professor of Old Testament
Department of Religion
Baylor University
Waco, Texas

William H. Elder, III, Pastor
Pulaski Heights Baptist Church
Little Rock, Arkansas

Thomas D. Lea
Associate Professor of New Testament
Southwestern Baptist Theological Seminary
Fort Worth, Texas

Daniel B. McGee
Professor of Christian ethics
Department of Religion
Baylor University
Waco, Texas

Libby Potts
Associate, Singles and Senior Adults
Christian Life Commission
Baptist General Convention of Texas
Dallas, Texas

Dick Rader, Dean
School of Christian Service
Oklahoma Baptist University
Shawnee, Oklahoma

W. David Sapp, Pastor
First Baptist Church
Chamblee, Georgia

D. Glenn Saul
Professor of Christian ethics
Golden Gate Baptist Theological Seminary
Mill Valley, California

Ronald D. Sisk, Pastor
Tiburon Baptist Church
Tiburon, California

Sid Smith
Manager, Black Church Development Section
of the Special Ministries Department
Baptist Sunday School Board
Nashville, Tennessee

William M. Tillman, Jr.
Assistant Professor of Christian ethics
Southwestern Baptist Theological Seminary
Fort Worth, Texas

David R. Wilkinson
Vice-President of Seminary Relations
The Southern Baptist Theological Seminary
Louisville, Kentucky

Contents

1

Why Study Christian Ethics?

William M. Tillman

Some time ago in response to my question, "Why should one study Christian ethics?" a student answered, "Because it's required to graduate!" Certainly fulfilling the requirements of a degree plan is a worthy motivation. Yet, it falls beneath some higher motivational and valuing levels.

This chapter will attempt to answer the question, "Why study Christian ethics?" with some positive suggestions toward the rationale for the study and application of this discipline. The outline essentially posits some of these reasons. The careful reader will be able to discern a definition of the discipline emerging as well. For the not so careful reader, the majority of the chapter involves delineating a description of Christian ethics. A final section will expand upon the normative nature of the enterprise that is Christian ethics.

Refining Decision Making

A rampant heretical assumption is that every Christian will know automatically (by virtue of his or her conversion) the right thing to do and will act out of that knowledge. This assumption virtually knocks the air out of the assertion which says every Christian should not only be about the business of learning the right but also acting upon what he or she knows is right.

A new Christian does not come fully mature into the life of the kingdom. Those with the most profound understanding of conversion to Christ's way of life still need cultivation and nurture in the ways of the Christian life.

Celebrity conversions often are given much attention, some-

13

times to the detriment of the individual who testifies of great changes of life-style. Observation of such persons over a long period of time reveals that these, along with those who have much quieter conversion experiences, should not be hurried in their understanding of the living of the Christian life.

Christian ethics is in one sense an emphasis study. That is, it, more than any branch of theological study, is geared specifically toward matters of virtue, character, rightness and wrongness, and application of such knowledge to the multiple circumstances of life in all of its personal and corporate relationships.

None of this is to say that a new Christian, or any other Christian for that matter, is incapable of making ethical decisions without a study of Christian ethics. Quite the contrary, anyone reading this material is already making ethical decisions. The point is to examine and evaluate decision making in light of the best resources which biblical materials, sociological data, and decision-making principles and skills can provide. To avail yourself of such knowledge and skills in application entails, at the least, proper stewardship of one's life, and, at the best, comprises what it means to follow the high calling of Jesus Christ.

Intellectually Comprehensive

Most who read this book will do so for academic reasons. Its contents will be assigned for readings, testing, and general knowledge. But why are such assignments made? One major reason is that people—theologians, ethicists, and curriculum experts—have determined over a period of centuries that a study and application of the Christian faith is a necessary part of the education for the person who would call himself or herself an accomplished and theologically educated individual. Well-rounded theological education demands that ethics be a part of the curriculum even for those who do not recognize the necessity of the study when they begin.

A characteristic mentality of many students is either-or thinking. Whether out of sociological background or psychological disposition, individuals come into educational settings ready to hear only one side of an issue or assuming every ethical concern has only one clear right and one clear wrong response. Obviously a student with these predispositions considers ethical reflection to be unimportant.

Yet the testimony of those who have invested themselves in ethical study is that Christian ethics provides a needed balance to other academic and practical studies. An understanding of ethics is essential to a full understanding of any other discipline, such as biblical studies, historical studies, theological studies, and practical studies; for ethics is integrally intertwined in each and all of these.

The matter of relating Christian faith consequently includes conversation with other disciplines or professions. A constructive view of ministry enables us to realize that contact with many professional spheres of life is imperative. While the Christian does not need to have special expertise in any or all of those areas, it is incumbent upon each of us to be aware of those areas in order to ask the ethical questions appropriate to those areas. An avenue for further witness and application of the gospel can sometimes be opened by the ability to dialogue with the ethical dilemmas of another vocational interest.

The Christian ethicist should be encouraged that so many professional fields are developing ethics courses as a part of their academic credentialing processes. Though many of these developments have come because of ethical laxness in the various professions, openness to a search for integrity provides new opportunities for Christian ethicists to act as consultants in previously closed arenas.

Medical ethics, business ethics, legal ethics, engineering ethics, educational ethics, political ethics, journalistic ethics are only a few of the burgeoning directions for ethical inquiry. In some ways ministers are no different than any of the professionals of these fields in functioning as responsible members of society. If for no other reason than their individual responsibility to society, ministers should study Christian ethics.

What Is the Right, the Good, and the Happy?

Discerning the right thing to do, determining the good over the bad and the not so good, and living in a state of happiness deal with explicit and implicit dimensions of ethics. The dimensions relate to the nature, exploration, and application of values.

What, more specifically, are values? Though there is much debate about their qualities, values are essentially those matters upon which we place some amount of worth or importance. With even so brief or inexact a definition, one should be able to see how large a portion of our lives are directed to making decisions based on concepts of values. One might say that life is a series of one value choice after another. Nothing about which we make any conscious choice lacks a value facet. As one picks out a place to live, a car to drive, clothes to wear, a school to attend, a preacher to hear, or subscriptions to magazines, value choices are made. As we vote or do not vote, relate to those like or unlike us, marry or not marry, have children or not, value choices are made. Finding a job or choosing not to work, considerations of the worth of others and the worth of oneself, all represent value choices. Theodore Hesburgh poignantly considered values to be "the constants of our existence . . . navigational aids . . . fixed points of reference that keep our human journey from aimless wandering."[1]

The search for the right, the good, and the happy is every generation's responsibility because moral crisis is every generation's problem. Without examination of values the possibility looms of a generation whose values are shaped by wandering from one crisis to the next. Without identification and application of values from one generation to the next, we "risk creating informed cynics and critics who know the price of everything and the value of nothing."[2]

Is this generation any worse than any other? Probably not, when all things are considered. Because of media attention and a larger world population, the effects of human perversity may be more pronounced. Indeed, the modern compulsion toward nostalgia may cause us to forget that sin has always been bad.

To say all of that does not remove the observation that those who read this chapter are living in an age of moral crisis and moral confusion. The problem for Isaiah is the problem for us all: Many are those who "call evil good and good evil, who put darkness for light and light for darkness, who put bitter for sweet and sweet for bitter!" (5:20, RSV). Moral dilemmas presented by technology will face each of us. Questions about the standards for measuring character and conduct are perennial. Breakdowns of family life, abrogations of human rights, questions of corporate and personal life-style, economic stress, religious liberty definitions—all these point toward a theme of moral anarchy in our midst. Thus, an examination and reexamination of the right, the good, and the happy is always appropriate for us.

Uncovering Ethical Fallacies

Much ethical decision making is done on the basis of what can be called ethical fallacies, or illogical or incorrect reasoning about ethical concerns. Rumors, "old wives tales," and emotive language usually constitute the core of the content of these fallacies. Taking note of some of them is necessary for the best ethical discourse of which we are capable.[3]

"What did you say?" Ethical conversation contains a great many words and phrases like, "That's wrong"; "It's against the law"; or, the sometimes overused, "This is clearly God's will." These are examples of the fallacy of ambiguity or lack of clarity with regard to how a word is used.

"What's the source of your argument?" Ethical arguments which attempt to undercut an opposing viewpoint's position by discrediting the source of that viewpoint can be called fallacious. Such arguments begin from statements like: "Well, there is more than a hint of socialism here." What should be apparent to the reader (or hearer) is a linking without basis in fact to a usually distrusted philosophy. Any argument then used by another which has any remote connection to that distrusted source in name or philosophy will be discredited by the fallacious argument.

"You are all alike." A slight turn from the previous fallacy, this one attacks the character of the person making the argument. This one is quite the opposite of a truer principle of addressing the principle and not the person. Such an argument is often heard in prejudicial statements related to age, sex, race, level or place of education.

"I don't care what you say." This fallacy arises out of a mind already made up. Facts will only prolong the decision to be made. This approach is used to lend legitimacy to power manuevers as some attempt to rise above accepted standards; for example, the statement, "No matter what he has done he is still the _____, and he should not be removed from office."

"This is the only way." Beware of expansive, exaggerated claims. Broad generalizations may garner crowd appeal, but they usually break down in credibility under close examination. People who use this approach will probably be subject to using the approach just mentioned. Theirs is often a narrow world view.

"Everybody else does it." This approach easily could fit into the fallacy of generalization category. However, it and its variants usually are heard as support for some wrongdoing by an appeal to an instance of similar behavior which received no reprimand. Parents are used to hearing it, but so do employers and church staff persons!

"Ethics is all personal/all social in application." This particular fallacy is peculiar to the study of Christian ethics, it seems. Though well meaning, many Christians have yet to make the connection that the Christian life has both personal and social ramifications. Henlee Barnette said it well:

> There is no such thing as a "personal" gospel as over against a "social" gospel. There is but one gospel which is both personal and social. Personal regeneration and social reconstruction are demanded by the gospel. The redeemed man must seek the redemption of the society in which he lives. He is the salt of the earth and the light of the world. The areas of marriage, industry, and state are, as is the individual, under the judgment of God. The Christian, therefore, is called not merely to live in these areas, but to do his part in bringing them more in accord with the will and purpose of God.[4]

To be fair, one qualification may need to be offered. Many of those accused of dealing with only individual ethics in the 1960s began to speak and act regarding larger, social concerns in the 1970s and 1980s. Rather than seeing a split between social and individual ethics, the contemporary scene may be presenting more of an image of compartmentalization. That is, life is divided into compartments for some people. These compartments are observed to have obvious social and personal dimensions and ensuing ethical questions. However, many folk simply are not aware of many of the compartments which this world presents us.

Other arguments from fallacious bases could be enumerated. Since many of them overlap with those already considered in some detail, only a list of them will be made: inconsistency; begging the question; arguments from ignorance; false appeals to authority; hasty conclusions. These are not as difficult to recognize as one might imagine. The difficulty enters the equation when you find yourself in dialogue with one who is expert in implementing these fallacies. Perhaps just as difficult is conversing with those who use such perspectives in ethical conversation *without* being conscious of the fallaciousness. Often their modus operandi is out of the context of another fallacy, an appeal to "but we've always done it that way." Such times call for the Christian ethicist to have the innocence of doves but the wisdom of serpents.

What Is Your Ethical Language?

Those who work in language analysis and story/narrative approaches have described how our language provides a key to understanding our system of values. One theological educator has said, "Give me an opportunity to listen to your language for a time, and I will be able to tell you a great deal about your theology." Indeed, there is much room for the exploration of personal language as we think about how our vocabulary indicates our world view and approach to circumstances calling for decision making.

Robert Bellah has presented one of the more intriguing ways of identifying our ethical language. In *Habits of the Heart* Bellah described two languages, a primary and a secondary, by which we articulate our values. Each of these has two parts.[5] Bellah's main title comes from the phrase used in *Democracy in America* by Alexis de Toqueville. De Toqueville wrote his book as an analysis of American customs and cultural values. Bellah's analysis of language provides a constructive key to how Americans think and do ethics.

The first or primary language, according to Bellah, is built around American individualism. The first facet of this language is called utilitarian individualism. It is cost-benefit language. It asks the questions: "Does it work?" and "What will this cost me in time and energy?" The vocabulary for this language is that of economic materialism. Models for decision making and implementing these decisions follow the corporate executive style. All of us, however, are relatively comfortable with this language in our vocational pursuits.

The second facet of the primary language, according to Bellah, is that of expressive individualism. Still individually based and ego centered, this language communicates the struggles of life. In a search for deeper expression of oneself this language reflects growth group vocabulary. Noted by how it wrestles with life, this language can be caricatured through contemporary soap opera plots.

Interestingly enough, many reading this portion of this chapter will notice no incongruity in these ideas about one's primary ethical language and what they call a Christian language. The tragedy is that Christians have bought heavily into what essentially is a primary language of their culture and not of the Bible. The primary language of their culture is marked by cash, convenience, and consumerism—values which hardly rank high on a stackpole of Christian values.

These two facets of the primary language lack the ability to explain the real commitments of life, however. They can, and do, make commitments, but they are precarious ones. For an integrated (or, what Bellah called a constituted self), we each need a second language to transcend our radical individualism. This calls for a language which organizes life with reference to ideals and commitments to those ideals.

Bellah's second language is identified through more corporate-

or community-centered vocabulary. Again two facets are noted. The first is called Jeffersonian ideals. Life, liberty, and the pursuit of happiness are common vocabulary here. Such vocabulary stems from the Age of Enlightenment and some of its chief architects: Rosseau, Locke, and Jefferson. The direction of application is noticeably social. There is heavy moral content to these concepts. At the same time, such ideas are divorced from the moral perception of these ideas in a biblical context. Attempts to wed these ideas usually climax in what is called civil religion.

The second facet of Bellah's secondary language is what he called a biblical world view and is based on the language of the Bible and the virtue ideas found there: love, faith, hope, righteousness, peace, justice, and so forth. The usage of these follows the content and ethical understanding of these words from a biblical perspective.

Both parts of the secondary language, according to Bellah, are carried on from generation to generation by what he called communities of memory. In the case of Jeffersonian ideals, our courts and legal system maintain the memory of the moral content. In the case of the biblical world view, Bellah found that churches act as the communities of memory.

Such communities of memory retell the story from generations past. Examples of men and women who embody and exemplify the meaning of the community are put forth. There are calls to alter evil and to turn toward the future for the sake of the common good.

Where the primary language works off a vocabulary of feelings and desires, the communities of memory language is marked by long-term commitments. Such commitment language gives individuals a sense of integrity as virtues are passed on and modeled by others. In addition, as individuals assimilate such virtues, a distinct sense of responsibility toward others is projected, a trait not necessarily recognized in the primary language set.

What's the Issue?

A standard approach to Christian ethics is to work through a list of issues or sociological concerns. After teaching Christian ethics for some time now, I have become more concerned about how some people deal with ethics in an issues-only approach. My concern is based upon the conviction that one needs first to deal with issues out of their sense of character and values rather than running headlong into the "issue."

Certainly many of those who are issues people allude to biblical texts. However, these allusions usually serve as no more than a backdrop or convenient jumping-off place from which one puts forth presuppositions on the matter.

With such an approach ethics becomes "issuism." Issues such as abortion, AIDS, divorce, homosexuality, nuclear war, parent-child relations, and a myriad of others become ends in themselves. Emphasis on the action becomes so overwhelming as to eliminate attention to the actor(s).

Thus, one of the primary issues of Christian ethics is to deal with basic character formation. What are the dynamics which bring one to make the decision the way he or she does? How do we figure in the factors of where one is born and raised? Who are the role models or heroes after which one has cast his or her style of life? What is one's framework of authority out of which he or she will base decisions? In other words, where is one's sense of worship focused? How has one processed the multiple grief experiences that are common to all of us and those which seem to strike unpredictably only some of us? How has one experienced and implemented power? How does one develop a sense of what the Bible so frequently addresses—being blessed?

An interesting maze to explore is how people move through stages of moral development. Major thinkers for the reader's investigation include John Westerhoff, Lawrence Kohlberg, and James Fowler.

Consider how individuals you have known and do know express their perspective on living the Christian life. Some people live almost exclusively out of a "thou shalt not" approach to life. They have comprehended an important level of ethical thinking; that is, some things are out of bounds for a Christian. People who base their decision making on this approach frequently proof text from the "Thou shalt nots" of the Ten Commandments.

You may have noticed also those people who live out of a kind of "thou shalt" approach. Indeed, this one is more positive than the former one. However, a person operating from this approach is still laying responsibility for decisions outside personal parameters of accountability.

A third approach individuals take to decisions is that of the "I must." This one has the constructive dimension of being a responsible decision maker. Note, though, that it is still heavily duty oriented. There is not much joy in the style or decisions made.

Some individuals follow another approach—"I shall." This one recognizes both the positive and negative imperatives of a Christian style of life. There is a sense of duty boundness, but there is more joy and hope in meeting the response called for in the decision. This response takes accountability into the mix and goes forthrightly to making the decision.

The final approach, dare I say stage, that may be followed is that which I call "I am." This one represents the picture the apostle Paul drew for us: the perfect man, the mature person in Christ. This individual has come virtually to personify the characteristics and actions of "one in Christ." He or she is the person of integrity, the one who *is* what one *does.*

Such thinking on issues still needs to call forth the matter of what a Christian addresses in this world. Are any issues off limits for discussion? I think not. Biblical examples abound where persons addressed nearly everything that could plague humankind ethically. What is not specifically treated at least has grounding in principles that can assist our contemporary decision making.

Whatever approach to decision making one follows, at least one caution must be raised. That is, the approach to issues must consider major matters over minor ones. We have only so much time and energy to give to things in this life. Too often we burn up our time and energy over inconsequential things to the exclusion of quite important ones. Another way of saying this is we take too much time with brush fires while the whole forest may be burning away.

Christian ethics deals with some matters which are perennial. Other matters build on the horizon and are at first like Ezekiel's cloud vision, no larger than a man's hand. Some of these issues faddishly fade away. Others build into thunderclouds, from which a storm follows.

How does one determine or forecast how issues will arise and build? One cannot forecast accurately every time, but at least two guidelines can be used to identify where ethical issues will emerge. When one sees a biblical ideal compromised (for example, justice), an issue will arise. When one sees a concern that will affect large numbers of people, an ethical matter will develop.

With these two guidelines in mind, one can be sure that peace-making concerns, church and state matters, and ecological crises will be in our future. Developments around the world show that the relationships of societies and the women in them will grow in intensity. This will be especially true in the United States. Countries with burgeoning numbers of senior adults and single adults will need to give more time and financial considerations to these groups.[6]

Christian Ethics and the International Community

Surveys among middle school and high school students have revealed that the students have little knowledge of their native land, the United States. Such a finding would not be difficult to duplicate anywhere in the world.

On a trip to Cambridge, England, my wife and I had the pleasure of eating dinner one evening at one of the colleges associated with the university. During conversation we learned that one gentleman had come to the university from a shire, or county, only thirty miles from Cambridge. Coming to the university constituted only the second time he had been out of his shire in his life. Though this student had a fairly good grasp of world events, his provincialism showed.

Christians are called to be world citizens. That does not necessarily imply that one is to be a world traveler, but that may ensue. The point is that one must begin to perceive the world from a global perspective. God's creation is an interrelated and interdependent one. What we do with what we have does make a difference to the rest of the world. Conversely, what happens in the rest of the world makes a difference on what options we have in Christian decision making in our own setting.

In many ways Christian ethics has become a solidly American discipline. Intellectual leaders abound in the discipline as one reels off North American names: James Gustafson, Stanley Hauerwas, Roger Shinn, Lewis Smedes, Ron Sider, Philip Wogaman, Max Stackhouse, Harvey Cox, Richard Mouw, Stephen Mott, James McClendon, Tom Beauchamp, James Childress, Charles Curran, or Southern Baptists' own Henlee Barnette and T. B. Maston.

Yet, Christian ethics is much more than a North American discipline. Liberation theologians/ethicists, particularly in Latin and South America, are putting forth some of the most provocative ethical thinking of our time. Gustavo Gutierrez, Hugo Assman, Leonardo and Clodovis Boff, Juan Luis Segundo, and Jose Miguez Bonino are professors and pastors who press the international community of theologians and ethicists to consider the application of the gospel on a huge scale. African theological/ethical thinkers Desmond Tutu and Allan Boesak are doing no less.

Moving from Transcendent Universals
to Historical Particulars

Most of this chapter to this point falls into the category of descriptive ethics. That is, a discipline and some observations concerning the discipline have been described. Such an exercise is imperative. Some problems can develop, however, when many begin and end with descriptive ethics, believing they have done all the job called for by Christian ethics.

One of these problems is treating ethics from the point of view that what the most people do must be right. Generally Christians use the phrase "just because everyone does it does not make it right." Increasingly, though, I am observing Christians substantiate ethical claims by an appeal to majority, or perceived majority, opinion.

One must be careful about building "majority-opinion" ethics. Too often the majority opinion is based on a cultural definition of what is the right, good, and happy. Basing one's ethics on majority opinion often has the effect of bringing ethical ideals down to a lowest common denominator. This begins to range dangerously close to equating ethics with morals, the customs or habits of a society. The Bible also cautions us about such a position. The people in the Bible who sounded the most ethical notes were usually in the minority.

Identifying values and applying them can still be difficult, however. A conversation which I had with a student a few years ago illustrats the point. She said, "I've been in this class all this time, and I have not heard any absolutes. I want to hear some absolutes!" My response was, "We have been talking about them every day. Look at the biblical material we have discussed. The value ideals are everywhere. But, we are talking about more than naming love, justice, and righteousness. We have been talking about the God who personifies these values."

This Christian had missed the fact that, unlike the Greek philosophers, Christians do not search out some kind of platonic, absolutized values treated as ends in themselves. Rather, we are about the task of coming to know better the God who is our objective source of absolute, transcendent values. That is difficult enough. What is even tougher is understanding how the values personified in God apply to our own history and understanding of reality.

Such work begins the move from strictly descriptive ethics to that of establishing norms for the living of life and the application of those norms to the best of our understanding. Such normative ethics also introduces the ethical categories of accountability, forgiveness, and courage.

The matter of accountability calls for one to take responsibility for one's attitudes and actions. Observations of people over a short period of time in business, family, or church settings reveal how sophisticated we have become at covering over a blown assignment or a poorly handled relationship. We are rather quick at handing blame over to someone else or sidestepping our part in what went wrong. The conclusion is that not many people can straight forwardly say, "I did it. It was my fault." Accountability calls for a level of commitment to ideals, ethical standards, and a willingness to act on that commitment in responsible action.

Forgiveness is another commodity talked about frequently in Christian circles. However, merely talking about it generally leaves it within the descriptive realm. Forgiveness extended and experienced falls solidly within the normative realm. Interestingly, a reciprocal relationship exists between our sense of forgiveness, in God's eyes and from our fellow human beings, and how we handle accountability. It appears that those who have the healthiest sense of forgiveness in their lives are also those who are willing to live with a sense of responsibility and accountability to others.

Courage is a kind of "also ran" among ethical virtues. Such a development is intriguing from one angle in that so much is discussed in the Bible about acting in courage; but, we give relatively little attention to it. More emphasis is needed to help individuals understand that to be able to describe the proper decision-making principles, even describe what would be the most ideal course of action, may be for naught—if there is lack of courage to act on those principles or ideals.

Which is most important in normative ethics—accountability, forgiveness, or courage? None of these can be rated over another. Each provides the glue for the other.

Another aspect of normative ethics is *how* the norms arrived at will be applied. Three basic styles or approaches generally are recognized: deontological, teleological, and relational. A fourth, intuitionism, is considered important enough for inclusion, as well.

The deontological approach is one which is grounded in acts, attitudes, and policies apart from their effects or consequences. These rules or duties become ends in themselves. A kind of deontological application is found in the statement, "Honesty is the best policy."

Immanuel Kant's "categorical imperative" is an example of deontological ethics. Kant's appeal was to discover, primarily through rational means, the right thing to do in a given circumstance. The key to its rightness was answering the question: "Could everyone do this and it be right?"

W. D. Ross, in some of the same spirit as Kant but with more specific intent, suggested some categories of duties called prima facie duties. Prima facie means literally the first look, or on the face of the matter. These duties, Ross viewed, were to be followed if no others could be discerned. They are duties of fidelity (signing a contract); duties of gratitude (relational bonds such as friendship); duties of justice (sense of fair play); duties of beneficence (helping those who cannot help themselves); duties of self-improvement (a stewardship and responsibility toward one's own self); and duties of nonmaleficence (no injury to others).[7]

A teleological style emphasizes the moral worth of actions by judging the consequences of the actions. This approach has a distinct utilitarian dimension. Suppose you had one hundred dollars you could use in a discretionary way. A teleological approach arrives at the decision of whether to give the money to a charity or make it a gift to a friend on the basis of the effect the use of the money would have on the most people.

Aristotle's summum bonum idea of searching for the highest good provides a distinctive and foundational part of teleological ethics. As one educational psychology professor once told me: "Learning is a joyful thing." This is an example of Aristotelian thinking.

A corollary of teleological ethics is that which is called utilitarianism. Early proponents of this were Jeremy Bentham and John Stuart Mill. Their system supported the acts or the virtues which would bring the most good for the most people. There is more than a little bit of what has come to be called hedonism attached to this philosophy.

A third response to the question of how we apply ethical values to our experience is the relational approach. A distinctive of this approach is its interest in human beings and what happens to human beings as ethical decisions are made. Its recognition of fellow humans as creatures made in the image of God brings a high level of appreciation for others' worth. Following this, an emphasis upon covenantal agreements and fidelity to those agreements is considered important.

This approach gained momentum with H. Richard Niebuhr's book *The Responsible Self.* Building on his earlier thought, Niebuhr considered our response to God's acts (creation, redemption, and judgment) in history to be a major key to our faithful acts of Christian character. According to Niebuhr, God is sovereign, but He extends Himself to us for purposes of relationship. Thus, a model is established for us to use in dealing with ethical problems in this world. We are to act out of our own character with a strong sense of responsibility and caring for the relational bonds we have established with others.

A fourth style of application is that of intuitionism. Where the former three rely heavily upon a rational, analytical plan of attack on ethical issues, intuition comes to an ethical decision with less appeal to conscious deliberation. Sometimes this approach travels under the disguised phrase, "I'm not able to give a rational response, but this decision doesn't *feel* right." Or, another way of identifying this approach is when we catch ourselves saying, "Aha" as we discover a resolution to a dilemma.

Some ethicists discount the place of emotions in any form and, therefore, discount intuition as a basis for ethical decision making. Certainly this style could be overused and taken to a dangerous extreme (as can be the others). Yet, serious decision making usually involves more than a little of intuition mixed in as our subconscious minds aid us in sorting through a problem.

Shaping Ethical Studies

Little rebuttal would come to the assertion that Christian ethical reflection is done (positively and negatively) in academic settings. Frequently not enough attention is given to the importance of ethical reflection in the local church. Thomas Ogletree considered this "ecclesial context" to be the primary base for beginning discussion on matters of morality and integrity.[8] It is imperative for theological scholars and church laypersons alike to realize that theological education is not just for the professionals.

The salient features of the suggestions made in this chapter and those which follow must find some form of expression in the educational and outreach processes of the churches. Are there any practical suggestions for such an attempt? A few follow. The hope is that they and those that can be mined from the other chapters will give the reader cause for much imaginative ethicizing.

Emphases in basic decision making.—Many ministers are surprised by the positive reception they receive when they emphasize decision making skills. People do want to make the best decisions possible. Chapter 4 in this text is an excellent beginning place.[9]

Developing hermeneutical skills.—Hermeneutics is the science of interpretation, which in the context of Christian ethics becomes particularly biblical interpretation. Several years ago James Smart posed an interesting idea with his book, *The Strange Silence of the Bible in the Church.* That idea is that too many ministers trained in theological seminaries fail to communicate their skills in hermeneutics to their people. The result is a continuing biblical illiteracy.

Some help can be extended to laypersons with such simple approaches as following the trail of the development of the English Bible and the development of particular versions of the Bible. Helping people understand the importance and variety of biblical genre is necessary. Exercises in identifying context—verse, chapter, book—will reap rewards. Last, but certainly not least for Christian ethics, is finding ways to apply the Scriptures to contemporary life.

Story/narrative.—An increasing interest in story and oral history, in general, is a part of our society. For some it may be only another nostalgia fad. Developing skills in communicating one's ethical pilgrimage and in listening to others' journeys in faith may well help us better to understand the communication world of the biblical characters.[10]

An assignment I make to many of my classes is what I call an "Autobiographical Ethical Reflection." Essentially this is the digested synthesis of notes made over the course of the semester related to ethical concerns. I do not assign the keeping of a journal, but suggest such an enterprise to help students stay up to date. By the end of the semester nearly every one of the students has begun to get a hint of his or her individual ethical story. The students have developed insight into some of the ways their character and sense of integrity has formed and is forming.

The creative ethicist will use ways of communicating ethical ideals the same way Jesus often did, telling stories. It is a rare child or adult who will not stop when they hear, "Let me tell you a story."

Gaming/role playing.—Following the story in interest building is the matter of decision-making games. Many of these are parlor games available commercially. Others can be concocted. Any age group benefits from such games as case studies are implemented to draw participants out of themselves temporarily. In the process new insights will come which probably would not have come through simple lecture.

Research.—Research may entail library work. Unfortunately, that conjures up too many musty memories for it to be of great effect for some people. Yet, there is no end to ethical resources once one begins to notice. An especially effective approach to research is to do interviews with those particularly affected by an ethical concern. Along this same line many people have benefited from tours of target areas, for instance, to notice economic or racial issues.

Pastoral integrity.—This is an encompassing term. It is meant to include pastor-preachers and all those who have any pastoral role in the local church. This broadens the number of people considerably as it includes Sunday School teachers, deacons, those who visit as no one else can visit, and the myriad of other "pastoral" people who make up our congregations.

These people are the front line of the ethically aggressive edge of a congregation. By word and deed they are proclaiming the truth and trustworthiness of the gospel. When their integrity breaks down, the gospel goes on trial for some. Out of these folk is formed the network of heroes and models all of us can name and designate as being instrumental in our realizing our own fascination and response to the calling of the gospel.

Conclusion

So, "Why study Christian ethics?" The hope is that after reading this chapter, you can answer that question. Some of you will probably have a teacher who will ask that question on some exam, minor or major. If he or she does, be assured that the question is meant to prepare you for those questions which come to you in real life, probing, prodding, sometimes even bludgeoning you at the point of your Christian values and character. It is a good question.

Notes

1. Theodore M. Hesburgh, in preface to Olive F. Williams and John W. Houck, *Full Value: Cases in Christian Business Ethics* (San Francisco: Harper & Row, 1978).

2. Frank Rhodes, president of Cornell University in November 15, 1986 address to Harvard University, as reported in *The Christian Science Monitor,* 30 January 1987, B9.

3. Vincent Barry, *Applying Ethics: A Text with Readings* (Belmont, Calif.: Wadsworth Publishing Company, 1985), pp. 20-36.

4. Henlee Barnette, *Introducing Christian Ethics* (Nashville: Broadman Press, 1961), p. 4.

5. Robert N. Bellah, et.al., *Habits of the Heart—Individualism and Commitment in American Life* (Berkeley: University of California Press, 1985), pp. 28-48, 152-154.

6. Considerable assistance can be found for further research in this idea of the shape of Christian ethics through examination of Edward LeRoy Long, Jr.'s materials. See his *A Survey of Christian Ethics* (New York: Oxford University Press, 1967); *A Survey of Recent Christian Ethics* (New York: Oxford University Press, 1982); *Academic Bonding and Social Concern: The Society of Christian Ethics, 1959-1983* (N. p.: Religious Ethics, Incorporated, 1984).

7. W. D. Ross, *The Right and the Good* (Oxford, Great Britain: Oxford University Press, 1946), pp. 19-21.

8. Thomas W. Ogletree, "The Ecclesial Context of Christian Eth-

ics," *The Annual of the Society of Christian Ethics* (Vancouver, B. C.: The Society of Christian Ethics, 1984), pp. 1-17.

9. Anyone wishing to consider narrative, theology, and ethics would be interested in James McClendon, "Narrative Ethics and Christian Ethics," *Faith and Philosophy,* Vol. 3, No. 4, October 1986. Appreciation also would be found for Terrence W. Tilley, *Story Theology* (Wilmington, Del.: Michael Glazier, 1985).

10. See chapter 2, "You, the Decision Maker," in William M. Tillman, Jr. with Timothy D. Gilbert *Christian Ethics: A Primer,* (Nashville: Broadman Press, 1986).

2
The Old Testament:
Source Book for Christian Ethics

W. H. Bellinger, Jr.

Introduction

I still remember the profound impact of learning as an undergraduate that the same kinds of things which happen to me also happened to Abraham and the other characters in the Old Testament. This realism is why the Old Testament can be such a powerful resource for living. The Old Testament speaks God's word and reveals God's relationship to life. This dual nature of the Old Testament—human book and divine book—is essential to its place as authority for faith and life. Much of human life revolves around making choices, making decisions. Most of us want our decisions to be ethical. How does the Old Testament relate to such decisions? This chapter explores the Old Testament as source book for Christian ethics.

Learning from the Past

Old Testament ethics is an interdisciplinary field. Two groups of people have produced work in the area: Old Testament scholars and ethicists. We will, therefore, look at how others have viewed Old Testament ethics to see what we can learn from those who have come before us.

Old Testament Studies

Johannes Hempel made perhaps the most significant contribution to the study of Old Testament ethics with his *Das Ethos des Alten Testaments.* He discussed the variety of ethical conduct seen in the Old Testament and commented briefly on the chief agents of its ethical teaching. Making full use of a sociological analysis, he treated the relationship between the individual and ancient Israelite society. He indicated that position in society often influenced ethical behavior in ancient Israel. Because the Old Testament frequently describes loyalty to God as the basis of right conduct, Hempel asserted that ethics prescribed in the Old Testament derive from faith. Hempel's work demonstrates the complexity of the subject matter, but he made a significant contribution in attempting to systematize the ethics of the Old Testament and to show the Hebrews' distinctiveness in the ancient Near Eastern world.

Another work of fundamental importance for the modern study of Old Testament ethics is Walther Eichrodt's *Theology of the Old Testament.* Eichrodt understood all of Old Testament faith to derive from ancient Israel's covenant with God. This relationship led to the prescription of basic moral standards, standards on a higher plane than popular morality. Only by way of a lengthy struggle with popular morality did ancient Israel come to understand that ethical living was part of the community's covenant obligation to God. Eichrodt's work demonstrates the importance of ethics for understanding the Old Testament.

On the American scene, the work of James Muilenburg stands out: *The Way of Israel: Biblical Faith and Ethics.* Muilenburg sought to show the various ways in which the Old Testament speaks to ethical conduct. This ethic is a religious ethic, coming primarily from the word or self-relevation of God.

Studies in Ethics

Studies in Old Testament ethics have also been attempted in the discipline of Christian ethics. Perhaps the most influential work is still that of T. B. Maston, *Biblical Ethics: A Survey.* Maston examined various ethical emphasis in each section of the Old Testament. The Hebrews divided their Bible, or canon, into three sections: Law, Prophets, and Writings. The first section includes Genesis, Exodus, Leviticus, Numbers, and Deuteronomy and is called the Pentateuch.

Maston's treatment of this material concentrated on legal texts

(The Ten Commandments, for example); he understood these passages to relate to covenant, holiness, and love. Maston then summarized the various prophetic writings and interpreted these texts as showing concern for righteousness, love, and justice, especially justice for the oppressed. In his section of the Writings, Maston spent much time on the Psalms and the various teachings which derive from the moral character of God. His volume overall provides helpful summary material on the Old Testament and its ethical implications.

Other ethicists have written on biblical ethics, but usually these books concentrate on the New Testament. Such an emphasis has seemed more relevant to Christian ethics because the New Testament reflects the ethics of Jesus and because some New Testament Epistles comment on ethical issues in early church communities. In his volume *Biblical Ethics,* R. E. O. White discussed the legacies of the Old Testament for Christian ethics. He concentrated on the law and the prophets and treated these texts as background for the New Testament. Thomas W. Ogletree's *The Use of the Bible in Christian Ethics* includes a significant section in the Old Testament. Ogletree was aware of the variety of material in the Old Testament but centered on covenant and commandment. Lewis B. Smedes's *Mere Morality* also emphasizes Old Testament commandments. These volumes demonstrate the need for and possibility of synthesizing the Old Testament's ethical content in order to make it available for the community of faith.

Conclusions

Probably the most striking result of this brief look at the history of scholarship on Old Testament ethics is the realization that few studies have been done. There are several reasons for this state of affairs.

The problem of relating the Old Testament to the church. Some ethicists think the Old Testament reflects primitive social standards and thus is not worthy to be considered in Christian ethics. This illustrates the tendency to separate the Old and New Testaments and accentuate the distance between the Old Testament and today's church. The Old Testament's *setting* in the ancient Near

East does include moral standards different from ours. Witness the merging of "church" and state in ancient Israel (as in the "holy" wars).

The difficulty of establishing Old Testament ethics. The Old Testament is not a systematic document. It reflects many concerns, life settings, and historical eras. In addition, the Old Testament is primarily concerned with faith. Its ethical content derives from that faith; this means that Old Testament ethics is often implicit and difficult to identify. Add to that the great variety of material in the Old Testament and the reason many have found Old Testament ethics to be a difficult topic is obvious.

The primacy of other matters. In part because of the first two reasons, Old Testament students have concentrated on matters other than ethics. Special interest has gone to Old Testament theology in recent years; perhaps this is part of the reason for the neglect of the study of Old Testament ethics.

Old Testament ethics, unfortunately, has not received the attention it deserves. The result is a community of faith which has little relationship to part of its heritage and canon. Many have discarded the Old Testament as far as ethical study is concerned. However, the few important studies which I have mentioned show that is not the only alternative. We turn now to more fruitful possibilities.

The Old Testament as Ethical Norm

I have identified one of the difficulties with studying Old Testament ethics as the problem of finding some way to synthesize the material. How can we approach the Old Testament in order to study its ethics? One way is to ask, "How does the Old Testament reveal its ethical standards?" Discovering a model for approaching the Old Testament on its own terms should aid our attempts to derive its ethical content. Several possibilities come to mind.

Approaching the Old Testament

We could approach the Old Testament as *a book of rules.* That is, we could list the rules or laws in the Old Testament; obedience to them would constitute ethical living. Following this approach, the Christian should not steal or commit murder, should demand "an eye for an eye," and should deal with slaves according to the laws pertaining to slavery in the Old Testament. The problem with this view is that it ignores the difference between Old Testament times and today; it also disregards much of the Old Testament which is not in the form of laws.

We could approach the Old Testament as a book of rules that have been superseded by the New Testament and Jesus Christ. Much of the interpretation of the Old Testament since the time of the Reformation has suggested that the Old Testament is a book of laws one followed to earn salvation; this contrasts with the gospel of grace in the New Testament. Such an understanding of the Old Testament essentially makes it irrelevant for Christian ethics. It also takes a view of Old Testament law foreign to the Old Testament itself. The Book of Exodus, for instance, describes God's law as instruction to a people whom God had already delivered from Egypt and chosen to be His own (20:1-2). In addition, this view of the Old Testament as a book of rules which has been superseded by the New Testament is contrary to Jesus' view of the law (Matt. 5:17).

So approaching the Old Testament as a book of rules does not provide a good basis for understanding Old Testament ethics for the Christian community. However, we must take into account the legal material in the Old Testament.

We could modify this approach but keep in mind some of its positive aspects and look at the Old Testament as *a book of principles.* This approach suggests that one look for the principle behind a commandment. This task is not always easy, but, for example, many would suggest that the principle behind the Commandment against committing premeditated murder (Ex. 20:13) is respect for human life. This principle can then be applied in various settings in the Christian life.

In addition, a story in the Old Testament might suggest certain principles, such as fairness and loyalty in relationships (the story of David and Jonathan). Old Testament stories, as well as Old Testament laws, are rich in ethical content. In some cases this approach is helpful; however, it may encourage the tendency to abstract principles from Old Testament texts and thus separate them from a historical setting in life. Such an approach is far from the spirit of the Old Testament, which is certainly enmeshed in its sociohistorical setting.

Another possibility is to approach the Old Testament as *a pattern for life*. The Old Testament presents a relevant, authoritative view of life. One could construct ethical standards and pursue ethical decision making on the basis of that overall view of life rather than on the basis of specific rules or principles. Such an approach understands the relationship between the Bible and Christian ethics in terms of a dialogue. The Bible presents a pattern for living; when ethical concerns arise, the believer is to ask how that pattern relates to the ethical issue. The pattern might center upon love and community, and thus the basic question for the contemporary person is how to live in community in a loving way.

This approach provides a framework for making ethical decisions. It uses the principles mentioned above to construct an overall pattern for life. With this approach, the Old Testament may become one of several authorities. As with the notion of principles, however, the use of a pattern tends to remove the Bible from its setting in life.

A fourth possibility is to view the Bible, and thus the Old Testament, as *a book for character building*. The Bible contributes to a person's character, to his or her development as an ethical thinker and decision maker. Persons pursue the life of faith and make ethical decisions. Thus the question for the use of the Old Testament is not about rules or principles or paradigms, but rather about its contribution to the development of ethical persons. These persons are then the ones who make ethical decisions.

A person will learn respect for human life as he or she develops in character. A mature person will also learn the significance of justice in life and apply that in various settings. This approach is interesting and certainly holds the value of keeping the Old Testament tied to real life. Such an approach, however, seems not only to concentrate on individuals to the exclusion of community but also to ignore the Old Testament's proclamation to all of creation.

The Old Testament does not speak specifically of character building that often; thus its application in this way could only be indirect. So while this approach has some promise, it does not appear to provide all we need.

The Old Testament As Story

Four models for approaching the Old Testament as ethical norm have been summarized briefly: a book of rules, a book of principles, a paradigm for life, and a book for character building. All of these models have some merit, but not one of them provides a wholly satisfactory approach. Another approach understands the Old Testament as story. This has the important advantage in of using a form—story—which is primary to the Old Testament itself. The Old Testament is essentially the story of God with ancient Israel. The story bears witness to the events in which God was revealed.

A story speaks to identity. It answers questions like, "How are we to view ourselves? How are we to view others and life and the world? How are we to live life? Who is this God who calls to us?" Stories give roots to persons and to communities; they provide challenge and sustenance throughout life. Thus, ancient Israelites remembered stories which became part of the ongoing story of God with the people—providing a script, a lens for the living of life.

The account in the Book of Jonah of God's deliverance of sinful Nineveh upon her repentance can challenge the community of faith to remember that God is the God of all people and the community in the living of its story is to relate to all people as creations of God. The story of God's deliverance of ancient Israel from oppression in Egypt reminds the community of faith that its life (story) is both gift and task; the Ten Commandments are also part of this story. Such stories can powerfully shape ethics.

So the Old Testament presents a story. It presents the idea that future generations of believers can continue to live that story. This approach to the Bible keeps it close to a life setting and attempts to understand the Old Testament on its own terms. Remembering the Old Testament story can provide perspective for our own contemporary stories.

Ethics in the Old Testament Story

Approaching the Old Testament as story has many advantages. It provides an umbrella for seeing the unity of Old Testament ethics and a way to apply Old Testament ethical content to today's church. However, the approach must be tested with the text itself. It is important to consider the various aspects of the story. The traditional divisions of the Hebrew canon are: Law (Torah), Prophets, and Writings. Ethical content is summarized in each section with comments on selected passages.

Torah

The first section of the canon of the Old Testament is the Law or Torah. There are essentially two types of texts here—law and narrative—but the first section of narrative is distinctive and calls for separate treatment.

Primeval history. Genesis 1—11 is known as the history of the first age, the primeval history, and treats the beginnings of humankind. God created the world and human beings in the divine image. Among other things, this image of God is closely associated with dominion over the created order; that is, men and women are to be God's representatives in supervising the earth and caring for it. The biblical story thus begins with the affirmation that life is gift from God and with the challenge to persons of faith to take seriously the task of stewardship of that life and of the world in which they pursue life. Genesis 2 continues this emphasis. Adam was created and placed in the garden as the gardener; he was to care for the garden: "The Lord God took the man and put him in the garden of Eden to till it and keep it" (v. 15, RSV). Adam also related to the animals and finally fulfilled the need for human community with Eve. In short, God entrusted all created life to humankind. These texts raise ethical issues: How do we best preserve life? How do we nurture creation and the human community?

The sin story in Genesis 3 provides some perspective on what happens when we deny the good place of humanity as creation of God. Adam and Eve broke the divine prohibition. The result in part was alienation from God, from each other, and from the rest of creation: "Cursed is the ground because of you; in toil you shall eat of it all the days of your life" (v. 17, RSV).

The emphasis on the growing power of sin continues in Genesis 4 but raises a new issue: What is our relationship to our brother? Cain and Abel were brothers but alienation in their relationship led Cain to kill Abel and, thus, become isolated from his family: "When you till the ground, it shall no longer yield to you its strength; you shall be a fugitive and a wanderer on the earth" (v. 12, RSV). Genesis encourages growth in, rather than destruction of, human relationships. However, the destructive tendency in the human story continues in the story of Noah and the Flood: "The Lord saw that the wickedness of man was great in the earth" (Gen. 6:5, RSV).

The story of the Tower of Babel describes the results of human attempts to take the place of God. Humanity was scattered and confused; community was in jeopardy. "Therefore its name was called Babel, because there the Lord confused the language of all the earth; and from there the Lord scattered them abroad over the face of all the earth" (Gen. 11:9).

These texts remind us that wholeness of life from God is fragile. It should be noted that in spite of the growth of the power of sin in these accounts, God did not abandon humanity, but continued to provide ways toward the fullness of life in community. Ethical living and decision making need to contribute to the good steward-ship of life by supporting growth and mutuality in relationships.

Narrative. The rest of Genesis is taken up with the narratives of the patriarchs and matriarchs. The narratives of the Pentateuch are rather diverse; they include the patriarchal/matriarchal sto-ries and the stories of the Exodus from Egypt and of the movement through the wilderness toward the Promised Land of Canaan.

The patriarchal/matriarchal stories center on God's promise of land and progeny to the descendants of Abraham and Sarah. In the important text Genesis 12:1-3, a significant ethical concern becomes clear: The purpose of the promise was not self-aggrandizement for the Hebrews but service to the human community. "I will make of you a great nation, and I will bless you, and make your name great, so that you will be a blessing" (v. 2, RSV). The last phrase emphasizes the purpose of the promise.

The remaining narratives in Genesis show how these Hebrews did, or did not, live on the basis of the promise and shared or did not share it with those around them. The text constantly confronts the ethical question of how we live in relationship with others: the story of Abraham and Lot, the story of Jacob and Esau, the story of Jacob and Laban, the story of Shechem and Dinah, the story of Joseph and his brothers and their relationship to the Egyptians.

These narratives are primary in the story of God with ancient Israel. They remind us that God calls persons to wholeness in life, and the narratives give guidance in the quest for that wholeness. These texts reaffirm that life is gift from God, often in the form of a promise—a promise which provides the means of faithful living and the task of sharing blessing with others.

The stories of the last generation of the patriarchs/matriarchs provide the transition for the next part of the biblical story: the deliverance from Egypt. The Book of Exodus begins with the Hebrew slaves in Egypt. They, though preserved in the midst of harsh oppression, cried out to God for help. God heard their cry and raised up Moses to deliver them. God demonstrated His ethical stance by squarely placing Himself on the side of the oppressed people and in firm opposition to the oppressive Egyptian empire.

> Then the Lord said, "I have seen the affliction of my people who are in Egypt, and have heard their cry because of their taskmasters; I know their sufferings, and I have come down to deliver them out of the hand of the Egyptians, and to bring them up out of that land to a good and broad land, a land flowing with milk and honey, to the place of the Canaanites, the Hittites, the Amorites, the Perizzites, the Hivites and the Jebusites. And now, behold the cry of the people of Israel has come to me, and I have seen the oppression with which the Egyptians oppress them" (Ex. 3:7-9, RSV).

God through Moses liberated the people from that oppression and made them into people of God.

As an example of a narrative text, look briefly at Exodus 1. The Hebrews had increased in Egypt. A political change had taken place in the empire, and those in power were no longer sympathetic to the Hebrews. The pharaoh feared their numbers and out of this fear sought to oppress them through harsh forced labor. Still fearing that a deliverer would be born among the Hebrews and lead a rebellion, he instructed the midwives of the Hebrews to destroy all males born to the Hebrews. The midwives, on the contrary, "feared God" (v. 17) and simply told the pharaoh that the Hebrew women gave birth before they arrived and they were unable to take the lives of the male Hebrew infants.

This chapter is an important part of the story of God and ancient Israel; the Hebrews could remember that God is on the side of those who are oppressed. People of faith are to resist, not contribute to, those powers in the world which oppress persons.

A third part of the narratives in the Torah relates to the wanderings in the wilderness. A frequent theme is the complaints of the people against the leadership of God and of God's chosen representative, Moses. They complained about food and about meat and about the route to the land of Canaan and about Moses' leadership (Num. 11—14). The ethical issue central to these texts is that life is to be lived on the terms of its giver. Life is not a possession of humans to be pursued in some self-aggrandizing way but a gift from God to be appreciated and celebrated. The people sought to control the course of life rather than live on the terms of the giver of life.

Law. The remainder of the material in the Torah can be classified as law, though in a rather different way than we often use the term. The legal texts are very much a part of the story of God with ancient Israel. In the Exodus from Egypt, God delivered the Hebrews and made them His people. In the legal material God gave them instruction for living as people of God. The laws in the Pentateuch were not legalistic means for earning salvation. They were rather a means of responding to God's gift of salvation and a means of deepening the relationship with God and with other members of the community of faith. The laws also revealed God and God's relationship to all of life. That is, the law codes were a part of the covenant relationship between God and ancient Israel.

Covenant is a way of describing God's relating to the people in order to enable fullness of life for them. God always initiated this relationship by saying, "I will be your God." The people responded with, "Yes, we will be your people." God then instructed them in how to live as people of God for there were consequences to their response. So the laws were instruction for the community of faith, instruction deriving from relationship with God. There several codes of laws.

THE TEN COMMANDMENTS are universal commands give. the basis of the Lord's authority. The first four Commandments deal with relationship with God, and the Fifth Commandment provides the family as a transition to relationships within the social order. The last five Commandments lay a foundation which enables the community to live together in wholeness: a just legal system (Ex. 20:16), fidelity in relationships (v. 14), and the preservation of life and property (vv. 13,15,17). Remembering and enacting such concerns is an important part of the ethical implications of the Old Testament's story of faith.

THE COVENANT CODE follows the Ten Commandments (Ex. 21—23) and applies the universal laws of the Ten Commandments to daily life. For example, the prohibition against murder was considered in cases related to accidental homicide, physical conflict, self-defense, and so forth. The code reflects concerns for justice and the preservation of life and property.

THE HOLINESS CODE, a collection of laws found in Leviticus 17—26, gets its title from the frequent injunction, "You shall be holy; for I the Lord your God am holy" (Lev. 19:2, RSV). God is holy and as people of God ancient Israel was to be a holy people.

Leviticus 18 reflects the understanding of holiness in this code. The key for understanding this chapter is found in its introduction (vv. 1-5), and its conclusion (vv. 24-30). These verses urged the community of faith to live as people of God, that was as a holy people. Such a life would bear witness to their difference from the Canaanites and Egyptians and other idolaters around them.

> You shall not do as they do in the land of Egypt, where you dwelt, and you shall not do as they do in the land of Canaan, to which I am bringing you. You shall do my ordinances and keep my statutes and walk in them. I am the Lord your God. (vv. 3-4, RSV).

The rest of the chapter gives exposition to this concern in the particular area of sexual ethics. It lists family relationships in which sexual intercourse is forbidden. The Chosen People were admonished to demonstrate their relationship to God by responsible sexual behavior.

Some other instructions relate to worship and some pertain to social relationships. There is provision for the poor:

> When you reap the harvest of your land, you shall not reap your field to its very border, neither shall you gather the gleanings after your harvest. And you shall not strip your vineyard bare, neither shall you gather the fallen grapes of your vineyard; you shall leave them for the poor and for the sojourner: I am the Lord your God. (Lev. 19:9-10, RSV).

Verse 18 of that same chapter contains the famous injunction, "You shall love your neighbor as yourself." This code also expresses concern for justice and ecology. As there was a sabbath for humans, there was also a restorative sabbath year for the land—a reminder that land and life are not owned by the people but a gift from God to be nurtured rather than exploited. In addition, every fiftieth year was a jubilee year in which slaves were to be released and property was to be returned to its original owner. In general, wholeness of life for the community had priority over individual needs to "get ahead."

A fourth law code is the Book of DEUTERONOMY. It is a restatement of the covenant instruction and urged the community of faith to live by the covenant and to love God. There is a strong emphasis on ancient Israel's ethical responsibility to love one's neighbor and to nourish family relationships.

Prophets

The law codes provided instruction as the people sought to live the story of faith. The next section of the Hebrew Bible is the Prophets. This section has two divisions: the Former Prophets and the Latter Prophets. The Former Prophets are the Books of Joshua, Judges, 1 and 2 Samuel, and 1 and 2 Kings. These books include the stories of several prophets, such as Nathan, Elijah, and Isaiah. The books also have much theology in common with the Latter Prophets. The Latter Prophets are made up of what we have come to know as the Major and Minor Prophets.

Former Prophets: History and Ethics. These books recount the history of ancient Israel from the time of their entry into the land of Canaan to the destruction of their kingdoms and the beginning of Exile in Babylon, an important segment of the Old Testament story. The people first entered the land in the Book of Joshua. They had trouble taking the land because of their disobedience or violation of covenant.

The Book of Judges provides insight into the time of the early settlement in the land and is concerned about ethical and religious confusion. This period has sometimes been called the dark ages of ancient Israel's history.

The Books of 1 and 2 Samuel tell the story of the movement toward a monarchy for the people. First Samuel reflects a profound ambivalence toward the notion of having a king in ancient Israel. Ethical concern is part of the debate, for the establishment of a monarchy in the land brought with it concerns for justice and the plight of the powerless. The power of those in charge in a monarchy brings with it the temptation for oppression. This concern did not become pressing until the time of Solomon. First Kings shows that Solomon brought great prosperity to the kingdom but supported his burgeoning empire with heavy taxation and forced labor. Thus the seed of oppression grew in the midst of the very people who were supposed to be the guarantors of justice and faithfulness to the God of justice—the divinely chosen line of rulers. The burden of this oppression was part of the reason the kingdom divided at the death of Solomon (1 Kings 12). The result of the division was two kingdoms, one in the north and one in the south.

The Northern Kingdom of Israel continually battled with syncretism, the mixing of the religion of the Lord and the religion of the idols. This conflict had powerful significance not only for worship and faith but also for ethical living. Along with the Canaanite idols came a different way of life and relationship in society. One illustration is the story of Ahab and Naboth (1 Kings 21). Ahab was king in the Northern Kingdom and sought to buy a vineyard from his neighbor Naboth. Naboth refused, saying, "The Lord forbid that I should give you the inheritance of my fathers" (v.3, RSV). This comment reflects the ancient Israelite custom of keeping the land in the family since it was a gift from the Lord.

Ahab still desired the land, and his queen, Jezebel, hatched a plot to get it. They had Naboth framed and executed for cursing God and the king. Ahab then seized the land. When the king went to view his new prized possession, he was confronted by God's prophet Elijah: "Have you killed and also taken possession?" (v.19). This unjust murder and oppression reflects the abuse of power sometimes seen among the kings in ancient Israel. They serve as a negative ethical example in the story of ancient Israel's faith.

Similar problems existed in the Southern Kingdom of Judah. Perhaps the worst offender was the evil king Manasseh who ruled a long time in Jerusalem. His reign included much idolatry and oppression: "Moreover Manasseh shed very much innocent blood, till he had filled Jerusalem from one end to another, besides the sin which he made Judah to sin so that they did what was evil in the sight of the Lord," (2 Kings 21:16; note also 2 Kings 24:4).

During the time of the divided kingdom, some kings did practice justice and righteousness in Judah. Josiah was one; Jeremiah described him in contrast to Jehoiakim:

Did not your father eat and drink and do justice and righteousness?
Then it was well with him.
He judged the cause of the poor and needy; then it was well.
Is not this to know me? says the Lord. (Jer. 22:15-16, RSV).

The history in the Former Prophets is an important part of the story of God with ancient Israel. The people remembered these accounts and came to understand that their identity as covenant people of God had implications for ethical living, primarily in terms of justice.

I have not mentioned the story of David, but we can also use the texts about him to illustrate the ethical content of the Former Prophets. David was a central figure in ancient Israel's history; he established the kingdom and dynasty. He was a good king and able politician. He kept his word and was kind to the remainder of the family of his rival Saul and his friend Jonathan.

However, David also had problems, many of them in family relationships. David's most famous sin was adultery with Bathsheba and the murder of her husband, Uriah. The king was confronted with this sin by the prophet Nathan and, to his credit, repented of this great injustice. This part of the memory of faith reminds the community that covenant relationship with God includes matters of justice and ethical living, even for the great King David.

Latter Prophets. The Major Prophets—Isaiah, Jeremiah, Ezekiel—and the Minor Prophets—Amos, Hosea, Micah, Nahum, Habakkuk, Zephaniah, Obadiah, Joel, Jonah, Haggai, Zechariah, Malachi—make up this division. The prophet Elijah has been mentioned already. Other early prophets also provided the antecedents for the Latter Prophets. This survey will cover major emphases found in the books of the classical prophets.

The prophets assumed that ancient Israel was to be a people of God and spoke words of judgment when the people failed to be so, whether their failure came at the point of improper worship or defective social ethic. So, the prophets were not primarily social reformers or creators of a new system of ethics, but speakers who echoed the word of God, a word which demands ethical living as a part of faith in the Lord. This word is an important part of the story of faith.

Amos was the first of the Latter Prophets; his book speaks of justice and righteousness. Hosea emphasized the mercy and love of God as a basis for mercy in social relationships. Isaiah, also in the eighth century, raised the clarion call for justice in community, a justice based on faith in a God of justice. Isaiah's words reflect common prophetic themes:

> Hear the word of the Lord,
>   you rulers of Sodom!
> Give ear to the teaching of our God,
>   you people of Gomorrah!
> "What to me is the multitude of your sacrifices?
>   says the Lord;
> I have had enough of your burnt offerings of rams
>   and the fat of fed beasts;
> I do not delight in the blood of bulls
>   or of lambs, or of he-goats.
> "When you come to appear before me,
>   who requires of you
>   this trampling of my courts?
> Bring no more vain offerings;
>   incense is an abomination to me.
> New moon and sabbath and the calling of assemblies—
>   I cannot endure iniquity and solemn assembly.
> Your new moons and your appointed feasts
>   my soul hates;
> they have become a burden to me,
>   I am weary of bearing them.
> When you spread forth your hands,
>   I will hide my eyes from you;
> even though you make many prayers,
>   I will not listen;
>   your hands are full of blood.
> Wash yourselves; make yourselves clean;
>   remove the evil of your doings
>   from before my eyes;
> cease to do evil,
>   learn to do good;
> seek justice,
>   correct oppression;
> defend the fatherless,
>   plead for the widow (1:10-17, RSV).

The prophets were often concerned with provision for the powerless: the widow, orphan, sojourner. To worship and confess faith in a holy God of justice entails living a life of justice in relationships and in the corporate life of the community. A similar sentiment was expressed by Micah in the same century:

> He has showed you, O man, what is good;
>   and what does the Lord require of you
> but to do justice, and to love kindness,
>   and to walk humbly with your God? (Micah 6:8, RSV).

The prophets pictured God as railing against injustice and oppression (Nah. 1). Faith and justice were a major theme of the Latter Prophets.

These prophets also emphasized righteousness. The term indicates right relationship or fidelity to a relationship. Right relationship with God is to be demonstrated in right social relationships. In righteousness is found wholeness of life.

> Seek the Lord, all you humble of the land,
>   who do his commands;
> seek righteousness, seek humility;
>   perhaps you may be hidden
> on the day of the Wrath of the Lord (Zeph. 2:3, RSV).

Jeremiah, in the seventh century, also called for righteousness.

> Behold the days are coming, says the Lord, when I will raise up for David a righteous Branch, and he shall reign as king and deal wisely, and shall execute justice and righteousness in the land. In his days Judah will be saved, and Israel will dwell securely. And this is the name by which he will be called: "The Lord is our righteousness" (Jer. 23:5-6, RSV).

The Latter Prophets of the eighth and seventh centuries BC cried out for a life of justice and righteousness as a part of faith in God. Their cry, central in the Old Testament story, went largely unheeded; destruction came as a result of injustice, unrighteousness, and unfaithfulness. The kingdoms were destroyed.

The destruction of Jerusalem and beginning of the Babylonian Exile had an important impact on prophecy. There was little vitality left in the movement after that corporate trauma. Of the prophets after the return from Exile, Malachi and Jonah have significant words related to ethics. Malachi forcefully reminded the people of the priority of the family in the growth of faith. He spoke strong words of judgment against those who would forsake their families for the sake of social, political, and economic expediency (Mal. 2:10-16). Jonah reminded the people that God is the God of all, even the wicked Ninevites, and desires all to have life. Jonah's message, then, is that the community of faith should join in sharing the divine gift of life with those outside its traditional homogeneous bounds.

You can easily see that the Latter Prophets were a powerful voice for social ethics in various settings in the life of ancient Israel. They spoke incisively for justice and righteousness as the very core of the life of faith.

Words from the prophet Amos (eighth century BC) can summarize what I have said about the prophets. The Book of Amos does not present a system of ethics; rather, it proclaims a word from God to the people of the Northern Kingdom around 760 BC, a word with the purpose of calling them back from a death-giving life-style. Amos called the people to act upon their identity as God's people; such an emphasis is central to the story. Amos began by pronouncing coming destruction on many peoples in the ancient Near East because of their cruelty in relationships. He concentrated God's word of judgment and warning on the Northern Kingdom of Israel because of its background in covenant relationship with God. The people had broken covenant by oppressing the poor:

> they sell the righteous for silver,
>   and the needy for a pair of shoes—
> they that trample the head of the poor into the dust of the earth
>   and turn aside the way of the afflicted (Amos 2:6-7, RSV).

The rich and powerful were living luxuriously at the expense of the powerless, and the poor had no recourse because of a corrupt

court system; the empty, established religion supported the rich
and powerful. Amos declared that God seeks wholeness of life for
all and that a national life-style of oppression would lead to destruction. The coming judgment would turn the tide. The prophet
as preacher of righteousness spoke his most famous words in
5:21-24:

> I hate, I despise your feasts,
>   and I take no delight in your solemn assemblies.
> Even though you offer me your burnt offerings and cereal offerings,
>   I will not accept them,
> and the peace offerings of your fatted beasts
>   I will not look upon.
> Take away from me the noise of your songs;
>   to the melody of your harps I will not listen.
> But let justice roll down like waters,
>   and righteousness like an ever-flowing stream (RSV).

Writings

The third section of the Hebrew Bible is the Writings. It contains a variety of books, but primary interest centers on the Wisdom books and the Psalms.

Wisdom Books. The books central to Old Testament wisdom
literature are Proverbs, Job, and Ecclesiastes; they reflect two
aspects of wisdom. Proverbs might be called pragmatic or practical wisdom because it presents practical observations on the moral
life. It encourages living the life of faith as God created it and
passes on observations to enable others to do that. With various
types of teaching sentences or proverbs, it seeks to help persons,
as a part of the story of faith, achieve the goal of life in healthy
community. It presents a general, positive view of life which is to
be celebrated, enjoyed, and shared in appreciation. The book offers
a sketch of righteous living in contrast to the wicked.

> Better is a little with righteousness
>   than great revenues with injustice (Prov. 16:8, RSV).

> A false balance is an abomination to the Lord,
>   but a just weight is his delight (Prov. 11:1, RSV).

The wise contribute to the community and learn through wisdom's instruction about such things as the use of speech and what to avoid in life or family relationships:

> Discipline your son, and he will give you rest;
> he will give delight to your heart (Prov. 29:17, RSV).

The wise life also includes justice:

> He who is kind to the poor lends to the Lord,
> and he will repay him for his deed (Prov. 19:17, RSV).

Proverbs then gives practical observations as guidance for living the wise, moral life as a part of the story of faith. Therein is found blessing.

The Books of Job and Ecclesiastes complement Proverbs; they react to a simplistic understanding of Proverbs by asking: What about ethics when life falls apart?

Job is an extensive dialogue in the wisdom tradition. It affirms that while there is sense to life, there are also unexplainable circumstances, such as the undeserved suffering of Job. Job was the righteous man who suffered great loss but rejected the notion that it was deserved punishment from God. Living the wise, moral life does not guarantee prosperity and success. What of the justice of God? The book does not give an answer to that question; it simply affirms that God, the Creator of all, came to Job in the midst of his deep struggle. Because God came to be with Job and demonstrated that God is the Creator, Job could continue in life with some sense to the struggle. This powerful dialogue suggests that righteous living does not guarantee success and that we cannot always judge who is blessed by God.

Job 31 provides a good illustration of a wisdom text and perhaps the highest ethical standard in the Old Testament. In this chapter Job protested for a final time his innocence of unrighteous living; he did not deserve the suffering he had endured. He avoided falsehood and lust, provided for his servants and for the poor, sympathized with those in pain, cared for his land, shared his prosperity, and lived honestly; and yet he suffered. This chapter affirms ethical living, living the life of justice, and describes specifics included in it. At the same time, it cannot guarantee that living such a life will bring prosperity or success; it rather affirms that God is somehow present to undergird such a life.

The Book of Ecclesiastes is a series of experiments searching for what gives life meaning but which do not find the answer. It affirms that humans do not control life—life is given by God—but still it encourages persons to make the most of the life they are given in community. These books struggle with the difficulties of life but affirm that there is generally sense to life and so ethical living makes a difference. At the same time, they are acutely aware of ambiguity in life and, thus, the difficulty of ethical living and decision making in the story of faith.

Psalms. The Book of Psalms centers on the worship of God and the relationship between God and worshiper in such an overpowering way that little attention has been paid to its ethical dimensions. However, the ethical application of faith is certainly present in these texts.

The notion of justice is central; God is described as a God of justice (Ps. 82; 89:14). Persons of faith are to live a life of justice, to demonstrate their identity (story) in ethical living. The psalms which press this notion are often the laments, those which cry to God for help in the midst of trouble. There are two aspects to the issue: worshipers call for God to enact His justice in life and cry out against those who perpetrate injustice (Ps. 7; 9;10;94).

In addition, the royal psalms reflect the responsibility of the Davidic king to guarantee justice in the nation.

> Give the king thy justice, O God,
>   and thy righteousness to the royal son!
> May he defend the cause of the poor of the people,
>   give deliverance to the needy,
>   and crush the oppressor! (Ps. 72:1,4, RSV).

Other psalms call on the worshiping community to live by justice:

> Depart from evil, and do good;
>   so shall you abide for ever.
> For the Lord loves justice;
>   he will not forsake his saints (Ps. 37:27-28, RSV).

Of particular note is the psalms' relation between the ethical life and worship. Psalms 15 and 24 speak of qualifications for worship, and they are all ethical:

> He who walks blamelessly, and does what is right,
> and speaks truth from his heart (Ps. 15:2, RSV).

In addition, the Book of Psalms is a prayer book. Psalm 1 characterizes the book as part of God's instruction in which the believer is to delight; the psalms are instruction in the honest dialogue of faith, an important part of the story of God with ancient Israel. Such literature on the dialogue of faith is one of the primary ways the Old Testament relates faith to the life of ethics. The joys of life were celebrated gratefully and the crises of life were brought into the context of faith and relationship with God. God, as Lord of life, is the one to whom crises were taken. The psalms of vengeance, often spoken out of a sense of injustice (Pss. 109; 137), worked this way. Rather than destroying the wicked, the worshipers took their concerns to God. The psalms then are one of the important ways the Old Testament integrates faith and life.

Conclusion: Ethics and the Life of Faith

Our survey of the ethical content of the Old Testament suggests that our understanding of the Old Testament as story is sufficiently broad to provide an umbrella for the study of Old Testament ethics. The story approach is also sufficiently powerful to provide a means for applying Old Testament ethical implications to the contemporary community of faith.

The Old Testament expresses a significant concern for creation, for life, and for relationship in community. To relate to God is also to move beyond the boundaries of the community of faith to share life with others. Within all this is a significant concern for the powerless in society—the widow and fatherless and sojourner—so that justice is enacted, a justice based upon need rather than upon any criteria found in our own social position. This ethical perspective on life grows from the identity of God as a God of justice and the identity of ancient Israel as a distinctive people because of their relationship with God. So the worshiping community is called upon to live a life (story) of social justice.

A final outcome of our study of Old Testament ethics is that social ethics is, in the Old Testament scheme of things, not peripheral or secondary or even derivative in the story of faith; it is rather at the heart of faith in God. Indeed, the two aspects essential to the life of faith are worship and ethics. Such a conclusion calls the community of faith to greater ethical issues.

Suggested Reading

Birch, Bruce C. and Rasmussen, Larry L. *Bible and Ethics in the Christian Life*. Minneapolis: Augsburg, 1976.

Clements, R.E. "Christian Ethics and the Old Testament," *The Modern Churchman* 26(1980): 13-26.

Eichrodt, Walther. *Theology of the Old Testament*. Translated by J. A. Baker. 2 vols. Philadelphia: Westminster, 1967. (2: 316-379)

Interpreter's Dictionary of the Bible, Vol. II, "Ethics in the OT," by J. Hempel.

Kaiser, Walter C. *Toward Old Testament Ethics.* Grand Rapids: Zondervan, 1983.

Spohn, William C. *What Are They Saying About Scripture and Ethics?* New York: Paulist, 1984.

3

Living to the Glory of God:
The Ethics of the New Testament

Thomas D. Lea

Dr. Nilson Fanini is pastor of First Baptist Church of Niteroi, Brazil. Fanini's church of over 5,000 members has organized 28 new churches since 1964. It has 92 missions and sponsors radio and television programs on 152 stations. In addition to this vigorous preaching, teaching, and evangelistic ministry, the church carries on an active program for meeting human need. The program emphasizes five areas: nutrition, health, education, housing, and salvation.

The church has nineteen clinics staffed with twenty doctors and six dentists. In 1985 members helped to build thirty-eight houses in the slums, and in ten years they have given away eight hundred tons of food. Committed Christians offer courses in sewing, manicuring, hairdressing, typing, electronics, and carpentry. Their goal is to incarnate the love of God through good work. They are seeking to live to the glory of God.[1]

Fanini's practices represent an effort to apply the ethics of the New Testament in a local church setting. The effort has proven remarkably effective.

The study of New Testament ethics is not merely an academic exercise. The goal of such ethics is to produce individuals and churches who can incarnate the love of Christ in their own sphere of life. The teaching of the New Testament aims at producing people who will live with enthusiasm for the glory of God (Col. 3:23).

As we look at the subject of New Testament ethics, we will begin by observing how people have approached the Bible in general and Christian living in particular. Then we will survey the ethical teaching of Jesus and of Paul, John, Peter, and other New Testament writers to learn their meaning and application. Finally we will examine one area of Christian living to learn what Christians over the centuries have done to glorify God in this area. We will look at the subject of slavery with an examination of Paul's Letter to Philemon.

Approaching the New Testament

In approaching the New Testament, we need to understand some of the methods which biblical interpreters have followed over the centuries. Many of the earliest Christian interpreters practiced allegory in understanding the New Testament. In this method the interpreter used a person, event, or teaching of the Bible to illustrate some idea which he saw as important.[2] Usually the interpreter ignored the historical sense of the Scripture. One Christian writer took the reference to the 318 servants of Abraham in Genesis 14:14 and assigned meanings to the Greek letters used in forming the number "318." His method led him to assert that the reference to the 318 servants is really speaking of Jesus and the cross and not merely of 318 servants. That interpretation goes far beyond the verse's historical meaning.[3]

Many Jewish interpreters of Scripture practiced an excessively literal method of understanding God's message. They were deeply devoted to the details of the text, but they frequently missed the essential truths of a passage and made a trivial reference into a major issue. Some Christian interpreters were influenced by their methods.

During the Reformation such interpreters as Martin Luther urged a return to a reasonable literal exegesis of Scripture and a departure from excessive allegory. In recent centuries some more liberal interpreters have questioned the appearance of the supernatural element in Scripture. Some have suggested that social conditions are the chief sources of theological beliefs and that the task of the interpreter is to understand the conditions behind the belief and not the belief itself.

Evangelical interpreters today accept the Bible as God's inspired message to humanity. They seek to understand a given passage in its normal or usual sense. They also use a knowledge of the customs and manners of biblical times to understand a passage better. They demand that an interpreter have an adequate justification for his interpretation without merely resorting to subjective feeling.

Those who use the New Testament to formulate ethics can approach the text in various ways. Many of these methods involve theological presuppositions. We can approach the New Testament in at least four ways.[4]

First, we may view the New Testament as a book of laws or codes to regulate human conduct. Those who follow this method view the Testaments as containing prescriptive laws in the form of commandments and ordinances. The truth behind this approach is the recognition that Jesus, indeed, gave His ethical teachings as commands and not as mere suggestions. The limitation of this approach is that it does not produce morally committed people but rather individuals who try to regulate the worst features of immoral behavior. Although this technique can provide some assistance in the field of personal morality, it will not give sufficient guidance in the area of social morality.

Second, we can look at the Bible as a collection of universal moral principles. We can emphasize that our responsibility is to learn specific moral principles from the New Testament. This approach does allow for a flexibility in the application of Scripture. This makes the Bible relevant for today. Its shortcoming is that it turns Jesus into a philosopher who spoke about various issues of moral significance. Also, it unduly magnifies the role of reason in deciding moral issues.

A third approach emphasizes that in making ethical decisions we can have a free and sovereign encounter with God through the Spirit. It is proper to emphasize the role of the Holy Spirit in guiding the individual Christian in decision making. However, this type of approach has the defect of making decisions too subjectively.

The final approach emphasizes that Christians should look at the facts of an ethical decision and determine the loving response to make in any circumstance. It contains a prescriptive statement in that it insists that the law of love must be applied in each situation of life. One limitation is that the term *love* becomes a feeling which can easily adjust to the toleration of any kind of behavior. Those who stress this kind of decision making often fail to realize that the call for love does not provide enough protection against human pride, arrogance, stupidity, and cruelty.

Each of these methods contains an element of truth. The first approach emphasizes that God has provided an authoritative source of guidance. The second technique underscores that the Bible contains flexible principles rather than tightly woven rules. The third approach suggests that the role of the Holy Spirit is vital in leading an ethically acceptable life. The final method correctly emphasizes the importance of a motivation of love in living a life which is pleasing to God. We should make use of the valid contributions of each approach as we apply the ethical teachings of Scripture.

Now we turn to examine the chief ethical emphases of the major portions of the New Testament. Our goal is to discover the principles which Jesus or the writer gave for making ethical decisions and to illustrate the principles.

The Ethics of Jesus

In this section we will study the ethics of Jesus as they appear in the Synoptic Gospels. The Synoptic writers, Matthew, Mark, and Luke, sometimes included different ethical emphasis, but each gave an accurate reporting of what Jesus said. This study will include the Sermon on the Mount, one of the most ethically significant sections of Jesus' teaching.

The ethical statements of Jesus deal more with personal ethics than with social ethics. For example, Jesus involved Himself more with personal directives about forgiveness (Matt. 5:21-25); love (Matt. 5:43-48); and materialism (Matt. 6:19-21) than with outlining a pattern of living for a community. He did speak about the importance of service (Mark 9:33-37) and duty to the state (Matt. 22:15-22), but these are not as numerous as His directives for personal behavior.

Principles of Jesus' Ethics

The highest incentive for ethical obedience in each Christian is the example of God's character. Jesus spoke about God's perfection (Matt. 5:48) and urged Christians to be as perfect as God is. Jesus urged His listeners to pray with hopefulness by focusing on the goodness of God (Matt. 7:11). In all that the Christian does he is to seek to be like God and is to glorify God.

Achieving an obedience like this is impossible, but the true disciple of Christ makes the attempt. Such a person has begun the journey toward the perfection which Jesus described. Jesus' initial call to His followers was an appeal to become disciples (Mark 1:17). A disciple was one who attached himself to a teacher in order to learn from him. Jesus' disciples accompanied Him on his travels (Mark 3:14), asked questions about His teaching (Mark 4:10), learned from Jesus' example (John 13:14), and received special ministries of teaching and preaching (Matt. 10:1-15). Jesus did not call His disciples to ease and pleasure but to self-denial and suffering (Mark 8:34).

The demands which Jesus made were oriented around the climactic work which God was doing in the life of Jesus. These demands had an eschatological orientation. Jesus clearly told His disciples that the kingdom of God had arrived in His ministry (Matt. 12:28). The knowledge that God was already fully at work in Jesus' actions gave an incentive of urgency to each Christian. In Jesus, God could meet the needs of each believer. Through Jesus, for example, believers could experience forgiveness and joy in daily life (Mark 2:10).

Jesus clearly practiced the level of commitment to the will of God which He demanded. He understood that His purpose in coming to earth was to minister to others and give His life as a ransom for human sinfulness (Mark 10:45). His followers recognized that He Himself demonstrated the quality of commitment which He sought from others (2 Cor. 10:1).

Jesus emphasized that love for God and love for neighbor were a fulfillment of all of God's commandments (Matt. 22:34-40). This love for God was not a mere emotional affair. It was a deep commitment of the human personality to do the will of God. God demanded the love of the entire personality.

Jesus also emphasized that love for neighbor demanded an obedient service to meet human needs. Jesus' disciples clearly grasped that love for human beings demanded actions and not merely talk (1 John 3:17-18). Christian living demanded a commitment which would glorify God.

Jesus and the Law

What did Jesus teach about the demands of God in the Old Testament? Did He ignore Old Testament law? Did He insist upon its observance in a legalistic sense?

Whenever Jesus mentioned the law, He stressed its validity (Matt. 5:17). He observed the law to the extent that it continued to express the will and intent of God (Matt. 8:1-4). He was not hesitant to set aside the demands of the law where it failed to reflect the intent of God. He relaxed the rigid enforcement of the dietary laws of the Old Testament when it became apparent that they no longer represented the will of God (Mark 7:19).

As Jesus made ethical demands on His hearers, He often brought out the original purpose for God's demands. This is especially true in the teaching of the Sermon on the Mount. In His teaching in the Sermon, Jesus encountered an interpretation of the Sixth Commandment (Ex. 20:13) which said that only murder was a violation of the will of God. He pointed out that God's original desire was to ban hatred as well as murder (Matt. 5:21-22). He also emphasized that God's original purpose for the sabbath included acts of healing and mercy (Mark 2:23 to 3:6) and not merely cessation of all activity.

Sometimes Jesus' declaration of God's purpose put Him in conflict with popular human interpretation. Popular Jewish thought seems to have understood that the command to love the neighbor authorized hatred for an enemy. The groups at Qumran near the Dead Sea authorized such an attitude.[5] Jesus swiftly rejected this interpretation and demanded that His hearers love, bless, and pray for their enemies (Matt. 5:44).

Whenever Jesus interpreted the law, He made its application

more radical than interpreters had traditionally understood it. Righteousness became an internal attitude and not merely an external act (Matt. 5:20). He condemned the lustful glance as sinful (Matt. 5:28). To those who had demanded an eye for an eye and a tooth for a tooth, He prohibited all revenge (Matt. 5:38-42). To those who had been content with their regular acts of prayer and fasting, He condemned the attitude of pride and pretense which motivated the entire display (Matt. 6:1-6, 16-18).

Jesus' treatment of the law of God dealt chiefly with the moral law and not with the ceremonial law. His moral demands led His hearers to condemn the attitude behind the act. Jesus did not completely dispense with ceremonies and traditions (Matt. 17:24-27), but He rejected them whenever they did not represent the will of God.

Jesus' Use of Hyperbole

One feature of Jesus' statements which causes much difficulty for interpreters is His frequent use of hyperbole. Hyperbole is acceptable exaggeration for effect. A mother uses hyperbole when she finds her son tracking outdoor mud into a room and says to him, "Get your shoes off! You're ruining the whole house with this mud." The fact is that the son may have ruined only one room of the house. No one will stop the mother to say to her, "You're not telling the truth. He is ruining only a single room." We regard her exaggeration as totally acceptable. Jesus frequently used hyperbole in making demands of His disciples.

In Matthew 5:29-30 he urged His listeners to pluck out the right eye or to cut off the right hand if it led them to sin. He meant that His hearers should show the same zeal in fighting the sin of lust as would be shown by removing the eye and cutting off the hand. He had no intention that anyone should lose hands and eyes in fighting sin.

In Matthew 6:3 He directed those who performed deeds of mercy to keep their left hand from knowing what their right hand was doing. Jesus' intent was to suggest that one be so secretive about publicizing deeds of kindness that one might try to hide it from oneself. To comply literally with this demand is impossible.

In both of these instances Jesus was using hyperbole. As we observe the radical nature of Jesus' commands, we can make a wiser interpretation if we observe the presence of the language of hyperbole.

The British biblical scholar C. H. Dodd has given us some assistance in properly interpreting Jesus' hyperbolical statements. Dodd focused on Jesus' command to turn the other cheek (Matt. 5:39) and suggested that Jesus' words described "the *quality* and *direction* of action" which will conform to the standard set by the love of God.[6] He indicated that the correct quality of response might be present only in a low degree. However, it is possible to observe the right direction of response even though the goal is still far off.

For example, if someone slaps you on the cheek, you might abruptly turn around and leave the scene of the encounter without saying a word. Perhaps you left in order to avoid a physical conflict. It would have been more significantly like Jesus' intent if you could have uttered the words, "I forgive you." However, your action, though present in a low degree, was moving in the direction which Jesus indicated.

Applying the Ethics of Jesus

Jesus linked ethical behavior with a new religious experience. Living the Christian life required renouncing self, experiencing a new birth, and demonstrating a new character. The obligations of love were not merely external. These obligations required personal self-denial. This new life was possible only through repentance and commitment to Jesus Christ (Mark 1:15,17).

Jesus placed much stress on the inwardness of moral behavior. In the Sermon on the Mount Jesus emphasized that anger was the sin from which came murder. He pointed out that lust led to adultery. He denounced both anger and lust as sin and warned His listeners to avoid them (Matt. 5:21-30).

The example of Jesus' own behavior toward the outcasts showed the value of the individual. Jesus accepted people viewed as insignificant by His society (Mark 1:40-45; 10:13-16; Luke

8:1-3). He gave worth and dignity to the sick, to children, and to women by His actions.

In Jesus' teaching, ethical behavior also demanded service. The call to follow Christ was not a call to a place of privilege but to a responsibility of service (Mark 10:42-45).

Jesus provided an incentive for obeying His demands by offering rewards for the obedient (Matt. 16:27). The rewards included both a deepened experience in this life and a final consummation in which the followers of Jesus would receive added blessing. Those who receive Jesus' rewards must not make them the motive for discipleship (Matt. 6:1).

The Ethics of Jesus in John's Writings

The ethical teachings of John's Gospel differ from those of the Synoptic Gospels in at least two ways. In the Synoptics Jesus set forth general principles, ideas, or concepts. In the Gospel of John we find ethical teaching presented through such terms as *life, light,* and *truth.*

Also, we find that Jesus used parables as a major teaching tool of moral truth in the Synoptics (see Matt. 13:1-52; Mark 4:1-34). John's Gospel has allegories, such as the vine and the branches (John 15), but contains few parables of the same nature as those in the Synoptics.

John's Epistles contain some of the same terms as the Gospel of John, such as *life, light,* and *truth.* Ethical teaching is more central in the Epistles of John than in his Gospel.

The Book of Revelation is a prophecy which aims at changing the behavior of its readers (Rev. 1:3). It does not contain a significant amount of ethical material. The book contains many warnings and appeals to wavering Christians (Rev. 2:7,11,17,29; 3:6,13,22).

Ethical Principles in John's Gospel

The Greek verb for *faith* appears nearly one hundred times in John's Gospel. It never indicates a mental assent or a passive agreement. It points toward a complete commitment to someone or something. Those who showed faith in Jesus acted upon His word (cf. John 4:50; 5:9). In John 6:35 Jesus called His listeners to a faith committed to Him. This type of commitment represented the first step in ethical behavior for John.

John also emphasized that ethical behavior is a normal and expected outgrowth of living in fellowship with Jesus. In John 15 Jesus indicated that He had chosen those who would serve as His disciples (v. 16). The purpose of that choosing was not for any special privilege but so that they might bear fruit. The fruit which Jesus had in mind included all of the results of living a life of full obedience to Christ. This involves service to others, the practice of evangelism, and the development of Christian habits and character. This fruit will be the normal expectation for the Christian so long as he remains in Christ.

John also stressed the supreme importance of love. In John 13:34 Jesus introduced the command to love and called it a "new commandment." The love which He described was not a mere emotion; it was an attitude of the will which demonstrated itself in unselfish conduct toward others.

Jesus took an old commandment concerning love (Lev. 19:18) and breathed new life into it. The motive for obeying this command to love was new. Christians are to love one another as God has loved them. A new result of obeying this commandment appears in verse 35. Loving others provides proof that a person knows Jesus. It is important to realize that words, promises, and kind thoughts do not prove to others that we know Jesus. Only the demonstration of love by unselfish deeds does this.

Ethical Principles in John's Epistles

The Epistle of 1 John emphasizes the importance of a right attitude and right action. The right attitude is love. This love shows itself in the demonstration of compassion for a brother in need (3:17). The right action is righteousness. This righteousness consists of obeying the commands of God. Righteousness is the assured outcome of being born of God (2:28-29).

In 2 John the apostle appealed for the demonstration of love in conduct (v. 5). A true love for God will show itself by an obedience to God's commandments (v. 6).

In 3 John the apostle called on his readers to practice the truth in moral living (vv. 3-4). John commended his reader Gaius for showing hospitality to traveling Christians (vv. 5-8).

Ethical Principles in Revelation

Many of the ethical emphases in the Revelation relate to social righteousness rather than to personal righteousness. In Revelation John faced the challenge of a state which demanded what belonged to Caesar and also what belonged to God (cf. Matt. 22:15-22). John's teaching indicated the importance of continuing to obey God even though the demands of the state were unwarranted (Rev. 6:9-11). However, nothing in John's statements indicates that he encouraged rebellion against the state. He called for Christians to serve God and expected that they would suffer the consequences of their disobedience. In the midst of persecution, Christians were to refuse to follow the idolatrous demands of the state, and they were to demonstrate patience and loyalty by following God's will.

The Ethics of Paul

Paul wrote letters to Gentiles who had recently been converted from paganism. They had no knowledge of the Old Testament. They lived among moral squalor and faced overwhelming temptations and problems. Paul stated theological principles and then applied them in the personal and social lives of the new Christians.

Some of Paul's instructions concerned women and their role in the life of the church (1 Cor. 14:34-36; 1 Tim. 2:9-15). Paul also gave principles regarding the eating of certain meats (Rom. 14:15-23) and guidelines about receiving an offering for the poor (2 Cor. 8—9). Because of the needs which Paul faced, we will find more specific applications in Paul than in Jesus.

Ethical Principles in Paul's Writings

Paul resembled Jesus in that he did not prescribe a code of laws for the Christian life. He outlined basic principles of behavior which an individual and a church could apply under the leadership of the Holy Spirit.

Like Jesus, Paul stressed that love was the chief moral principle of the Christian life (Gal. 5:14). This love obviously was first of all a love for God (2 Cor. 5:14). It also included a love for neighbor and especially for those in the fellowship of faith (Gal. 6:10). Paul considered that love began within the household of faith and extended outward.

In emphasizing love as the driving force of the Christian life, Paul did not intend to deny the value of law. He affirmed the continual validity of the law (Rom. 7:12). He warned against an expression of Christian freedom which encouraged sin and disobedience. The new freedom which believers had in Jesus Christ was to become an opportunity for serving others through love (Gal. 5:13-15).

Paul also emphasized the example of Christ as a principle of ethical living. Christians were to follow the example of Christ's humility (Phil. 2:5). They were to imitate His generosity and love (2 Cor. 8:9). Christians could not literally copy Jesus, but by the power of the Holy Spirit they could reproduce His moral power, inner convictions, and spiritual concern.

Incentives for Christian Living in Paul

One of the important incentives for ethical living in Paul's writings is the Christian church or community of believers surrounding the individual. Paul emphasized that Christians constituted one body (1 Cor. 10:17), and he underscored the mutual dependence of one member of the body on another (12:14-26). Furthermore, he stated that a chief consideration in the matter of ethical choices was the effect of an action on the body and the members of the body. All things were to be done for the purpose of edifying one another (14:26).

Paul stressed the importance of an "in Christ" relationship in the Christian life. He had been brought into a life-changing relationship with Christ, and this relationship provided the divine strength to glorify God (Gal. 2:20).

To be in Christ is the same as to be in the Spirit of God (Rom. 8:9-10). The relationship of being in Christ brings the individual Christian into the position of receiving the power of the Holy

Spirit. It is this power which provides the divine dynamic to become holy and pure in the sight of God (v. 13).

Paul expected that Christians would observe certain accepted standards of behavior. On the positive side he emphasized such demands as an exemplary family life, a work ethic, and a life which received respect from those outside the church (1 Thess. 4:1-12). On the negative side he presented lists of sins which Christians were to avoid specifically (Gal. 5:19-21).

According to Paul an underlying motivation in all that the Christian did was to seek to please God. The ambition of the Christian was to learn what pleased the Lord (Eph. 5:10) and to direct life so as to achieve this aim. The glory of God was the aim of Christian service.

As an incentive for obedience, Paul appealed to the coming judgment of God. He indicated that God would reveal His wrath against the unrighteous (2 Thess. 1:3-10). All human beings would reap what they sowed (Gal. 6:7). Christians could also expect to appear before God's judgment seat to receive the reward for what they have done in this life (2 Cor. 5:10).

Handling Debatable Issues

One of Paul's unique contributions is his discussion on dealing with ethical issues which are debatable. Paul fully recognized that Christians would disagree over some specific issues of ethical behavior (Rom. 14:1-2). Paul insisted that the chief goal of a Christian in all of his actions was to bring glory to God (1 Cor. 10:31; Col. 3:17). Within the demands of that one requirement, there is much freedom in deciding issues about which Christians might differ.

Each Christian must avoid actions which would defile or injure his own conscience. Some actions, not wrong in themselves, may interfere with personal communion with God or dull spiritual concern for others. If that is true, the Christian must avoid these actions (1 Cor. 6:12). The Christian can determine his actions with reference to some things not specifically mentioned in Scripture by following this principle.

No Christian should place a negative example before a weaker believer. Our liberty to participate in a certain act is limited by the effect which it produces upon another believer (1 Cor. 8:9). One Christian may react so strongly against immaturity in other believers that he himself moves into areas which are objectionable. By this behavior he may entice a weaker believer into an act which defiles the conscience (Rom. 14:13-16).

No aspect of Christian behavior should lead to bringing reproach upon the gospel. The behavior of the Christian must not cause the non-Christian to become more confirmed in his actions (1 Cor. 10:32-33). Our behavior must be such that we will not put any needless offense before an unbeliever who desires to come to the Savior (1 Pet. 2:11-12; 3:15).

Christians must avoid entering into practices and activities with unbelievers for mutual purposes and aims (2 Cor. 6:14 to 7:1). This prohibition applies to marriage, but it also has application to business relationships and other areas of potential common action. It is impossible for two individuals who have radically divergent purposes for their lives to have a mutually beneficial relationship.

There were occasions when Christians adapted their conduct to conform to local customs as a spiritual benefit and witness to others. Modesty and Christian decency required that Christian women in Corinth cover their heads (1 Cor. 11:2-16). Irregularities in the services of worship required that the privileges of women for speaking be closely regulated (1 Cor. 14:34-36). However, there was no universal ban on the speaking by women in such services (1 Cor. 11:5).

The Ethics of Peter

In 1 Peter the apostle made reference both to the actions of Jesus (2:21-25) and, in a subtle sense, to the teachings of Jesus (5:6; cf. Luke 14:11). In 2 Peter the apostle again made a clear reference to the actions of Jesus (1:16-21). Although the influence of Jesus' teaching is not as clear in 2 Peter, such a passage as 3:10 has similarities to Matthew 24:43.

Two principles of ethical behavior are particularly significant in 1 Peter. First, Peter made use of a "grace" ethic. Because of the actions of God in Jesus Christ, Peter urged his readers toward a behavior which was committed and obedient. The appearance of the gospel mentioned in 1:3-12 leads to an appeal for holiness in verses 13-21. The experience of regeneration mentioned in verses 22-25 leads to an appeal for holy living in 2:1-2. The promise of Christ's return in 4:7 leads to an appeal in the same verse for wise, prayerful living. These appeals for ethical behavior are based upon the acts of God. God's grace leads to human action.

Second, Peter urged an ethic of submission based on the example of Christ. Peter called for readers to submit to their government (2:13-17) and for Christian servants to be subject to their owners (vv. 18-25). He appealed for wives to be submissive to their unsaved husbands in order to win them to Christ. (3:1-6). This appeal for submission will fall strangely upon modern ears, but Peter did not state his appeals as mere laws. He called for them as voluntary acts. Submission is a spiritual principle of life by which we serve God and relate to one another.

In the Epistle of 2 Peter the apostle attacked the false teaching that faith in Christ and holy living were unrelated. The appeal to the practice of the Christian virtues in 1:3-11 assumes that the readers were themselves believers. Based on their faith in Jesus Christ, Peter urged readers to behave with self-control, patience, love, and diligence. Peter mentioned that false prophets were leading his readers into moral evil, and he wrote to prevent this mistake.

The problems which the apostle faced in 2 Peter sound very contemporary when we compare them with modern teaching that suggests that what we believe need not influence how we live. Peter firmly emphasized that wrong belief led to evil actions (2:1-3).

Other New Testament Emphases

The chief ethical emphasis of the Epistle to the Hebrews appears in its repeated exhortations to show endurance and loyalty in the service of Christ. Exhortations appear in Hebrews in such passages as 2:1-4; 3:12-15; 6:1-4; and 10:26-31. In each of these exhortations, the author fervently urged his readers to persevere in their loyalty to Christ without turning aside (6:11-12; 10:36).

These appeals of the author indicate the importance of warnings, encouragements, and earnest concern in leading believers to live ethically.

The Epistle to the Hebrews also mentions such basic Christian virtues as faith (11:6) and love (6:10, 10:24; 13:1). There is an appeal to follow the example of Christ (12:1-2), who becomes the pioneer of our faith.

The Letter of James overflows with ethical content. Its teaching provides many similarities to the teaching of Jesus recorded in the Gospels (cf. 5:2-3 and Matt. 6:19; 5:12 and Matt. 5:34-37). In form it bears resemblance to the Book of Proverbs in the Old Testament.

James emphasized the importance of being "doers of the word" (1:22-25). The type of obedience which James urged consisted of works of compassion and mercy to the needy (1:27; 2:14-17).

James also denounced the practice of partiality in vogue in the churches in Palestine (2:1-13). He compared those who practiced partiality to evil-thinking judges (v. 4) and labeled the deed as "sin" (v. 9).

An unworthy use of the tongue by some who were teaching prompted James to warn potential teachers that they needed to control their tongues and personalities (3:1-12). A tongue had great potential for accomplishing good (vv. 3-5), but out of control it could be a source of contention and confusion (v. 6).

The use and abuse of wealth finds frequent mention in James. In at least one instance the "rich" who are mentioned were Christians (1:10), but in two instances these wealthy people were unbelievers who seem to have oppressed poor believers (2:6-7; 5:1-6). James accused wealthy unbelievers of injustice, wanton living, and murder (5:4-6) and threatened that God would remove all of their riches (5:2-3).

Practical Application of New Testament Ethics

No writer of the New Testament has given us a systematic summary of ethics. The principles which a writer used in making ethical decisions were worked out as he faced a specific need or challenge. Paul's statements in Philemon, for example, have much application to the practice of human slavery. However, Paul did not state his beliefs about slavery in Philemon in a systematic manner. He articulated and refined them as he faced the challenge of urging Philemon to receive again graciously his runaway slave Onesimus.

Paul penned the letter to Philemon to smooth the way for the runaway slave Onesimus to return to his master (vv. 14-15). Paul asked Philemon to accept Onesimus as a brother in Christ and not merely as a slave (vv. 16-17). Paul's method of approaching the problem provides an interesting illustration of his proclamation in Galatians 3:28 that in Christ all ethnic distinctions are abolished.

Paul's response to Philemon did not attack the essential elements of slavery. What he said contributed to revolutionizing the thinking of Christians on the subject. In Colossians 4:1 Paul had warned slave owners that they had a responsibility toward their slaves. In Colossians 3:22 Paul addressed slaves as responsible moral beings who were to fear God. In Philemon Paul did not condemn slavery, but he presented Onesimus as a Christian brother instead of a slave (v. 16). When an owner can refer to a slave as a brother, the slave has reached a position in which the legal title of slave is meaningless.

Christianity laid the foundation for a new relationship between owner and slave. Paul attempted to link Philemon and Onesimus with Christian love so that emancipation would become a necessity. He related both owner and slave to one another in the body of Christ. The owner and the slave were to conduct their relationships in the light of belonging to the same Lord. By exposing slavery to the light of the gospel, the institution of slavery could only shrivel and die.

The practice of slavery made people appear as things and not as persons. Paul was proclaiming that one's status in society and one's ethnic background made no difference before God spiritually. What God had done in Jesus significantly altered the relationships between slaves and freemen in society.

Paul was not primarily interested in social structures but in relationships. If two individuals were Christians, they could overcome the social difference of freeman and slave by the quality of personal relationship.

In Philemon Paul spoke about Onesimus as a responsible person. In the instructions given to women, children, and slaves in his house codes (Eph. 5:22 to 6:9; Col. 3:18-25), Paul addressed all of these groups as responsible people. He did not attempt to promote a head-on confrontation with slavery. Instead he tried to raise the level of personal relationships within the existing structures of society.

We do not know just how Paul's exhortations to Philemon affected Onesimus. Perhaps Philemon freed him. Perhaps he continued as the slave of Philemon and worshiped with Philemon as a spiritual equal. All that we can say is that Onesimus's relations with Philemon and those of Philemon with Onesimus became considerably different.

There are few available materials to indicate fully how the church in succeeding centuries responded to the practice of slavery. In the second century it was widely held by Christians that slaves should be treated kindly. Second-century Christian writers did not denounce slavery, but they urged Christian masters to treat their slaves kindly.[7]

Augustine often urged Christians to treat their slaves with kindness. He never went so far as to see the Christian faith as a threat to the institution of slavery. He emphasized that the gospel brought freedom from the tyranny of sin, but he did not stress political freedom.

In North America the growing of cotton led to the usage of slave labor in growing and harvesting the crop. As conditions in parts of North America made the keeping of large numbers of slaves untenable, and as Christians looked again at the Scriptures, some prophetic voices lifted an effective challenge to the institution of slavery. The church struggled to apply the truth that both social and spiritual freedom are inherent in the Christian message.

In America a crusade for the abolition of slavery began in earnest in the 1840s and 1850s. Evangelist Charles G. Finney founded the town of Oberlin, Ohio, as a location for training evangelists. Later, the town became a main link on the "Underground Railroad" by which slaves were transported through the Northern United States to Canada. Finney himself stumped the state and spoke to abolitionist societies. He proclaimed a gospel which would save souls, revive the church, rebuild society, and end slavery and poverty.

In a Lincoln's Birthday speech in February 1987, President Ronald Reagan noted that "racism is still with us, North and South." New incidents of racism in Howard Beach, New York, and Forsyth County, Georgia, focused the attention of the country on the continuing specter of racial discrimination.

Today Christians face additional challenges in taking ethical teachings inherent in the gospel, such as these about race, and applying them in their own lives and institutions. We must provide a climate by our preaching and teaching so that we affirm the worth of each individual. This can provide an opportunity for greater freedom and personal growth. It can bring glory to God.

Notes

1. Reported in *Decision*, December 1986, p. 23.

2. An excellent discussion of the effects of allegory in biblical interpretation appears in Bernard Ramm's, *Protestant Biblical Interpretation* (Boston: W. A. Wilde Company, 1956), pp. 24-45 and in Robert M. Grant's, *A Short History of the Interpretation of the Bible*, 2nd ed. rev. (Philadelphia: Fortress Press, 1984), pp. 52-62.

3. The reference to Genesis 14:14 appears in *The Epistle of Barnabas* 9:7-8. This epistolary title is a pseudonym, and the writing is usually dated in the early second century. The use of numbers in this way reflected a Jewish practice known as "gematria" in which the numerical value of the letters in a word was important.

The Greek letters involved were the letter which represented the figure 300 and the letters which total eighteen. The shape of the letter resembles the cross, and the letters are the first two letters in the Greek word for *Jesus.*

4. Richard Longenecker, *New Testament Social Ethics for Today* (Grand Rapids: William B. Eerdmans Publishing Co., 1984), pp. 1-9.

5. Donald A. Carson, "Matthew," *The Expositor's Bible Commentary,* ed. Frank E. Gaebelein (Grand Rapids: Zondervan, 1984), 3: 157.

6. C. H. Dodd, *Gospel and Law* (Cambridge: Cambridge University Press, 1951), p. 73.

7. For a brief but helpful discussion of the church's response to slavery see Longenecker, pp. 60-70.

Suggested Reading

Barnette, Henlee. *Introducing Christian Ethics.* Nashville: Broadman Press, 1961.

Henry, Carl. *Christian Personal Ethics.* Grand Rapids: William B. Eerdmans Publishing Company, 1957.

Maston, T. B. *Biblical Ethics.* Cleveland: World Publishing Company, 1967.

Verhey, Allen. *The Great Reversal: Ethics and the New Testament.* Grand Rapids: William B. Eerdmans Publishing Company, 1984.

Wirt, Sherwood Eliot. *The Social Conscience of the Evangelical.* New York: Harper and Row, 1968.

4

The Ethics of Decision Making

D. Glenn Saul

A couple wants to know what's wrong with living together before marriage. A family is troubled because a loved one is being kept alive by a respirator in an intensive care unit. A church member wants to know if he should report the misappropriation of funds by his boss. A young mother asks if she should file suit against a hospital that acted irresponsibly in treating her. These are serious questions of ethics and Christian faith.

Other ethical questions are related to Christian life-style. How should one thousand dollars be spent which has come unexpectedly? Should a family move into a larger house simply because they can afford it? Is it enough to give a tithe of personal income to the church? Is it legitimate to make as much money as one can and enjoy the life-style which that will afford? These are individual decisions.

Some choices for Christians have corporate or social implications. Many of them are made difficult because they are also political issues. Should a Christian support a national defense buildup at the expense of social programs? Are laws that favor one minority group worthy of support? Would a constitutional amendment banning all abortions infringe on the rights of some women in extreme situations?

In this chapter we will consider how ethicists have approached decision making. No one particular method will be advocated. Nevertheless, it will be important to make some evaluations as we go along. Some of the descriptive categories will be somewhat artificial. The decision-making process is more complicated than can be summarized in a short chapter. Important questions must be asked. Is it possible to know what is right? Can we as Christians have a ready answer for the decision that we have to make? How can we know God's will? Let's look at how some have answered these questions.

In the first section of the chapter we will explore the basic responses that ethicists have given to decision making. Ethics focusing on laws, principles, contexts and situations will be briefly discussed. Henlee Barnette and Lewis Smedes will exemplify approaches using a combination of the preceding categories. From the Book of Romans we will consider a biblical example of decision making, using Paul as a model.

The second focus of the chapter will take note of some ethicists who major on community and character. James McClendon's ethics of narrative will serve as an example of this approach. A biblical parable of Jesus will also help us consider ethics of character. Finally, a conclusion will summarize the chapter.

Follow the Rules

One of the oldest and most basic approaches to decision making is the one which suggests that we follow the rules. For example, the writer of Ecclesiastes said, "Let us hear the conclusion of the whole matter: Fear God and keep his commandments: for this is the whole duty of man" (Eccl. 12:13, KJV). This would suggest that we are not left without specific guidance in the world. We are to follow God's laws. Rules (laws, commandments) were introduced early in the life of the people of God at Mount Sinai. The Lord said, "You are to perform my Judgments and keep My statutes, to live in accord with them, I am the Lord your God" (Lev. 18:4; cf. Deut. 7:11-13, NASB). This was followed by rules governing all areas of Hebrew life. The term *law* or *Torah* in Hebrew means "instruction" or "to teach." The Old Testament law was important because the Hebrews knew the God behind the law. God's word was authoritative. Since He had delivered them from Egypt, they were to be responsible to Him. The law involved a sense of accountability to the God who had delivered them.

Following God's revelation through His Word then is a means of decision making. We can call this law ethics or, as some prefer, prescriptive ethics. For many the Bible is the source of ethical wisdom and guidance. In this view, the Bible reveals God's will in the form of propositions or prescriptions.

Carl F. H. Henry wrote, "God has spoken clearly and propositionally to man in the Bible. Man has no trustworthy norm for moral behavior apart from revelation."[1] The norms in this view are objective and are not open to question. "Both the Old Testament and the New are very careful to define in great detail the content of Christian ethics."[2]

Even a person as certain as Henry about the ability to find specific guidance in the Bible is not unaware of the difficulties in this approach. He admitted that there is often a distinction between perpetual obligations (laws) and temporary rules.[3] The difficulty is in making distinctions between what is permanent and what is temporary. Who decides that? How can one make a distinction? We also are faced with differences of language and customs between the earliest recipients of God's laws and ours. The recipients of Scripture did not ask some of the questions about moral decision making that we are forced to ask. Their culture and practice eliminated many of the questions that face modern persons.

All that is to say that even the clearest commands of God have to be interpreted and applied. One danger of law ethics is that there have to be rules to interpret the rules. For example, in Jesus' day there was conflict over the Commandment, "Remember the sabbath day, to keep it holy" (Ex. 20:8, NASB). Certain interpreters of the law over the years had added their understanding to what the Commandment meant. Jesus had a different idea and was accused by scribes and Pharisees of misapplying and breaking the law (Mark 2:27-28). In turn, Jesus charged the scribes and Pharisees with missing the point of the Commandment.

Legalism is the temptation of law ethics. The external keeping of the law or rules can become more important than the main issues of life. As seen in the misuse of the sabbath Commandment the law of God, which was intended to be a blessing, can become a burden. In legalism, rule piled upon rule is often necessary to make room for exceptions that might arise. A casuistry develops which seeks to prescribe rules for every conceivable choice. External aspects of law keeping may neglect internal virtues and character development. The letter of the law may get in the way of the spirit of the law.

Principles for Decision Making

Another way of doing ethics is by using principles which act as guides to decision making. Principles are not as binding as laws. While principles point a person in the right direction, they do not always give specific guidance. The Bible, in this view, contains the answers to the basic needs of persons but does not always offer specific answers for an issue.[4]

Some ethicists use other terms for principles. Lewis Smedes used the term *command* or *commandments.* "My point of view is that the commandments are guides to grace-filled living, invitations to the good life within the grace of God."[5] Smedes found in the Ten Commandments guidelines for a basic human life-style.[6] He turned the negative "thou shalt nots" into positive commands. For example the Commandment, "Thou shalt not kill," becomes a principle to respect human life. The prohibition against adultery becomes a principle of respect for the sacredness of covenant.

Philip Wogaman in *A Christian Method of Moral Judgment* posited certain presumptions (principles) which give guidance to decision making. Those moral presumptions are built on a theological basis and, according to Wogaman, can help steer the Christian between perfectionism on the one hand and situationism on the other.[7] Wogaman's premise is that these presumptions serve as a basis for initial attitudes in decision making. Any deviation from what these presumptions affirm must bear the burden of proof.

The presumptions or principles which Wogaman listed as positive are: (1) the goodness of created existence, (2) the value of individual life, (3) the equality of persons in God, and (4) the unity of the human family in God.[8] Included in the decision-making process is the consideration of negative moral presumptions. These negative principles are human finitude and human sinfulness.[9] The negative presumptions are to remind decision makers of their own fallibility. Wogaman's model includes other presumptions (polar, ideological) which are to be included in the moral calculus which gives insights into ethical dilemmas.

Wogaman's basic thesis seems to be that the content of Christian ethics can be summed up in these principles. Decision making grows out of rational deliberation using these principles. The presumptions in Wogaman's system are to be consonant with God's kingdom of love and justice. However, Wogaman pointed out that one may decide that what is presumed to be the better or worse may not be so at all. In that case one must be free to follow actions outside those presumptions.[10]

Most principlists agree generally that the two primary principles of Christian ethics are love (*agape*) and justice. Mott emphatically wrote that "a Christian ethic, and with it a Christian basis for social action, obviously must be established in love."[11] The command to love God and neighbor forms the heart of the New Testament ethic. T. B. Maston called attention to the importance of love in the Christian life. "The crowning virtue and the guiding principle in every area of human relations should be love."[12] Love is both a virtue and a principle. It is a virtue in that it is a character trait of Spirit-filled individuals (Gal. 5:22). It is a principle in that it is commanded.

All of the Commandments and the teachings of the prophets depend on the law of love, according to Jesus (Matt. 22:36-40). That means that all the Commandments of the Old Testament would be fulfilled if one truly loved God and one's neighbor. Love is the true spirit behind the laws of God. Love is best defined for us in the self-giving, self-sacrificing life of Jesus Christ. In Him we see love in action and the nature of God revealed.

All the ethicists who can be defined as principlists insist on the primacy of love. Love, however, becomes problematic when attempts are made to translate it into social policy. Reinhold Neibuhr spoke of love paradoxically. He saw the command to love as an "impossible possibility." It is possible in that human beings have enormous potential in their being for becoming like their Heavenly Father. It is, nevertheless, impossible because of the persistence of human sin and finiteness. Neibuhr saw the value of the love command in that it keeps us in tension between what is and what ought to be. The love command serves both to judge us and to call us to a higher level.[13]

When Reinhold Neibuhr moved to talk about politics and economics or social ethics, he preferred to talk in terms of justice. Justice is the expression of love in society. Justice seeks to balance the claims of individuals and groups in society. It seeks to bring harmony through fairness and equity, thus, creating order. One can never say that justice fulfills all the demands of love, nevertheless it is a step in the right direction. Seeking justice, especially for those on the social, economic, and political bottom of society is one way to carry out what love motivates.

Beyond love and justice, principlists find other themes which are to be applied in decision making. These themes include freedom, crossbearing, obedience, hope, and faith. Such principles are used to make an intelligent analysis of concrete ethical decisions. As well the ingredients of reason and faith are included in principlists' methodology.

There is great variety within the family of those ethicists who fall under the umbrella of the principled approach. Some emphasize principles for the delineation of the proper goals or consequences. Paul Ramsey, on the other hand, wanted to emphasize the importance of right conduct. The goal or the consequences, in his mind, were not as important as how one does things. Principles are very useful in making decisions. Some of the perils of legalism can be avoided, and at the same time, the perils of subjectivism are omitted.

Relational Ethics

A third methodology for moral decision making can be called relational or contextual. This response-type ethic is not concerned so much with the good (the end) or the right (means) as with what is fitting.[14]

Contextualists shun principles or laws because they generally believe that what appears to be right in one context may be wrong in another. Rather than simply apply the rules or principles in a given context, one must seek to relate to the activity of God. For example, Bonhoeffer believed that the command of God cannot be heard and known apart from a concrete context. Richard Neibuhr posited the premise that God is acting in all actions upon you so you must respond to God's activity. For Neibuhr, God was present and acting as Creator, Governor, and Redeemer.[15] The Christian is to discern what God is doing and respond appropriately to God's activity. Decision making is not so much the issue here as is acting responsibly within the context of God's activity.

Paul Lehmann also stressed the relational motif in his contextual ethic. For him Christian thinking about ethics started from within the Christian *koinonia*. From the context of Christian community persons can ask, "What am I, as a believer in Jesus Christ and as a member of his church to do?"[16] God is in the process of creating conditions that make it possible to keep human life human. Christians are to join in what God is doing.

Relational ethics affirms that being in a relationship with God or others calls for responsibility to that relationship. Every relationship brings some obligations or claims with it. It is also true that persons should act faithfully to the demands engendered by that relationship. For the Christian, "right" is a relational matter; it is to value what God values.

Relational ethics has much to commend it. Love of God and a faith relationship to Jesus Christ provide a perspective on life that is positive. However, relational ethics does not provide much concrete help in the task of choosing among a variety of competing values and choices. Because of this, it has a relativistic aspect at its heart. This is inevitable as long as one maintains that ethical norms are to be derived from the particular circumstances in which decisions are to be made.

Situation Ethics

Situation ethics as taught by Joseph Fletcher is a step closer to antinomianism than contextual or relational ethics. Antinomians or existentialists see little or no connection between one moral moment of existence and another. Decisions are made in an impromptu manner with very little help from past actions or decisions. Professor Fletcher frequently stated, "In the utmost seriousness that Christian obligation calls for lies and adultery and fornication and theft and promise breaking and killing—sometimes, depending on the situation."[17] There was no normative principle of conduct which is universally and unexceptionally obliging, according to Fletcher.

Situation ethics posits love as the only absolute and intrinsic good. Love in Fletcher's language is "good will." Only love decides in each circumstance what is the right thing to do. Principles, maxims, or general rules may serve as illuminators for the decision maker. However, all of them may be rejected if love is better served by violating them. Only the end can justify the means. In deciding love's need, situational variables count every bit as much as laws or constraints. In this view circumstances may alter rules or constraints.

Paul Ramsey, in a devastating critique, charged that situational ethics has not a word to indicate that the Christian life has or can find any forecastable course.[18] This, in his opinion, meant that there is no way to distinguish situation ethics from antinomianism or existential situationism. Fletcher seems to have been too optimistic about the ability of human beings to be able to determine the most loving thing to do. Sin, repentance, faith, and the long heritage of the Christian community have little if any place in situation ethics. Fletcher reminded us, however, that rules do not always cover the circumstances of Christian decision making.

Let us now look at a couple of models in which a combination of some of these methods are used. First we will consider Henlee Barnette and then take a brief look at Lewis Smedes.

Two Examples of Decision Making

Henlee Barnette in his book *Exploring Medical Ethics* offered *contextual principled-agapism* as a model for decision making. A brief look at Barnette's model may give a useful example of how one may apply a method to contemporary decisions. First, the terms of the model. Barnette meant by contextual the whole background, situation, or environment to a happening.[19] Not only must the secular context be taken into account, but the context of faith is also important. For the Christian it is "faith working through love" (Gal. 5:6, NASB). Barnette insisted that ethics for the Christian must be tied to personal faith in Jesus Christ.

Barnette drew a clear distinction between principle and rule. Rules give specific guidance in a situation. Principles give direction like a compass. "Agapism" includes the idea of trust and obedience to God as well as the well-being of other humans. "Principled-agapism" is love expressing itself in basic principles which provide it with structure, concreteness, and direction.[20] Justice, truth, trust, care, forgiveness, servanthood, and fair play are just a few of the principles which help define love. Love may go beyond these principles but does not consider violating them unless they conflict with one another.

How did Barnette apply his contextual principled-agapism? We can see it at work in his discussion of physician-patient relations.[21] First of all, Barnette stressed the physician-patient relationship as a covenantal relationship in the sense of willing the well-being of the other. Love, then, would be the primary principle of relationship and action.

Several principles which would guide the physician and patient in covenant can be derived from *agape*. These include honesty, acceptance of responsibility for one's own health, and caring and trust between physician and patient. Both the professional insight and skills of the doctor and the patient's will to get well would be involved. The context of the patient's illness and the physician's skills calls for such a covenant relationship. Within the context of the patient's illness and the covenant relationship with the physician, decisions would be made regarding treatment. These decisions would draw from medical science and from the principles which structure love.

Barnette's method can be observed in his statements regarding euthanasia. he identified his position as *"Kalosthanasia,"* a death that is "morally right, dignified, and does not shock one's esthetic sense."[22] This position does not absolutely rule out either the passive or active method of dying. An openness to the patient and the circumstances help to make the decision. In citing examples, it becomes clear that Barnette would not favor the resuscitation of a hopelessly ill elderly patient. In some instances he would favor

all withdrawal of extraordinary treatment to keep a person alive
and give only drugs to ease the pain.[23] Efforts to keep a patient
alive, in this view, are legitimate as long as there is reasonable hope
for recovering with a decent quality of life.

Barnette's decision-making process, according to Ron Sisk,
consists of four actions: (1) a definition of the issue or problem,
(2) an analysis of relevant data, (3) application of theological
principles, and (4) specific guidelines.[24] There is a careful attempt
in Barnette's ethics to walk between legalism and a situationism
that is unprincipled. The guidance of the Holy Spirit and one's
own faith commitment are essential ingredients in Barnette's ethics.

Lewis Smedes ingeniously combined several of these approaches to moral decision making. In his book *Choices: Making Right
Decisions in a Complex World,* Smedes laid down the guidelines
for making solid decisions. While not putting the guidelines in a
specific Christian context, Smedes's own faith commitment shines
through. The guidelines advocated by Smedes are: sort out the
categories, face the facts, respect the rules, consider the consequences, and be responsible. Each chapter is filled with apt illus-
trations and questions which can help a person in the complexity
of moral decision making.

The final chapter in Smedes's book is the most provocative of
all: "Being Wrong Is Not All Bad."[25] It is a plea for humility, for
an awareness that one cannot always have the right answer or
know all the facts. Even the most mature among us are likely to
make mistakes and errors of judgment. An awareness of our sinful
humanity should keep us from being cocksure that what we're
doing is right. The best word of all, according to Smedes, was a
word of forgiveness. "Morality is the need to make right choices.
Forgiveness is the freedom to make wrong decisions."[26] This is a
helpful reminder that ultimately we are dependent upon the grace
of a loving God who "bears" us right or wrong.

A Word from Paul

The church has always had to deal with conflictual and controversial issues. Paul spent much of his time dealing with varied

controversies. Romans 14 presents us a glimpse of Paul's decision making. In Romans 12 thru 15, Paul laid down the ethical guidelines for Christian behavior. He summed up the moral law by admonishing that "he who loves his neighbor has fulfilled the law" (Rom. 13:8, NASB). Christians must "put on the Lord Jesus Christ" (v. 14, NASB) in order to protect themselves from the lust of the flesh.

Roman Christians seem to have been quarreling over three issues within their fellowship. Food (Rom. 14:2), observance of days (v. 5), and the drinking of wine (v. 21) were the causes of a rupture within the fellowship. Some seemed to have no scruples about food, wine, or failing to observe certain days. Others ate only vegetables, observed special days, and shunned alcoholic beverages. The problem was that some considered themselves to be superior Christians and set themselves apart from their weaker brothers and sisters.

Paul, speaking to the problem, used several principles that believers ought to consider in their relationship to one another. First, he warned them not to set themselves up as judges of others (Rom. 14:4,10,13). Only one person is ultimately qualified to judge—that is God. Instead of judging one another, believers are to remember that each one will be held accountable by God (v. 12). We are responsible for our own attitudes and not those of others.

Rather than judge one another Paul suggested that each one should determine "not to put any obstacle or a stumbling block in a brother's way" (14:13, NASB, cf. v. 21). This is obviously a principle growing out of love. Further, within the community of faith, believers are to pursue the things that lead to peace and that build up one another (v. 19).

Some have called Paul's ethic an ethic of accommodation. He called upon believers to give up behavior that in and of itself is not wrong in order to be supportive of other Christians. He used principles that can be applied in a number of contexts rather than laying down hard and fast rules. "It is good not to eat meat or to drink wine, or to do anything by which your brother stumbles" (v. 21, NASB) is a principle that leaves room for a variety of responses. Paul was willing to accommodate his own behavior for the well being of others. He also recognized that there may be different convictions on these issues (v. 22).

Paul was always concerned about the well-being of the church and the spread of the gospel. Personal rights and freedoms were to be subordinate to the good of the cause of Christ. To insist on one's rights might cause something that which is moral by itself to be spoken of as evil (v. 16). The kingdom of God is more than eating and drinking. It is righteousness, joy, and peace in the Holy Spirit.

This brief example taken from Romans is not to be seen as an exhaustive study of Paul's moral decisions making. Rather it is offered as one example of how Paul dealt with conflictual issues.

Now we must turn to a different set of considerations in ethical decision making. Our focus will be on the ethics of community and character.

Ethics of Community and Character

Some ethicists in recent years have sought to change the focus in ethics. From ethical methodologies built around decision making, attention has been given to ethics of character and community. This shift has occurred because of the realization that decisionism cannot give a complete enough account of the moral life. Too often, ethical decision making has ignored the self and its development. It has also failed to give adequate place to the role of the faith communities.

A person does not simply approach an ethical decision from a neutral stance. Rather each person brings the dispositions, experience, traditions, heritage, and virtues that he or she has cultivated. In other words, a person has character, which means that a person usually can be counted on to respond predictably. Character can be defined as that "basic moral orientation that gives unity, definition, and direction to our lives by forming our habits and intentions into meaningful and predictable patterns that have been determined by our dominant convictions."[27]

According to Willimon, character is formed in several conscious and unconscious ways. It is formed in a community or a social setting. The moral self is shaped ethically within the Christian context. What results from that community may or may not be useful. (Think of the churches which reinforced racial prejudice.) One cannot, however, isolate an individual from the community or society of which he or she is a part.

Because character is shaped by a community, the church must seek to be a community of faith and integrity. In fact, Hauerwas saw this as the first task of social ethics. "The first task of Christian social ethics, therefore, is not to make the 'world' better or more just, but to help Christian people form their community consistent with their conviction that the story of Christ is a truthful account of our existence."[28] If the church as a community is going to help shape Christian character, it must be a life-giving and life-affirming community. It must be a worshiping, witnessing, serving, growing community under the lordship of Jesus Christ.

Character is shaped in the second place by a lifelong cultivation of virtues.[29] Virtues are those habits which we practice until they are ingrained in our lives. Virtues become dispositional tendencies which give consistency to our being and doing. Paul continually urged his fellow Christians to get rid of destructive habits and put on new virtues. For example, in Colossians he urged:

> But now you must get rid of all these things: anger, passion, and hateful feelings. No insults or obscene talk must come from your lips. Do not lie to one another, for you have put off the old self with its habits and have put on the new self. So then, you must clothe yourselves with compassion, kindness, humility, gentleness, and patience. Be tolerant with one another and forgive one another (Col. 3:8-10,12-13, GNB).

If a person has grown up with the conviction and practice that lying is wrong, one can expect that habitually such a person is going to tell the truth. Each new situation will be approached with a strong disposition for truth telling. The decision to lie or to tell the truth basically will have been made. Virtues which become characteristic of persons are the fruit of the ethical life. Maturity is evidenced in that a person has practiced or cultivated a virtue until it becomes a part of her.

Christian character is formed by the sharing of the Christian vision.[30] A person's character is shaped by the way he or she sees things, by the vision they have. Vision is our perspective on the world and our perspective of how we see ourself in relation to the world. It is related to our sense of authority and our convictions.

For example, if I see the world as something to be shunned because it is evil, my response may be to surround myself with a Christian community. Withdrawal as much as possible from the world may become my style of life. If, on the other hand, I perceive (see) the world to provide opportunity for ministry and service then my life-style will be quite different. It all depends upon my vision and how I perceive the world.

Convictions form an important part of our vision. Convictions are deep-seated beliefs to be held on to tenaciously. We are usually willing to commit ourselves to something about which we have convictions. The community of faith helps to shape our vision as we experience its convictions. From our vision and convictions we shape our intentions toward the future. This is the map that charts our pilgrimage into what we will become in the future.

Besides the convictions of our own faith community, what else helps to shape our vision? This is an important question if we want to help people be moral. The Bible is an obvious answer to this question. Faithful study of the Word of God will help us to view God, the world, and persons in a new way. A careful study of the Bible will give new insights into our selves. It will also put us in contact with God's future for us in Jesus Christ.

Vision is also expanded by observing the lives of people who live out the faith in a unique and powerful way. In every generation, persons of vision inspire and motivate others. Often as we hear, encounter, or read about these persons there is something in our spirit that responds to their spirit. We may be changed because someone has helped us to see a new way.

The value of character ethics lies in the importance of paying attention to the formation of the moral self in its community and continuity.[31] It is a less individualistic way of doing ethics. By recognizing the moral self in community, there is more possibility for feedback and criticism. The narrative aspects in character ethics (which will be discussed next connects the decision maker with the whole people of God. Moral development is enhanced by the disciplines of worship, service, discipleship, and mission, which is the church's task. The loyalties and values of that fellowship must be passed on from one generation to another through the character of its members.

Narrative Ethics: A Model

James William McClendon in a significant book on ethics set forth a methodology which he calls narrative ethics. The book, *Systematic Theology: Ethics,* was written from the perspective of a "baptist" theology (McClendon insists on using the little *b*). According to McClendon, Christians are a people formed by their shared convictions and bound together by moral convictions about God and neighbor, self and community.[32] It is the task of ethics to reveal the structures of this shared life.

The phrase *narrative ethics* comes from the Bible's "realistic" or "history like" content. In the biblical narratives McClendon saw a coming together of the three elements that make up the structure of Christian morality. People experience the world in terms of their embodied selves, in their social setting of customs and practices, and in the eschatological aspect of faith.[33]

Ethics is to investigate, analyze, and criticize the way of life that makes up this story-formed community.

> Its task is the discovery, understanding, and creative transformation of a shared and lived story, one whose focus is Jesus of Nazareth and the kingdom he proclaims—a story that on its moral side requires such discovery, such understanding, such transformation to be true to itself.[34]

The effort to know this story and relate to it makes up "narrative ethics."

McClendon, by his emphasis on narrative, went to great pains to show that ethics cannot be reduced to propositions or principles. One cannot separate moral norms from the narrative or story in which they appear. The Christian ethic in this approach is a way of life. The Gospels were particularly important for McClendon. "The Gospels do convey moral teaching by identifying characters

(Jesus and the disciples) and a realm or setting (the coming kingdom)."[35] The gospel story unites these characters and the realm. As believers identify with the story, they receive moral guidance and hear the moral demand of the gospel. It becomes their story as they recognize the one they called Christ as Lord and acknowledge themselves to be among the disciples of the kingdom. "So to recognize, confess, be born into the kingdom is to take up the way of life called Christian: it is Christian morality."[36]

In a way that was more mystical than propositional, McClendon called for a recognition that the church now *is* the primitive church. The call of discipleship to Jesus' disciples is our call to discipleship. Jesus of Nazareth who taught, healed, loved, suffered, and died is the one who reigns now as the resurrected Christ. Commands addressed to Jesus' followers are directed to us. The story then and the story now are linked by the risen Lord.[37]

McClendon wished to take very seriously the historicity and the relevance of Jesus' life and teachings. By joining our lives to the ongoing story, we cannot dismiss the demands of His way of life. Loving enemies, forgiving one another, accepting suffering is what is expected from Jesus' followers. Discipleship means a life transformed and lived out in obedience to Him.

Rather than a lack of moral guidance, as some have maintained, narrative ethics offers a call to radical obedience in which the life and teachings of Jesus are normative. Rather than reducing Jesus' teachings to principles or values, costly witness is called for. It is to live in the liberty that the new age has dawned in Christ. What is necessary is an uncompromising commitment to Jesus' way of life in the here and now. It is to be a member of a community of faith that shares and lives out the vision of the new age.

T. B. Maston, seemed to be moving in the same direction in his book *To Walk as He Walked.* While not calling his ethic a narrative ethic, Maston did call attention to the fact that many Christians neglect the historic Jesus and the life He lived. According to Maston, the recurring question for us is, "How much do we walk as He (Jesus) walked?"[38] Much in the same fashion as McClendon, Maston said that Jesus' life-style was not only challenging to His original disciples but also is equally challenging to us. Maston found it inconceivable that Jesus could or would approve of a life-style which was incompatible with His life and teachings.

The narrative or story form of ethic can also be seen in Maston's call for a recovery of the nature and the character of the early Christian fellowship.[39] To call for a distinctive life-style modeled on Jesus is to take seriously McClendon's claim that this (today's church) is that (the primitive church). By emphasizing the life and teaching of the historic Jesus, and the necessity of being related to the risen Christ, Maston showed an awareness of the biblical story as our story. Another point that joins Maston with character ethics was his belief that the outward expression of the Christian's life will reflect what he or she is inwardly.[40] It was his way of saying that a person's character comes out in the day-to-day decisions and activities of a Christian.

We must not try too hard to force Maston into the character ethics or narrative ethics method. He has been considered a principlist over the many fruitful years of his teaching. Nevertheless, *To Walk as He Walked* emphasizes Christian morality as a way of life, not principles or values. Maybe we could say that the seed of narrative ethics were sown by Maston. (McClendon called him his "first and best teacher of ethics.")[41]

A Word from Jesus

Matthew 25 contains one of Jesus' most illuminating parables. It is the parable of the last judgment (vv. 31-46). The nations are separated by the Son of man, some on the left and some on the right. Those on the right are invited to inherit the kingdom of the Father which has been prepared for them. The reason for their reward is their faithfulness in ministering to the king. "For I was hungry, and you gave Me something to eat; I was thirsty, and you gave Me drink; I was a stranger, and you invited Me in; naked and you clothed Me; I was sick, and you visited Me; I was in prison, and you came to Me" (vv. 35-36, NASB).

Notice the surprise of the righteous, "Lord, when did we see you . . . ?" (v. 37, NASB). The King's response is "to the extent that you did it to one of these brothers of Mine, even the least of them, you did it to Me" (v. 40, NASB). Why is there surprise on the part of the righteous? Could it be that they have had no second thoughts about ministering to the hungry, thirsty, naked, imprisoned human beings with whom they came in contact? They had not given it a second thought because to do those things did not require a decision on their part. Ministry was simply a part of their nature.

To follow Christ *is* to feed the hungry, give drink to the thirsty, and visit those in prison. To do such is a result of Christian character. As the righteous went about their business and found opportunities to minister, they simply did what came naturally. William Booth of the Salvation Army recognized the reason for this kind of action. Speaking about the poor and needy, he said, "If these people are to believe in Jesus Christ, become the servants of God, and escape the miseries of the wrath to come, they must be helped out of their present social miseries.[42]

It was hard for him to imagine how Christians could see the plight of the needy and ignore them. How could they do anything else?

People can do many other activities. They can go about their daily lives without seeing those who are in need. It is possible to live one's life without an awareness that the poor, lonely, and hungry are the brothers and sisters of Christ. This seems to be the surprise of those on Jesus' left. They saw the same needs as the righteous, but did nothing to alleviate them. In the end, it was clear that they did not belong to Christ. "And these will go away into eternal punishment, but the righteous into eternal life" (Matt. 25:46, NASB).

A Christian is not someone who decides to participate in Live Aid or Farm Aid now and then. A Christian is one who walks in the footsteps of the One "who went about doing good" (Acts 10:38, NASB). "The good man out of the good treasure of his heart brings forth what is good" (Luke 6:45, NASB). That is the very essence of being a Christian.

Conclusion

In this chapter we have looked at various methodologies for Christian decision making. Laws, principles, relationships, and the context of decision making were considered in the first part. Examples of a particular methodology was illustrated from Henlee Barnette and Lewis Smedes. An illustration from the Bible was taken from Romans 14.

Beginning with the section on character ethics, questions were considered which are prior to decision making. James McClendon was used as an example of one who eschews decisionism and prefers to emphasize narrative ethics. Finally, a brief look at Matthew 25 considered the fruit of Christian character.

Have we settled the issue of Christian decision making? Can we give a definitive nod to either the ethics of doing or the ethics of being? Do we have to choose, for instance, Barnette or McClendon? Obviously, the answer is no to all of the questions. If we could solve ethical issues simply, books like this one would be unnecessary. The fact is ethical decision making is a complex process. It involves an understanding of the self and its formation. The history of the people of God is revealed in Scripture adds to the mix. Contextual consideration informed by the social sciences and other disciplines are valuable decision-making allies. The perfectionism of Jesus' ethics must be taken seriously as we heed His call to discipleship. Out of these factors and others, the servant of God is equipped to walk in a manner worthy of their calling in Christ Jesus (Eph. 4:1).

Notes

1. Carl F. H. Henry, *Personal Ethics* (Grand Rapids: Eerdmans), p. 245.

2. Ibid., p. 258.

3. Ibid., p. 267.

4. T.B. Maston, *Why Live the Christian Life?* (Nashville: Broadman Press, 1974), p. 58.

5. Lewis Smedes, *Mere Morality* (Grand Rapids: Eerdmans, 1983), p. 14.

6. Ibid., p. 12.

7. Philip Wogaman, *A Christian Method of Moral Judgement* (Philadelphia: The Westminster Press, 1977), p. 40.

8. Ibid., pp. 62-104.

9. Ibid., pp. 106-110.

10. Ibid., p. 237.

11. Stephen Mott, *Biblical Ethics and Social Change* (New York: Oxford University Press, 1982), p. 42.

12. Maston, p. 154.

13. Reinhold Niebuhr, *An Interpretation of Christian Ethics* (New York: Meridian Books, 1959), pp. 109-112.

14. Edward LeRoy Long, Jr., *A Survey of Christian Ethics* (New York: Oxford University Press, 1967), p. 118.

15. H. Richard Niebuhr, *The Responsible Self* (New York; Harper and Row, 1963), pp. 27 *ff.*

16. Paul Lehmann, *Ethics in a Christian Context* (New York: Harper and Row, 1963), p. 124.

17. Joseph Fletcher, "Situation Ethics," *Toward Authentic Morality for Modern Man* (Nashville: Christian Life Commission Proceedings, 1970), p. 18.

18. Paul Ramsey, *Deeds and Rules in Christian Ethics* (New York: Scribner, 1967), p. 152.

19. Henlee Barnette, *Exploring Medical Ethics* (Macon, Ga.: Mercer University Press, 1982), p. 2.

20. Ibid., p. 23.

21. Ibid., pp. 31-40.

22. Ibid., p. 130.

23. Ibid., p. 131.

24. Ron Sisk, "The Ethics of Henlee Barnette: A Study in Methodology" (Unpublished Ph.D. dissertation, The Southern Baptist Theological Seminary, 1980), pp. 173-181.

25. Lewis Smedes, *Choices: Making Right Decisions in a Complex World* (San Fransicso: Harper and Row, 1986), p. 115.

26. Ibid, p. 121.

27. William Willimon, *The Service of God* (Nashville: Abingdon Press, 1983), p. 28-29.

28. Stanley Hauerwas, *A Community of Character* (Notre Dame: University of Notre Dame Press, 1981), p. 10.

29. Willimon, p. 32.

30. Ibid., p. 34.

31. Ibid., p. 35.

32. James McClendon, *Ethics: Systematic Theology* (Nashville: Abingdon, 1986), p. 62.

33. Ibid., p. 66.

34. Ibid., p. 332.

35. Ibid., p. 346.

36. Ibid.

37. Ibid., p. 332.

38. T. B. Maston, *To Walk as He Walked* (Nashville: Broadman Press, 1985), p. 9-11.

39. Ibid., p. 91.

40. Ibid.

41. McClendon, p. 63.

42. General William Booth, *In Darkest England and the Way Out* (Hapeville, Ga.: Tyler and Company, 1942), p. 266.

5

The Church and the World

Bob E. Adams

Explore with me what the Bible teaches about the relationship between the church and the world. Since the church does not appear in the Old Testament, how can we do this? We can by using the terms, *people of God* or *community of God*. The people of God, the community of God, in the Old Testament were the Hebrews. The people of God, the community of God, in the New Testament was the church.

God created both communities. From Abram, God began to form the people called the Hebrews. Later, they were called the Jews. From Jesus of Nazareth, He began to form the church. God was the author of both. He set the rules for both. He gave to each its goals. He related to both in special ways. He walked alongside both in their journeys. Each was formed from within larger communities which were called the *world*.

Now we can talk about the Hebrews and the world which surrounded them, and the church and the world which surrounded it. Later, we can talk about different groups which called themselves churches and the world which surrounded them. Finally, we can talk about ourselves and the world which surrounds us. In each case, the *world* is made up of other groups of people, other communities, with their rules and goals, their ways of relating to each other, and their ways of relating to God's special people. These other people, who made up the world, also had some relationship to God. They had not been abandoned by Him when he formed His special people. The same thing is true today regarding the world's peoples. For example, when Paul preached at Athens, he told the Greeks that they worshiped God "ignorantly." Even though a group of people might not worship at all, they are still part of God's creation, and He relates to them as Creator to creation, even if not as Redeemer to redeemed.[1]

The Hebrews and Their World

The Hebrews were aware of the world which surrounded them because they were aware of themselves through the identity God gave them. They knew the world by first knowing themselves. The Hebrews had a life-and-death struggle, but it was not primarily with the world. It was with themselves over becoming what and who God wanted them to be. In this struggle, they saw that the world behaved in ways that God did not want them to behave. They saw that the world believed things that they could no longer believe and remain true to what God revealed to them.

The Hebrews had a special relationship with God. Unfortunately, it was all too easy for them to forget that God had chosen them out of grace, not because they were special or unusually deserving. Their relationship to God and His revelations to them determined their relationship to the world.[2] Let us look at some of those relationships.

A relationship of identity.—These people's self-identity was established and increasingly defined by God's calling.[3] Their identity in relationship to geography, the land, was defined by God Himself as He gradually directed them to the special land which He had chosen for them.

A relationship of rules and norms.—Long before Moses, God began to reveal rules by which He wanted His people to live. But these became much more explicit during the time of Moses. The Ten Words, Ten Commandments, formed a kind of constitution by which the people were to live. The first four (in the numbering given by the Jews) had to do with their relationship to God. These spelled out basic duties in worshiping God. The fifth formed a kind of bridge between their upward look toward God and their horizontal look toward family and neighbors.

A relationship of names and words.—The Hebrews understood that words had power and must not be misused. Misusing God's name, that is, using it for selfish purposes to call down a blessing on oneself, on one's friends or families, or to call down a curse on one's enemies, was always against God's will and purposes.

Image relationships.—Images for God were verbal and not visual. The only allowable visual image was one that God Himself had made: human beings. God wanted no other visual image to remind His people of Himself, and this image was definitely not to be worshiped!

Time relationships.—Some times were specifically set aside to spend primarily with family, to enjoy one another's company, and to meditate on God. These times were called "rests," sabbaths. Some were as short as a day. Others were as long as a year and in such a special case as the "Jubilee" may have been two years long.[4]

God-parent-child relationships.—These relationships formed a kind of bridge between two sets of Commandments, the first four and the last five. We have to remember that these Commandments were not given to children, but to adults. Those adults were supposed to honor their more aged parents. Children of those adults learned to honor them in the same way that they saw them honoring their aging or aged parents.

In a real sense, parents represented God because, in the structure of the Hebrew people, parents were the ones who instructed their children about God. If the parents failed in this duty, God had established no other way for children to learn of Him.

Human life.—No human on his own initiative was permitted by God to take the life of another. No individual was worth more than another.

Husband-wife relationships.—Sexual relationships within marriage were to be with one's spouse only. This husband-wife relationship also reflected how God felt about Israel and how He would treat her: as though she were His wife!

"Things."—Land, animals, garments, cooking utensils, and the right of an individual or family to possess them were regulated by God. Taking a thing that another human possessed, by force, by stealth, or by misrepresentation was prohibited by God.

Truth.—Lying was also prohibited by God. The language of this Commandment refers specifically to a court of law. If the truth were not told in court, no one, especially rulers-judges, could ultimately be trusted.

Inner correspondence to outer rules.—Desiring something or someone that was already possessed by someone else, with the intention of taking that thing or person away from its possessor, was also prohibited. This is the only Commandment which deals with intention or desire and not with an observable act.

Besides these Ten Words which formed the rules or norms by which God wanted His people to live, God also gave to His people certain goals. The primary goal was that they, in their behavior, should reflect God's behavior. In that way, they would become more and more "made in God's image." Also, other peoples who did not know God fully could come to know Him better by observing His people's behavior. This goal-oriented behavior, coupled with the rules by which they lived, distinguished the Hebrew people. When asked why they lived that way, their answer was to be, "Because this is the way God wants us to live. This is the way He is."

Sometimes the Hebrews obeyed. At other times they rebelled. God never abandoned them. Even His punishment was corrective and redemptive. God's goal for them was that they should grow to be like him: "You shall be holy; for I the Lord your God am Holy" (Lev. 19:2, RSV). To the extent that they obeyed, they would be a blessing to other peoples who did not know God as they did. Their very living would be a missionary force.[5]

The Early Church and Its World

The church was first formed among Jews (descendants of the Hebrews of Old Testament times) who followed Jesus of Nazareth and who believed that He was God's Anointed One, the Messiah/ Christ. They trusted that in Him God was fulfilling all the promises that He had ever made, both to the Hebrews and to all other peoples. Their intention, in the way lived, was simply to obey the Christ. Soon non-Jews, Gentiles, began to form part of the church and became a vital part of its life.[6]

That new life was radically and drastically different. It was also costly. In four areas the church was different from the world.

Primary loyalty.—The church's first loyalty was to the Christ and to fellow believers. This meant that a new community came into being. Its intention was not, first of all, to be different from other communities. Its first intention was simply to be itself. Its norms and rules, its goals, worked out of its relationship to and loyalty to Jesus, its Lord.[7]

Family.—The desire of every follower of Jesus was that his or her own father and mother, sisters and brothers, wife or husband, children and all other human family members, would also become followers of Jesus. They could not be coerced because that was not the way faith worked. But if a choice had to be made between being loyal to the Lord, Jesus, or following what human families dictated, believers were to follow the Lord. In any case, the new community, the church, became family. Doubly blessed was the follower of Jesus whose human family also became part of his or her spiritual family.

State.—Only one overarching political system existed in the time of the early church: the Roman Empire. Jewish followers of Jesus experienced conflict between their loyalty to the Jewish faith and its political expression and what the Roman Empire often demanded of them. For the followers of Jesus who had never been Jews, the empire was the only political reality they had known, and somehow they had to relate to it.

Could there be conflict between what their new faith in Jesus as Lord and the community of that faith, the church, asked and what the empire might demand? The answer was found in what the empire demanded.[8] Christians everywhere were urged by their spiritual guides to pray that God might bless all governing authorities. Christians were also urged to obey the same authorities, as long as what the authorities demanded was not contrary to what God, in Jesus, wanted. Each demand would have to be weighted by itself, to see if it was in accord with Jesus' precepts.

Economics.—God guided His people of the Old Testament in their use of material goods. He also guided His people of the New Testament in their use of material possessions. Not much new was added to the Old Testament teachings about possessions. In both cases, as long as anyone in the community had anything to eat,

everyone had something to eat. Things were to be used for the
benefit of all. No one could claim exclusive right to anything that
he possessed. There was no sophisticated theory of economics, no
primitive capitalism nor primitive communism. The church was
not trying to lay down rules for society in general. It was attempting to live out God's rules as they applied to material goods.

History After the Early Church

The church had to live in the world. It did not have to follow
the patterns of the world. The world believed in many gods. The
church confessed that there was only One and that He had made
Himself known in many ways to and through the Hebrews. The
church also staked its very life in its conviction that God had made
Himself known supremely in the person of Jesus of Nazareth; but
the church also wanted all the people of the world to share this
conviction. Therefore, it had to proclaim the good news in the way
its members lived and talked.

Three Centuries of Proclamation (AD 100-400).

The church witnessed. The world listened. It also persecuted.
Some people believed and became part of the church. The church
had a clear definition of itself; the world had a clear definition of
itself. A person could not live at the same time by the norms of
the world and by those of the church, as though those norms were
automatically the same.

Families in the world abandoned their unwanted babies on the
town dumps. The head of the family, according to Roman Empire
law, could banish or have killed any unwanted newborns.

The emperor was the head (*Pontifex Maximus*) of the official
religion. Every state official, especially those in the military, had
to swear ultimate allegiance to him.

The empire sustained itself on the institution of slavery. It was
always greedy for more land and more people; for on them it lived.

The empire was orderly. It functioned by laws, which were
inexorably enforced. Its laws determined, first of all, each human
being's place in a class-structured society. Then, when any law

was broken, the penalty for the guilty person varied according to the class to which he belonged.

Such was the world in which the church found itself. Its norms and rules were different. Some of its members had dual citizenship: in the kingdom of Heaven and in the Roman Empire. As long as the two did not conflict, Christians obeyed the laws of the empire as well as those of the kingdom. When they did conflict, the penalty for disobeying the empire's laws could be death.

Twelve Centuries of Accommodation and Adjustment (AD 400-1500)

The Roman Empire was in trouble.[9] It needed loyal defenders. Christians had always prayed for political leaders, even when those same leaders persecuted Christians. But Christians had not been willing to defend the empire with lethal force. However, some Christian leaders began changing their minds about the use of force to defend the frontiers of the empire. This change of mind was related to change in theology that defined how one became a Christian and the very definition of *Christian.*

Sacramentalism, sacerdotalism, and Christendom. Gradually many Christians came to believe that every person, when born, was headed for endless perdition. Even newborns were "lost." The church also came to believe that salvation was not truly initiated until a person was baptized.[10] These two beliefs were somehow combined. The result was that the church wanted to baptize every person as soon after birth as possible. Whether at a later time that person would consciously accept or reject the Christian faith was a bridge to be crossed at that time. The church also believed that it was the only agent of salvation. The church came to believe also that a person participated in salvation by taking communion, which could only be celebrated by an official representative of the church.

As a result of these beliefs, the church had increasing numbers of members who had never made any personal commitment to Jesus Christ as Lord and Savior. It became extremely difficult to distinguish between church members and nonchurch members, as far as beliefs and loyalties were concerned. The world was successfully invading the church.

The world, in the form of the Roman Empire, also needed the support of the church in its defense of empire territory. By this time, people in the church in the empire were identifying and confusing empire with church. They believed that in defending one they were also defending the other. Church had been given a geographic definition: to be born within this territory meant that one had also been baptized. To be baptized meant that one was a Christian.[11]

Many people outside the empire, who were attacking it, also believed themselves to be Christians. So, "Christians" were attacking and killing other "Christians" in the name of Christ.

Finally, the empire and its "Christians" won out over the heathen (who, in many cases, also were "Christians"). The empire "Christians" believed that they formed the kingdom of God. Thus, the church saw no conflict between the kingdom of God and the empire. The conflict was between the Christian Empire and all other empires.

In this way, sacramentalism (the idea that baptism gave entrance into salvation and that the Lord's Supper provided necessary sustenance in salvation) was coupled with sacerdotalism (the idea that the church, through its representatives, the priests, provided the only door to legitimate baptism and continuing salvation). These two were combined with the idea of Christendom (a political and geographic concept of Christianity). The results of this particular combination of theology and ethics was disastrous for the Christian faith.

Christendom in action. From the fourth century AD until the sixteenth, this geographic concept of Christianity generally prevailed in Europe. There were always individuals and groups who did not accept the concept or who believed that their geography and its church was the correct one and all others were to be combated. The principal thrust in Europe was that of a geographically defined Christianity.

One response to the problems that Christendom presented was to withdraw from contract with the world into either an individualism or an enclave, living there by "Christian" rules.[12] Thus, monasticism offered an escape from the low ethical level that the majority of Christendom lived on; at the same time, it did not condemn as wrong the concept of Christendom. The various monastic orders saw themselves as lighthouses, as islands of true Christian living. Indeed, in many cases, they did keep learning, reading, and writing alive in a largely illiterate world.

Islam became the principal threat to geographic Christianity. The peoples and lands who fell under Islam's dominion many times were better off physically than many people in "Christian" lands. The physical sciences, medical arts, and philosophy flourished in Islamic territories. Spain succumbed. Eastern Europe fell. Europe itself was threatened. The military aspect of that threat was finally staved off.

But the threat was not merely military. In the realm of ideas and philosophy and theology and ethics, Thomas Aquinas successfully defended geographic Christianity and its concepts. He was so successful that the Roman Catholic Church, foremost proponent of geographic Christianity, felt no need to change his basic concepts. Rather, it developed his concepts rigorously.

Three Kinds of Reformation (AD 1500-Present)

Many Christians became increasingly dissatisfied with the status quo. Their reasons for dissatisfaction varied from theological to political to ethical.

Three kinds of reform manifested themselves.[13] One was headed by leaders like Martin Luther and John Calvin. The second was effected by the dominant church itself. The third did not have individual founders as did the first. It was more a peoples' movement.

Magisterial Reform. Martin Luther and John Calvin represent one kind of reform. At first, they might have been satisfied if the Roman Catholic Church had made drastic changes in its theology and practices that depended on that theology. However, they began changes so deep-seated that separation was necessary. These changes were primarily theological. There were some changes in ethics, particularly in the area of family. Calvin's reform also led to changes in the way his followers related to economics.

What these two Reformers, and others like them, did not change was the way their churches related to the world. This world was primarily the political organization, the state. The Roman Catholic Church had developed the doctrine that the church should be the conscience of the state and should guide the state in all matters that had to do with salvation. In the final analysis, nearly all matters relating to state and everything else had to do with salvation.

According to this viewpoint, the state should enforce all the "spiritual" advice of the church with coercion and physical force when necessary. Neither Calvin nor Luther abandoned this doctrine. Each believed that there could be such a thing as a Christian state and that all the citizens of that state could be Christians, or at least they should be made to behave as though they were Christians. Ultimately, there would be no room in either a Calvinistic or Lutheran state for a person or a group that persistently and willfully rejected the Christian faith. The idea of Christendom, of geographic Christianity, prevailed with Calvin and with Luther.

Lutheran and Calvinistic reformers are sometimes called Magisterial Reformers. This is because they believed that they needed to depend on the magistrate (state power, or state officials) to defend and protect their church. They also believed that the magistrate could and ought to depend on the church to keep certain citizenship records and should authenticate those records to the state when asked to do so.

For instance, when a baby was born, he would be baptized and a record kept of his birth and baptism. The baptism and recording were done by the church. In that way, the baby began the Christian life and became a citizen of the state at the same time. Babies who were not baptized and whose births were not recorded in such a way were not citizens. The "state church," whether Roman Catholic, Lutheran, or Calvinistic (or, in England, Anglican) had this responsibility.

Also, when a couple decided to marry, both the ceremony and the recording of the marriage was done by the church. Any "marriage" not so done and recorded was not considered legally or theologically a valid marriage.

In addition, when a person died, the death was recorded by the church and the burial made in a church cemetery. The death record was also the official state record. Any person not buried that way could have had his estate confiscated so that his heirs could not claim it.

The three cases just mentioned were common practice in those states or territories where the system of Magisterial Reform prevailed. If any other kind of church were formed, it simply would not be recognized by the state. Therefore, citizenship rights of the church members would be lost, one could not legally be married, and any property one might accumulate could finally be confiscated.

Roman Catholic counterreform. The Roman Catholic Church began its own kind of reform which, from the perspective of ethics, consisted of little more than trying to consolidate its position and power. It corrected some of the ills that its own clergy considered to be abuses. The position and power of the pope was consolidated.

The third way. There was a third reform.[14] Until recently, it has either been ignored or belittled. Many small groups were part of it. It has been called the Radical Reform movement or believers' church. Among those small groups in Europe were the Anabaptists and Mennonites. Some of the early Baptists in England were very much like the Anabaptists and Mennonites in their view of the relationship that should exist between the church and the state. That view went something like the following.

A person became a Christian as a result of personal decision. That decision consisted of repenting of one's sins and voluntarily trusting Jesus as Christ, Lord and Savior. The decision itself was a result of God's grace coming to the person. In the same way that one voluntarily accepted Christ as Lord and Savior, the voluntarily decision was made to identify publicly with a group of those who believed the same way. Public identification was through baptism. Consequently, a church formed along these lines was a "believers' church."

The concept of Christendom was foreign and repugnant to this

kind of reform. In it, the state had no task either in the propaga-
tion or maintenance of Christian faith. True faith could not be
obliged nor coerced into existence. Neither could such faith be
maintained by legal obligation or coercion. In God's design, state
and church had different functions, which were not to be mixed.
Where the demands of the state did not conflict with the claims
of conscience, the state was to be obeyed.

The Radical Reformers, when they thought of Christian conscience, did not think primarily of it as a result of individual effort
alone, but rather as a common effort of all believers as they col-
laborated voluntarily in the reformation of their consciences. Conscience formation was the task of the church as it responded to
God. Radical Reformers were not anarchists, although the other
Reformers many times thought that they were.

Because the Roman Catholic Church, as well as the other Reformers' churches, both Lutheran and Calvinistic, wanted only
their kinds of Christians in the territories that they either ruled or
advised, people like Anabaptists and Mennonites were forced to
leave. They became wanderers. They moved farther westward, to
Canada, to the United States, and to South America.

Some contact was made between English Baptists and
Mennonite-Anabaptists in Holland in the early seventeenth century, and perhaps intimate contact even earlier in England. Early
Baptists in England had their own distinct beginnings and received somewhat different treatment from their government.
However, their ideas about believers and believers' churches were
very similar to Anabaptists and Mennonite ideas.

It is easy to understand why the Radical Reformers' churches
often felt persecuted by other churches: They were persecuted!
Since the Magisterial Reform churches did not consider the Radical Reformation churches to be churches at all, most of the time
the Radicals' churches were declared illegal. People attending
them were often jailed. Some of them were killed.

Radical Reformers took Jesus' words in the Sermon on the
Mount quite literally. Consequently, they did not believe that a
person could be a "magistrate" (official representative of the state)
and conscientiously be a member of a believers' church at the same

time. All the nation-states in Europe during the seventeenth century were called "Christian states" and enforced by law their interpretation of the Christian faith. They would not allow any other interpretation within their borders.

For the European Reformation churches, the world that surrounded them called itself Christian. Radical Reformers could not agree that it was, indeed, Christian. Eventually most English Baptists came to share this negative opinion of the world, although never quite so strongly. The treatment they received in the land of their physical birth was not as harsh as that suffered by the European Baptists.

In the early history of British colonies in North America, Baptists were often treated in the same way as their Radical Reformation brothers had been treated in Europe. One colony, Rhode Island, was founded with the purpose of giving refuge to those who could not accept the idea of the state church. While other colonizers accepted land from the British crown as gifts or contracted with the crown to secure titles to their colonies' lands, the founders of Rhode Island bought the land from its inhabitants, the Indians. Then the colonizers secured a legal right to it from the English crown. Rhode Island's founders did not want Indians to be treated as they had been treated. They wanted all people to have the same rights that they wanted for themselves.

For many years, the colonists disagreed over the place of a church in the political organization of the colony. As some of the colonies formed themselves into the United States, one of the bitterest struggles was over this question. And although the Bill of Rights settled most church-state questions for the federal government, many individual states continued with an official state church relationship for decades.

Differences in Ideas: Church and State Relationships

When the idea of *world* is thought of in terms of *state*, there is a clear difference between the thoughts and practices of the Radical Reformers on the one hand and the Magisterial Reformers and the Roman Catholic Church on the other hand. The Radical Reformers, believing that faith could not be coerced and that response to God had to be voluntary and free of human restraint, never believed that state support of a church or church support of a state could be right. Separation of church and state is a necessary consequence of this belief. Other Reformers evidently could not conceive that a church could flourish nor maintain itself without such support. Not only that, they evidently believed that a state and a church should mutually support each other as institutions.

In many Latin American and Eastern European countries where neither the Roman Catholic Church nor some form of Magisterial Reform church has ever had to face Radical Reform concepts, separation of church and state has never come about as a result of what Christians have sought. It has become reality in some areas as a result of other political or ideological pressures, as has happened in Russia and in China.

Other Historical Examples

Since the time of the Reformation in the 1500s, other Christian groups have arisen. One is the Methodist Church. As with Luther in Germany, neither John nor Charles Wesley originally envisioned the formation of another church. They simply wanted to organize methodically heartfelt religion. In the United States many other Christian groups have organized themselves as churches. In many cases, the new organizations were due more to personality conflicts among strong leaders than to doctrinal or ethical differences. Although such churches generally began their organized lives taking for granted the idea of a believers' church, many times they have not thought through all its implications.

However, with the advent of Pentecostal, or Holiness groups, in the early 1900s, another kind of reformation seems to have occurred. Most of these groups apparently arose to meet a need in the area of either personal experience or worship patterns. They include what some church historians see as a twentieth-century extension of the sixteenth-century Reformation. These groups are growing faster than most others. What their ideas are about the world has not been resolved. At first, they defined *world* in negative terms of activities in which a true Christian would not indulge. Drinking alcoholic beverages, dancing, and other forms of amusement were taboo. But they did not see *world* as *state*. They have tended to understand the relationship between church and state much as did the Magisterial Reformers and have seemed to believe that there can and should be a "Christian state." However, there are significant exceptions to this unconscious acceptance of a Magisterial Reformation view of a "Christian state."

The Present Situation

Television has spawned the "electronic church," and it is the specialty of preachers and groups with either Baptist or Pentecostal leanings. Television Christianity is passive, with two exceptions: money and political participation.

Probably few people who contribute to the electronic church give large sums of money at any one time. Like other mass-marketed products, small contributions/small profit margins make large totals when volumes of these small contributions are received.

During the 1970s, and more so in the 1980s, the real power of the electronic church has manifested itself in political influence, in its relationship to the state. This is the very area in which the Radical Reformers took a costly and opposite stand. It is also the area in which the newer, Pentecostal-type television churches are historically unaware or ignorant.

The mass media, particularly television, does not lend itself to a rational analysis of issues. Electronic church leaders are masters at evoking prejudgments, the way people deep down already feel about issues. The medium itself determines how the message can be presented, and it comes across on a feeling level. Electronic church leaders are also masters at compiling mailing lists of those whose prejudices have been evoked and at using those lists for many purposes. One such purpose is to construct a profile of the kind of religious or political leader whom many people in their subconscious want. Then they can tailor a projection of a person who fits that profile.

How the new "electronic church" will affect Christian ethics and theology, we do not yet know. The concept of "mass Christianity" is closely akin to the concept of "mass media." Mass Christianity has never been a concept acceptable to Radical Reformation thinking, unless each one of the mass has made some kind of personal commitment in a rather small group setting. That setting has always been on a face-to-face basis.

Issues: New and Old

In this chapter, we have ignored the relationship of church to family and to economic relationships. Concentration has been on world as state, as politics. Obviously, real life is not like that. All that we do and think relates to everything else that we do and think. Life is really a seamless garment. We cannot tear pieces of it off in order to examine individual relationships.

The most important issue for a Christian is his relationship with God through Jesus Christ. Since the knowledge of God through Jesus Christ came to the person through a community, the nature of that community is crucial. The relationship, the knowledge, and the community are linked together like life. That community is church.

Identity Crisis

Before any definition of world can be given, the church must first discover its own identity. As with Israel of old, self-knowledge and self-identity preceded world knowledge and world identity. Self-knowledge and self-identity grew out of relationship with God. That relationship was established in God's way, not in Israel's nor the church's. Israel had no identity before God began to form her. He took the initiative, and identity began to take shape. So it was, and is, with the church. It did not exist before God called it into being.

Foundational Crisis

The first task of the church is that of knowing its own foundation document: Scripture. Knowing and studying is not only a task for the pastor and the seminary or university but also for every member of the church. Each needs to know the Book for his own sake. He needs to know for the sake of, for the health of, the church. He needs to know for the sake of the world. With this knowledge, identity begins to shape itself.

Another knowing task of the church is to know history. What happened in the past between church and world? This is not just the task for the specialist. It is for everyone. The individual who does not know his own family past cannot easily have self-identity. The same is true spiritually. Church members need to know their spiritual genealogy, both in its widest and in its narrowest senses.

The church has the task of teaching this document and this history to the children of its members. Such knowledge will not make them Christians. But it will help them to know what the real alternatives are when the time comes for them to make the crucial decision voluntarily.

We-They Crisis

In a sense, what we have been talking about is a we-they situation. What the church should want is that all people, and every individual within those people who is capable of making a real decision, become a part of the *we* of the church. This is the essential missionary identity of the church.

A problem arises when they hear and see the message but do not receive the message. What should be the attitude of the church in this case? It must be open to those who reject the gospel. Our tendency is to reject those who have rejected us. This tendency is not in keeping with the gospel. The church does not know everything. It cannot know when or if it is too late for an individual or a people, as long as they are in this life. Thus, any church or any Christian would be highly presumptious to write off a person because at a given time that person rejected the gospel offer.

Options and Alternatives

The church is not by its nature an enemy of the world. Once the church has its own identity, its relationship to the world is largely marked off by the world. This does not necessarily mean that the church has been passive; but it has always begun with a response mode. Historically, church and world have worked out three basic alternative relationships.

Enmity

The world really did want to rid itself of the church. The fierce persecutions of Christians in the earliest centuries of the history of the church, military opposition to Christendom in the heyday of the Crusades, the opposition of the world of Christendom to groups like Mennonites and Anabaptists in Europe in the sixteenth and seventeenth centuries, the opposition of other religions to any kind of Christianity during the modern missionary movement, the antagonism of most kinds of Marxism to Christendom, and, indeed, to most kinds of Christianity illustrate the first possible alternative: antagonistic relationships. Enmity emanating from the world was fierce, and many times it was reciprocated by the church.[15]

Identification

A second alternative is identification. In this way, the church sees itself and the world as heading in the same direction, with basically the same set of guidelines and loyalties. All the world needs is guidance and a good example. Individual Christians, and perhaps even the church, should lead the way. From the world's perspective, it can hardly object to another group's existence when that other group shares the same norms, ideals, and goals as those it proposes. Modern Protestant ecumenical ethics is a contemporary example of this alternative, as were (and are, where found) the many kinds of Christendom that began during the time of the Magisterial Reformation.

Accommodation

The third alternative has been some kind of accomodation between church and world. They might coexist on different levels or planes. This was basically the thought of Thomas Aquinas, although some interpretations of Thomism have not gone in the same direction. Or, one might dominate the other, as the Roman Catholic Church has dominated the areas where it has not had to face a Reformation movement, such as in Latin America. In Eastern Europe the Orthodox Church has been dominated by the world (state).

Conclusion

If the church is conscious of its own identity, secure in its voluntary, uncoerced faith in God as revealed in Jesus Christ, it first of all does not desire enmity with the world. Neither does it identify itself with the world to the extent that it loses its own identity. It must, in some sense, accommodate itself to the world. That is, historical reality is such that church and world occupy the same planet. What does this mean in practical terms?

It means that the church is open to the world and to the people of the world. It is open to the world's hurts, worries, and injustices. What the world suffers, in a sense the church suffers also. The church has no secrets. What it does have, the message of salvation, it shares gladly. And it seeks to live by the entire gospel.

This does not necessarily mean that the world is open to the church. But the church by its very nature must be open to the world. Historically, the world has always sought to influence the church. If the church is open to the world, it also opens itself to being influenced by the world.

Since the church is open to the world, and receives people (repentant, faith-exercising people) from the world, the church experiences in miniature what the world experiences on a larger scale. The church, with its own particular identity, should try to solve within itself those problems that are brought into it from the world. In this sense, it can be a model for the world. Where it is successful in solving those problems, the world may decide to do what the church did.

Out of concern for hurting people churches established hospitals. Out of concern for ignorant people churches and Christian individuals began universities. The "cure of souls," counseling hurting people, began as a Christian ministry. Quakers first freed their own slaves before becoming active in the antislavery movement. Practice has preceded advice giving, and the advice was heeded in many cases.

How should the church respond when the world, particularly

the state, demands by law that Christians participate in activities that the church has condemned as wrong? The church should expect those affected to be true to their consciences. It should also stand with them and be willing, in its entirety, to suffer whatever the consequences might be. In the words of the Jesus in John's Gospel, "in the world, but not of the world" should be the church's stance.

Notes

1. That God is Lord of all, even of those who do not recognize Him, is a clear teaching of Scripture. The implications of this lordship are many times not drawn out.

2. Millard Lind, *Yahweh Is a Warrior* (Scottdale, Penn.: Herald Press, 1980), draws this out in a very specific way.

3. Norman Gottwald, *The Tribes of Israel.* (Maryknoll, N.Y.: Orbis Books, 1979), even from a radical reconstruction setting, makes the point forcefully.

4. Yoder, Sloan, and Ringe present varying interpretations of the implications of the Jubilee celebration. John Howard Yoder, *The Politics of Jesus* (Grand Rapids: William B. Eerdmans, 1972) and *The Priestly Kingdom: Social Ethics as Gospel,* (Notre Dame: University of Notre Dame Press, 1984), takes the Scripture seriously from the contemporary Radical Reformation perspective and successfully corrects the impression that such a position lacks a social perspective. In his Ph.D. dissertation, *The Favorable Year of the Lord: A Study of Jubilary Theology in the Gospel of Luke,* at the University of Basel under the supervision of Bo Reicke and Markus Barth, Robert Sloan presented a theological critique of Yoder's social ethics. Sharon H. Ringe, *Jesus, Liberation, and the Biblical Jubilee* (Philadelphia: Fortress Press, 1985) is a background biblical study necessary for any interpretation and application of biblical ethics.

5. What *mission* or *missions* may have meant to the Hebrew people has been and is being debated within Judaism. See also Wittmayer Baron, *Historia social y religiosa del pueblo hebreo,* Volumen I: Epoca Antigua, Parte I (Buenos Aires: Editorial Paidos, 1968).

6. Kenneth Scott Latourette, *History of the Expansion of Christianity*, 7 vols. (New York: Harper & Brothers, 1937-1945).

7. Wayne A. Meeks, *The First Urban Christians: The Social World of the Apostle Paul* (New Haven: Yale University Press, 1983) is a far cry from Troeltsch, but very aware of him, and gives ample discussion of this matter, particularly from the standpoint of the ordinary people in the churches.

8. For one crucial aspect of what the empire demanded, see Jean-Michel Hornus, *It Is Not Lawful for Me to Fight* (Scottdale, Penn.: Herald Press, 1980).

9. For example, see Stanley Lawrence Greenslade, *The Church and the Social Order: A Historical Sketch* (London: SCM Press, 1948).

10. Albert Henry Newman, *A Manual of Church History*, volume 2 (Philadelphia: American Baptists Publication Society, 1931), gives a Baptist perspective on this kind of sacramentalism.

11. See Otto Pfleiderer, *Primitive Christianity: Its Writings and Teachings in their Historical Connections*, volume IV of *Library of Religious and Philosophical Thought* (Clifton, N.J.: Reference Book Publishers, 1965).

12. Ernst Troeltsch, *The Social Teachings of the Christian Churches*, 2 vol. Chicago: The University of Chicago Press, 1960. This excellent English translation of *Die Soziallehren der christlichen Kirchen und Gruppen*, first published in 1911, is obligatory reading for any serious student of the history of Christian ethics. It was the springboard for the classic work of H. Richard Niebuhr, *Christ and Culture* (New York: Harper & Row, 1951).

13. Troeltsch, and then H. Richard Neibuhr's interpretation of Troeltsch, are the classical works. Yoder is not in accord, nor is George Wolfgang Forell, *History of Christian Ethics*, vol. 1, from the *New Testament to Augustine* (Minneapolis: Augsburg Publishing House, 1979). Forell's volume is the first of a three-volume projection. It is written from a distinct Magisterial Reformation perspective. The reader learns about valuable resources as well as the impossibility of writing an objective, impartial history.

14. See George Hunston Williams, *The Radical Reformation* (Philadelphia: Westminster Press, 1962).

15. The Russian constitution at least gives lip service to separation of church and state; the 1982 Constitution of the People's Republic of China guarantees it, and the country now seems to practice it.

Suggested Readings

Beach, Waldo and Niebuhr, H. Richard, Eds. *Christian Ethics: Sources of the Living Tradition,* second edition. New York: The Ronald Press Company, 1973.

Kasdorf, Hans. *Christian Conversion in Context.* Scottdale, Penn.: Herald Press, 1980.

Mouw, Richard J. *Politics and the Biblical Drama.* Grand Rapids: William B. Eerdmans Company, 1976.

Webber, Robert E. *The Church in the World.* Grand Rapids: Academie Books, 1986.

6

Politics And Christian Discipleship

William H. Elder, III

Boundaries of Christian Citizenship

Begin this study of Christian citizenship with a simple, functional definition. Such a definition correlates well with the essence of Christian citizenship. Christian citizenship is not a complex intellectual phenomenon but rather a straightforward, basically simple function. A person who takes his Christian citizenship seriously is one who applies the gospel to his world through responsible involvement in the political process. Christian citizenship involves applying the insights and principles of biblical faith to our world with its local, state, national, international, even global structures, through responsible, active participation in the political process.

A responsible citizen is one who: (1) understands the way his group, whatever its size or complexity, is structured in order to make corporate decisions and, thereby, create public policy, establish social systems, and allocate resources; (2) participates in decision making and course charting. Notice that authentic citizenship demands both understanding and participation. If one leaves either ingredient out, the result is either misguided or apathetic citizenship, both of which undermine citizenship's goal (i.e., participatory group advancement).

A Christian citizen is not only a good citizen in that he understands the process and actively participates in it but also in that he participates in it from a particular perspective, a Christian perspective. His bottom line in evaluating public policy options is not whether the particular possibility would advance his personal

123

or group holdings or coincide with his own or his group's preferences or prejudices, but whether it squares with God's will for His world.

A Christian citizen is a person who allows his political decisions to be not only influenced by but also dominated by the teachings, principles, and implications of the gospel. A Christian citizen is a person who applies Christian principles to political issues in order to discover the position he must take and who then goes on to promote that position through active participation in the political process. A Christian citizen is one who allows his Christian perspective to affect his politics but not vice versa. Christianity and politics are not equal partners for the Christian citizen. Faith is the beginning and the master; politics, the servant. Politics is simply one of many means a Christian has available to him for implementing the will of God in the world.

However, the Christian citizen recognizes the fact that politics is not suited for implementing the entire Christian agenda. It is important for shaping and leading society toward peace, justice, compassion, truth, integrity, and the whole panoply of ethical values which are totally at home under the roof of biblical righteousness. But, the political process is counterproductive for carrying out the most essential agenda of our faith: evangelism. When Christians try to use politics to effect the personal commitment of conversion, they undermine both the biblical witness and the Constitution. When politics is used to evangelize, it becomes poor politics and even poorer Christianity.

The Bible makes it quite clear that God is interested first and foremost with salvation, with the redemption of sinful people and their fallen world. Redemption is available to all who will freely receive it, to all who choose to become junior partners in covenant relationship with Jesus. But for that covenant to mean anything, the decision to enter the covenant must be made in freedom. Coercion undermines the freedom that is essential for creating a true covenant of faith. Thus, God tries very hard to attract and persuade, but He refuses to coerce. He will not force, for such an approach undermines the goal and dooms the whole evangelistic endeavor to failure.

Political power is not persuasive: it is coercive. Law is pure force. It is not suggestion. Whenever political power becomes the handmaiden of religion, the tables are turned in a very short time. Politics will reign. The secular consumes the sacred. Constantine tried it in the fourth century by simply mandating that his pagan soldiers become "Christian" in name only. The covenant that needed to be birthed in the womb of liberty was aborted. Christianity became the established religion and, at the same time, ceased to be the authentic vital faith of Jesus. Historians call the result "the Dark Ages."

Christian citizenship is the right tool for working on social issues and social problems. It is the wrong tool for calling people to commit their lives to Christ, through seeing it in operation may well stimulate nonbelievers to inquire further as to its motivation. To that extent, Christian citizenship can be oblique evangelism.

Up to this point I have been establishing the definition and outer boundaries of Christian citizenship. The outer boundaries need to be drawn because some people go too far and, thereby, undermine their own primary objective. However, the greatest threat to Christian citizenship comes not from the camp of the overextenders but from the much larger camp of the underinvolved. The underinvolved remain on the sidelines of the political process entirely or may run onto the field once in a while, just long enough to vote on election day, after which they return to spectator status. Those who do not go far enough are the most serious bane to Christian citizenship. Some of them refuse to get involved in politics at all. Some of them refuse to let their faith inform or influence their politics. Both postures are destructive to the dynamic of Christian citizenship. To this destructive nonengagement, the rest of this chapter seeks to speak a challenging, "engaging," word.

Barriers to Christian Citizenship

At least six common assumptions about Christian citizenship are the primary excuses people employ to explain why they are not more involved in applying the gospel to the world through involvement in the political process. Their positions are capsuled and captioned in the following mottoes.

"My Religion Is My Personal Business."

For faith to be real, it must be personal. Religion that is social convention provides no substitute for personal faith. Going to church and going through the motions because it is simply what "well-respected, good, successful" people do may be a step above hypocrisy, but it is a far cry from vibrant, soul-centered, heartfelt, will-committed faith.

The faith that Jesus demonstrated and propagated was always a personal faith at base. It began with a person's internal commitment to receive Christ as God's gift and to follow Him on the way of salvation. But, while the faith the prophets called for and the faith Jesus proclaimed was based on personal experience, it always led to a public demonstration. In fact, Jesus made the public acknowledgment of one's commitment the acid test of faith itself. He said, "Whoever acknowledges me before men, I will also acknowledge him before my Father in heaven. But whoever disowns me before men, I will disown him before my Father in heaven" (Matt. 10:32-33, NIV). The point is that so-called "personal faith" that is kept private is simply not authentic Christianity.

Jesus also said, "Not everyone who says to me 'Lord, Lord,' will enter the kingdom of heaven, but only he who does the will of my Father who is in heaven" (Matt. 7:21, NIV). In an earlier section in the Sermon on the Mount, Jesus challenged His followers to be "the light of the world" and reminded them of how ridiculous it would be to put a lighted lamp under a bowl. He said, "Let your light shine before men, that they may see your good deeds and praise your Father in heaven" (Matt. 5:16, NIV).

Having a personal faith does not exempt one from being an active Christian citizen. Indeed, quite the opposite is the case. Faith propels one into the world to demonstrate the authenticity of one's personal relationship with the One to whom all authority in heaven and on earth has been given (Matt. 28:19).

"Politics Is Dirty Business;
It's Meant for Dirty People."

Opinion polls continue to show that for a large majority of American citizens politics is seen as "dirty business." Politicians always fall at the bottom of the scale when people are asked to rank the professions in terms of levels of trust. There are even those who refuse to support candidates for public office unless they have some dirtiness to them, on the notion that clean people will not function effectively in the mirky waters of politics.

This "dirtiness" is really nothing but an unfortunate caricature which should be challenged. Politics is essentially an organized way of making corporate decisions. There is nothing inherently dirty about that. No one has suggested that the Constitution of the United States is corrupt. For politics to be inherently dirty, such would have to be the case.

To be sure, where the process is disregarded and distorted in the actual decision making, dirt enters the system and housecleaning is called for. Elections, investigations, and the courts are all ways that housecleaning can be carried out. If politics has dirt in it, as few would challenge, the solution is not to give in to skepticism and embrace the dirt, but rather for clean people to get their political mops and brooms out of the closet and go to work.

Politicians are not all crooked. In fact, very few of them are crooked. Most politicians are just ordinary people who work very hard, often at the expense of their own families and their own health, in order to make their personal impact on their group or to contribute something to the common good or to make their mark in the history books. They are people who make sacrifices because they believe in their causes or because they like to be where the corporate action is or because they enjoy and find stimulating the power that flows through the political process. Some politicians are very bright. Some are very dull. Some are highly competent. Some are totally incompetent. Most are just ordinary people who are doing the best they can to carry out their responsibilities. They deserve neither disdain nor devotion.

"Let George Do It; George Is a Pro."

Some people sideline themselves from the political process because they really do not understand the process or the issues. In an apparent effort not to make a mistake or muddy the waters, they stay out of the picture.

This approach may masquerade as humility, but it is nothing but pure slothfulness. According to the Bible, sloth is as much a sin as is self-idolatry. We err when we think too highly of ourselves, and we also err when we think to lowly of ourselves. We are not God, but neither are we worms.

Professionalism is the curse of the church. It is also the enemy of personal spirituality. The faith Jesus taught and demonstrated called for full participation by all, ordained and unordained alike. Churches that depend on ministers to carry out all the church's ministries will not only burn out those ministers but also will lack the spiritual nourishment that comes only as a result of active participation in worship and ministry.

Our system of government is based on the same participatory principle. It is a government "of the people, by the people, for the people." If the people allow it to be "of the pros" and "by the pros," be assured it will be "for the pros" in the end, rather than for the good of all the people. One does not have to be a professional politician to listen, read, evaluate, speak out, write letters, support candidates, and vote. All one must be is an interested and committed American.

"I Vote!"

The problem here is that a host of people feel that voting is fulfilling their obligation in the area of Christian citizenship. That would be like saying, "Sure, I'm a Christian; I go to church on Sunday morning." Going to church on Sunday morning is one very small part of what it means to be a Christian. If this is all a person does, his Christian faith will not come close to fulfilling its potential.

Voting fulfills the barest minimum in Christian citizenship. Citizenship involves so much more: aggressive study and analysis, communication with office holders, lobbying, campaigning, and coalition building.

"My Patriotism and My Christianity Are One and the Same."

Some well-meaning Christians do not see the difference between their faith and their patriotism. They are proud to be Americans, and they are pleased to be Christians. They have always thought of America as a Christian nation. They go about their business in a positive and uncritical way. They do not ask whether a government policy squares with the gospel. When someone else challenges a policy decision, the uncritical are bothered by the disturbance to the smooth status quo and, deep down, wonder about the critic's patriotism and his faith. This leads to the "America! Love It or Leave It" mentality.

Americanism and Christianity are not the same thing. They are not even equals. To be true to biblical faith, one must be a Christian first and an American second. The principles of the Christian faith must be the standards by which public policy options are evaluated. Those who fail to distinguish between patriotism and Christian discipleship will never be instruments for the engagement between gospel and world which God asks.

We do not live in a Christian nation. We live in a nation in which great pains were taken by its founders to guarantee religious liberty by disestablishing religion. In other words, our national forefathers wisely saw that for people to be free to practice their faith, there must be no state, or established, religion. Thus, the religious liberty clause of the First Amendment makes it very clear that America will have no state religion and that American citizens should be free to practice their faith without interference from government.

We live in a religiously pluralistic and free nation. That is worth celebrating and safeguarding. It also reminds Americans that their political options and decisions are not to be regarded as automatically possessing divine sanction. Laws must be studied and evaluated in light of God's will, as best we can discern it. Where those laws do not correlate to His will, we must work to shape them accordingly. This will not happen as long as we regard Americanism and Christianity as two sides of the same coin.

"I Believe in the Separation of Church and State."

Unfortunately, many Christian people are not involved in the political process because they interpret the doctrine of "separation of church and state" in such a way as to preclude Christians from engaging in government. They assume that this separation is absolute and mutually exclusive. It is neither. They assume that since the state is prohibited from interfering with the church the reverse is also prohibited—that is, the church, or Christian people, should not get involved with the affairs of state. This sounds fair-minded and reasonable at first, but on second examination it comes up lacking.

The "separation of church and state" doctrine is the established guideline for the practical incorporation of the religious liberty clause of the First Amendment of the United States Constitution. That clause reads, "Congress shall make no law respecting an establishment of religion, or prohibiting the free exercise thereof." We have already looked at the "nonestablishment" provision—no state church. It is balanced by the "free exercise" provision. Both are absolutely crucial to religious liberty. People must be free to choose to be religious, and they must be free to practice their religion even when that practice includes political activism. In other words, where one's faith has a social dimension, as is clearly the case with Christianity, the believer must not be prohibited in any way from full participation in the political process.

Historically, Baptists made major contributions to both the fields of government and religion by their efforts to birth the First Amendment. Because of Isaac Backus, John Leland, and other Baptists who lobbied their representative delegates to the Constitutional Convention long and hard, the religious liberty clause of the First Amendment became a reality. The prime reason those Baptists worked so hard for this constitutional guarantee was because they wanted to ensure their rights to engage, shape, and influence government according to their faith-informed consciences.

Thus, the free exercise clause of the First Amendment makes it appropriate for Christian people to become full-fledged participants in the political process. However, the separation of church and state does mean that the state must not become unduly involved in the affairs of the church. It does not mean that Christians, or any religious group, must distance themselves from the affairs of state.

There are surely many other barriers to Christian citizenship. These six have appeared time and time again, but they ought to be dispensed and overcome by those who understand the dynamics and the rationale involved. Having dealt with reasons some people do not fulfill their Christian citizenship, turn now to reasons for involvement and benefits of active Christian citizenship.

Benefits of Christian Citizenship

Christian citizenship brings significant benefits in two major categories. It benefits our nation. And it benefits ourselves as Christians.

Benefits for America

Christian citizenship fosters fundamental values.—Even in light of the deistic beliefs and tendencies and personal shortcomings from the standpoint of the Christian faith of our founding fathers, no credible historian would deny the fact that, as a group, our national progenitors who conceived and hammered out the outlines of the American system of government did so from the perspective of a religious faith. Indeed, the very values upon which our nation is based, values like liberty and justice for all, arose consistently from the soil of theological conviction. In other words, those key moral values were argued by our forefathers as being values worthy of enshrining in the law of the land because not only were they sensible, practical, civilized but also divinely established in the warp and woof of creation.

The Declaration of Independence preceded the Constitution. This Declaration began with a theologically based justification for the break with England.

When in the Course of human events, it becomes necessary for one people to dissolve the political bands which have connected them with another, and to assume among the powers of the earth, the separate and equal station to which the Laws of Nature and of Nature's God entitle them, a decent respect to the opinions of mankind requires that they should declare the causes which impel them to the separation.

The Declaration continues with this very familiar statement: "We hold these truths to be self-evident, that all men are created equal, that they are endowed by their Creator with certain unalienable Rights, that among these are Life, Liberty and the pursuit of Happiness." The framers of the Declaration of Independence understood the values they cherished to be divinely sanctioned and, therefore, doubly worthy of support.

Other examples are available of how our fundamental societal values had religious underpinnings for those who originally put them forward and for those who have fostered them throughout our history. Christian people who also appreciate the sacredness of such values should be contemporary champions of those values at a time when commitment to many of them seems to be waning.

Patriots Rather than Nationalists

For our political system to work properly and remain healthy, citizens are needed who love and respect our nation but refuse to deify it. Our nation is best served by those who care enough about it to stand up and speak out when it appears that we are moving in the wrong direction. True patriotism is authentic leadership, and leadership demands loving criticism. Leaders are people who are constantly alert to the safety and security of the group they are charged to lead. If the group seems determined to move in a direction that is dangerous and counterproductive, the true leader, the true patriot, is willing to stand up and face the resistance in order to engineer a correct course, rather than simply reflecting the group consensus and courting public praise while the group rolls down the hill toward oblivion.

Nationalists are people who feel that whatever their country does must be right, simply because their country does it. That kind of circular logic is dangerous. When it becomes the basis of public policy, it can be catastrophic, especially when the public happens to be a superpower.

Christian citizens who live within biblical teaching of having no gods other than God the Father of our Lord Jesus Christ are sensitive to the dangers of all kinds of idolatries, including nationalism. Because they will not allow their country to be first in their allegiances, reserving that spot only for God Himself, they are better able to evaluate government and politics from an objective perspective. That objectivity is crucial if a healthy future for our nation is to be safeguarded. Christian citizens would change the nationalistic slogan "America! Love It or Leave It" to "America! Love It and Lead It."

Power Servants Rather than Power Brokers

Politics is power. No doubt about it, when you put together the decision-making authority of many people and the willingness of those people to abide by the decision of the process, you have power. Indeed, the fact that politics is power is what attracts many people to political activism. It is exciting to be where the action is, where history is being made, and where impact for the better is made on people's lives and livelihoods. Power is exciting, but it is also an addicting narcotic of the psyche. Some people become so hooked on it that they would sell their very souls to be elected or selected to serve on some prestigious office holder's staff in a decision-making position.

We have all heard the phrase "political animal." Unfortunately, some politicians and political activists have become just that. They sacrifice their humanity just to stay in positions of power. They fight and struggle, they do things they never imagined themselves doing, in order to beat their opponents and live under the intoxicating influence of political power.

Needless to say, people who become hooked on political power for the thrill it brings them emotionally will often abuse the power they have to advance their own interests. Political power exists not to be used selfishly but to be entrusted to those who can be counted on to advance the public good.

Most people who are corrupted by political power entered the political arena in hopes of filling a void within. Their ego needs are generally enormous. Political power becomes their way to enhance their self-esteem. Consequently their use of political power is selfishly directed.

Christians are people who are supposed to know the full acceptance and approval of God Himself. The void within is filled with the presence of the Holy Spirit. Their direction in life is clear as they walk according to the commands of Jesus. They are people who need not prove themselves to anyone. They are not driven. They are at peace with God, with their fellow human beings, and with themselves. Because of these personal characteristics, they are excellent candidates for handling political power responsibly. Because they are followers of Jesus, they have accepted the servant role in life. That is exactly the right attitude and orientation for handling the power that derives from the people that is entrusted to public "servants" for appropriate administration of that power. They are ideally suited to be "power servants" rather than "power brokers."

Therefore, for at least these three reasons, our political system could be significantly improved if more authentic Christians became full participants in the political process. So, there are real benefits for our system of government that come via the door of Christian citizenship. Turn now to the benefits that accrue to the Christian who decides to take his or her citizenship responsibilities seriously.

Benefits for Christians

It Is Biblical

A Christian matures as he brings his life more and more into line with biblical principles. Christian citizenship squares beautifully with several dimensions of biblical thought.

The Bible challenges the Western mentality of stark individualism. "Am I my brother's keeper?" (Gen. 4:9) was entirely the wrong response to God's inquiry about Abel. Cain showed by that response that he had lost his sense of oneness with his brother. He was taking his stand on independent individualism. He did not want to be bothered with his brother, so he had murdered him. The Bible shows throughout that the "I can stand alone" mentality not only is misguided and misinformed but also is a departure from the will of God, who created people for each other, for fellowship, for relationship. The first thing God declared to be "not good" was that man should be alone (Gen. 2:18). The prayer of Jesus recorded in John 17 is a high-priestly prayer where Jesus prayed so intently for those who would carry on His ministry. He returned four times to the petition "that they may be one."

Jesus clearly taught that we are responsible for one another. We are not afforded the luxury of just taking care of ourselves and those closest to us. We are to give ourselves and our resources to meeting the needs of those around us. *Agape* love, fulfilling love, is expressed by the giving of one's self to another so that in the giving God is able to fulfill both. Discipleship is a corporate experience, not just in the sense of the disciple being in relationship to the Master, but in the sense of the disciple being in relationship to others. Jesus said, "All men will know that you are my disciples, if you love one another" (John 13:35, NIV).

Citizenship is corporate activity. It is a way we express our oneness as Americans. Thus as Christians work in the political process to accomplish good things for their fellow human beings, they are putting into action the biblical call to community.

The Bible also teaches that people of faith must work against evil, not only in its personal internal manifestation but also in its corporate, systemic manifestation. Thus, the prophets stood up to the kings and their whole political entourages with the word of the Lord. The prophets risked themselves in every respect as they proclaimed the prophetic message. Because they dared to take the risk, the work of the Lord was consistently heard. Consequently a faithful remnant remained even in the worst of times. Because the prophets spoke up, authentic faith was nurtured and the nation had opportunity to be rescued and restored.

We also have the example of Jesus in this regard. We do not often think of Jesus as being involved politically, even though He was crucified by Rome for sedition. That charge was trumped up under the urging of the Sanhedrin, but it was in the Sanhedrin that the real political system of the Jews existed. When one reads the Gospels, it becomes clear that Jesus was constantly confronting the structures of His society, the Pharisees and the Sadducees, with the word of the Lord. As His followers, we must do the same. Hence, Christian citizenship is an essential dimension of Christian discipleship.

The Bible also teaches that it is the responsibility of the faithful to be champions for right and to be people who meet needs. These are clearly major planks in God's platform for the world. They are indispensable ingredients for believers who seek to carry out His will. Sometimes we are not quite sure about what God would have us do. In standing for what is right and in meeting the needs of hurting people, we can be absolutely sure we are carrying out His will. Our system of government is supposed to be dedicated to these same ideals. Thus, it is appropriate for Christians to be involved in the political process. In this case we can see that by so doing we are working not only for a better world but also are carrying out our Lord's agenda.

It Fights Segmentalization

Some people of faith fall into the error of thinking that they can segment their lives. Thus, they divide their lives into neat little compartments. They have a family life, a vocational life, a recreational life, a social life, a political life, and, of course, a religious life. However, the Bible makes it clear that one's faith must not be compartmentalized. Faith is not to be treated as one among many responsibilities. If it is authentic, faith functions as the integrating focus of all that one is and does.

The prophets constantly challenged the segmentalizing tendencies in Israel. They spoke out boldly against those who could go to worship and offer lavish sacrifices while never realizing that God was offended by such actions when they were carried out by people who failed to apply their faith in all the other areas of their lives. Amos, in the middle of the eighth century BC, gave the Israelites this message from God:

> Away with the noise of your songs!
> I will not listen to the music of your harps.
> But let justice roll on like a river,
> righteousness like a never-failing stream!
>   (Amos 5:23-24, NIV).

In the last judgment scene described by Jesus in Matthew 25:31-46, God is not satisfied with religious jargon. There will be people who call Him Lord who will not inherit the kingdom of heaven because their knowledge of His lordship has made no impact on their lives. In other words, they have called Him Lord with their mouths, but they have not demonstrated that He is truly Lord of their lives by acting according to His mandates in their day-to-day conduct. Otherwise they would not have been able to have seen people hungry or naked or sick or in prison or alone and done nothing to help. The simple fact is that a real relationship with God *must* show itself in literally every area of a person's life. Faith is a wholistic, total commitment.

In this light then, as people apply the principles of faith in the political arena, they are defeating the pernicious tendency toward segmentalization. The more that tendency is defeated the more meaningful and fulfilling faith becomes.

It Enhances Spirituality

Spirituality is the ability to perceive and experience God. It is the lifeblood of personal faith. Without a growing spirituality a person ceases to mature as a Christian. The more one encounters God, the more one is aware of His presence elsewhere. We know He is present everywhere and at all times, but whether we are able to see Him and hear His voice depends on the vitality of our spirituality. Therefore, sure encounters are spiritual benchmarks. We can be sure that where people are gathered together to worship He is there. Jesus said that wherever people are involved in meeting needs God is there. "Inasmuch as ye have done it unto one of the least of these my brethren, ye have done it unto me" (Matt. 25:40). Nearly six centuries before Christ, Jeremiah, in speaking to King Jehoiakim, said that God could be encountered in meeting needs and in working for what is right in society (Jer. 22:15-16).

We want to use our corporate resources to help those in need, and we want to structure a society in which the highest ethical standards are honored. Our system of government has been fashioned with both of these objectives in mind. Therefore, as Christians work through the political process to be a voice for people in need, who are usually a people without much of a voice, and as they work to create a more just and peaceful society, they are engaging in actions that are not simply political and humanitarian but powerfully spiritual.

Christian citizenship is good for the Christian because of its biblical correlation, because it helps undermine the destructive temptation to segmentalize our lives and compartmentalize our faith, and because it can be for people of faith a significant spiritual catalyst. The final question is, What does it really take, on a very practical level, to carry out one's Christian citizenship? To that subject we now turn.

The Mechanics of Christian Citizenship

To determine what is involved, we need to recall our basic definition. Christian citizenship is applying the gospel to our world through *responsible* involvement in the political process. To carry out this function there must be relevant information and responsible involvement.

Relevant Information

The relevant biblical principles.—As we have seen already, Christian citizenship begins with the gospel. The Christian citizen decides where he stands on the issues based upon biblical insight. If his political preferences and prejudices do not square with the Bible, too bad for those preferences and prejudices. He must change his position to coincide with biblical truth. No other option is open for those who take biblical authority seriously, and Christian citizens take biblical authority seriously.

Therefore, Christian citizenship begins when an issue is encountered and the Christian goes to the Bible and to Christian thought to determine his position on the issue. To be able to do this effectively and efficiently, he needs to be familiar with the Bible. He needs to understand something about the many tools of Bible study so that he can study the relevant passages in their overall historical, literary, and theological contexts, thereby letting them speak to him rather than simply using them to endorse his presuppositions. He needs to be familiar with the best biblical commentaries, introductions to the Old and New Testaments, and Bible dictionaries. Many of the issues that arise have already been treated by scholars from the standpoint of Christian ethics, and the Christian citizen will find real assistance in analyzing and evaluating in light of biblical principles in many of these works.

The Facts

Discovering the relevant biblical principles that should apply to a given issue must be done concurrently with discovering the raw facts of the issue. Indeed, the raw facts will determine the course of biblical investigation, and knowing those facts will preclude many a wild goose chase and many a misconceived conclusion. Too many people make poor Christian citizenship decisions because they assume rather than investigate. When the facts are clearly known, then and only then can the relevant biblical principles be determined and applied.

There is another benefit for the Christian citizen in accurate fact gathering. It comes at the point of making one's voice heard or championing one's position. Much of Christian citizenship is urging, convincing, persuading legislators to move in a desired direction. To do this effectively, knowledge and credibility are indispensable. One sure way to undermine one's credibility with a legislator is to show that one is ignorant of the facts. Most legislators do not feel that it is their duty to educate those who come to them with an opinion. They expect the one doing the urging to know the relevant facts if he or she expects to be taken seriously. Know the facts if you want to use the Bible appropriately and if you want to be heard.

The Dynamics of the Political Process

One other major category of information needs to be encountered and mastered by the Christian citizen, and that is information about the political process itself. One needs to know how the political process is supposed to work. For that information the various constitutions (national, state, and local municipalities) are helpful sources. Textbooks dealing with government and politics are also quite helpful. Citizenship resources produced by groups like the League of Women Voters or by the two national political parties are readily available on request. It is important to know how a bill becomes a law. It is crucial to understand how the committee system works, how to secure an invitation to present testimony at a committee hearing, how the various branches of government balance each other.

It is important to know the way government is supposed to work. Sometimes it works the way it is supposed to work. Sometimes it does not. Most of the time it works somewhere in between, on the basis of unwritten canons, forged on the anvil of time and practicality and in the oven of key personalities. In other words, the system works the way people, real people, make it work. The Christian citizen needs to become educated in practical as well as theoretical politics. Who is the big power on the committee? Who owes whom favors? Who gave the most to the governor's last campaign? Indeed, never forget the fact that government and campaigning are two sides of the same coin. A legislator never stops being a campaigner until he retires, and to be an effective Christian citizen one must understand the very practical and often muddy business of campaign politics. Naivete about that dimension of government has undermined many a well-intentioned, highly principled, even well-informed Christian citizen.

Responsible Involvement

Christian citizenship demands education in biblical thought, on the issues, and on the political process and action based on the synthesis of pertinent information. Involvement is the proof of the pudding. There are many ways and many levels in which to become responsibly involved.

Voting.—As noted earlier, voting is minimal citizenship, but it is not to be minimized or overlooked. According to our system of government, every citizen can express his or her opinion through the ballot box. For our system to work, the citizens must speak. For God's will to be done in society, God's people must speak out through the voting booth. People who do not bother to vote are not only poor citizens but also poor Christian citizens in that they choose to remain silent and inactive while significant decisions and serious problems go begging for Christian insight and impact.

Lobbying.—Lobbying is simply making one's opinion known to a legislator with a view toward convincing the legislator to act in accord with that opinion. This expressing one's view can be done through letters, postcards, petitions, phone calls, and personal visits. Be assured, these contacts do make a difference. Especially powerful is the personal visit. It shows high level commitment. Time, money, and energy have been expended; legislators pay attention to such things. Next in terms of impact is probably the personal letter. In the mind of the legislator, that spells "grass-roots movement"; politicians pay great attention to such happenings. Many people never contact their elected representatives, assuming that their little efforts would have infinitismal impact. That is a flawed assumption that leaves the field to the professional lobbyists. The complaint is often heard, "The special interests dominate politics; the little guy doesn't count." That is both true and false. It is false because the little guy does count. It is true because the special interests do dominate. But the special interests dominate because the little guy stays home and keeps his mouth shut. The system responds to those who speak up and become active.

Campaigning.—"We are a government of laws." That sentence often appears on the lips of some reporter as he or she comments upon investigations of government officials by government officials. The idea is that the laws rather than the people are the central focus of the political process. While it is certainly true that their law-making prerogative makes legislators important, there is no way to minimize the crucial function the lawmaker as a human being plays. Our government and our laws will be a direct reflection of the individuals hammering out those policies and laws. If we want better government, we must elect better people to govern. That is where campaigning comes in.

We are fast approaching a television democracy. That is a system whereby the candidate with the most appealing commercials that are seen by the greatest number of people the greatest number of times gets elected to the office. The voters just sit back in their recliners, forget about the issues, and decide for whom they will vote on the basis of product packaging. That just about ensure that the wealthiest candidate will win. With enough money and a highly skilled advertising agency, it is not outside the realm of the possible that a baboon could be elected to Congress.

To ward off a television democracy or a rule of the rich, to encourage the best candidates to be able to run and be elected, Christian citizens ought to be able to run and be elected, Christian citizens ought to be involved in the campaign process. That means taking the time and expending the energy to research the candidates and study the issues. That means selecting one's candidates and supporting them through word-of-mouth recommendation, through contributing financially to their campaigns, volunteering to work in campaign organizations, posting yard signs, wearing buttons, using bumper stickers. As silly and inane as all those things may sound and look, they are all part and parcel of the campaign process. If more people got involved, the prize of election would not as often go to the most wealthy but rather to the most qualified.

Candidates become lawmakers, but they never stop being candidates. They do not forget their friends. Their supporters have access to them at the very highest level. When their supporters speak, they listen. This is why campaign politics and lobbying will always be the right and left arm of political activism.

Coalitions and Groups

It is popular to decry the influence of so-called "special-interest groups." But special-interest groups are a vital part of the political process. When people come together to promote a particular cause, they often gain much more strength than they might otherwise have had, had they opted to work independently. Pooling their resources allows them to plan better, strategize more effectively. It cuts down on waste and duplication. There is nothing inherently wrong with political action in groups. If the groups use ethical tactics in urging their cause, they are good mechanisms for political involvement. So, the Christian citizen should seek out political action groups whose causes he can support and participate in their efforts.

Running for Office

Finally, running for office is certainly a possibility as an authentic expression of one's Christian citizenship. We live in a country where anyone can present himself or herself as a candidate for public office. Christian people who understand the process, who want to serve rather than rule, who love their nation but refuse to worship it, who can handle power well and do not need it to fill some ego void, who want to fashion a just and compassionate and free society for all people, who will do what is right rather than what is expedient or what feathers their own nest, are desperately needed in all levels of government across our nation and around our world.

Conclusion

Christian citizenship is applying the gospel to our world through responsible involvement in the political process. According to the Constitution, Christians have every right to be fully involved in every level and function of government. According to the Bible, Christians have every responsibility to be involved in shaping the world in light of the Father's will for it. Christian citizenship is a mandate, not an option, nor an elective, for all who take seriously their call to discipleship by our Lord Jesus Christ.

Suggested Reading

Bennett, John C. *When Christians Make Political Decisions.* New York: Association Press, 1964.

Braidfoot, Larry. *The Bible and America.* Nashville: Broadman Press, 1983.

Gaddy, C. Welton. *Proclaim Liberty.* Nashville: Broadman Press, 1975.

Gilkey, Langdon. *How the Church Can Minister to the World Without Losing Itself.* New York: Harper and Row, 1964.

Hays, Brooks. *Politics Is My Parish.* Baton Rouge: Louisiana State University Press, 1981.

Mouw, Richard J., *Political Evangelism.* Grand Rapids: Wm. B. Eerdmans Publishing Co., 1973.

Stringfellow, William. *An Ethic for Christians and Other Aliens in a Strange Land.* Waco: Word, 1973.

Valentine, Foy. *Citizenship for Christians.* Nashville: Broadman, 1965.

7
Preparing for Multiethnic Ministry

Sid Smith

Clearly the opportunity for multiethnic ministry exists in unprecedented dimensions for the current generation of church leaders. If churches are to meet the challenge of multiethnic ministry adequately during the remainder of the twentieth century, leadership, especially pastors, must be prepared. This chapter deals with some areas of understanding deemed necessary for successful multiethnic ministry.

On Defining Ethnicity

What is ethnicity? At present, *ethnicity* is difficulty to define academically. A dearth of research in the area resulted in the following statement by a faculty member in a university department of multiethnic studies: "We teach ethnic studies, but I don't know that we have defined ethnicity, and there are no books on our shelves that speak to that problem."[1] Even the dictionary definition is not satisfactory: *ethnicity*—"ethnic quality or affiliation."[2]

For purposes of this inquiry, the definition of Dr. Wilma S. Longstreet is borrowed.

> Ethnicity is that portion of cultural development that occurs before the individual is in complete command of his or her abstract intellectual powers, and that is formed primarily through the individual's early contacts with family, neighbors, friends, teachers, and others, as well as with his or her immediate environment of the home and neighborhood.[3]

She lists five aspects of ethnicity: verbal communication, non-

145

verbal communication, orientation modes, social value patterns, and intellectual modes.[4] Ethnicity, then may be defined as the totality of one's group experience and style, which is distinctive from the group experience and style of others.

In the context of Christian ministry, this definition of ethnicity yields several conclusions. First, ethnicity is an inextricable part of human existence which means that every person is an ethnic. Second, whatever ministering is done will be from the context of an ethnic experience. Third, a decision will be made on whether to minister to more than one's own ethnic group members. In other words, the question is not whether a church will be involved in ethnic ministry. It is whether it will be involved in multiethnic ministry.

Biblical Bases for Multiethnic Ministry

Major questions arise for churches at the point of determining a biblical approach to the question of multiethnic ministry. In this age of philosophical and theological pluralism, sincere inquirers fall on different sides of critical issues such as: Can a church be faithful to the implications of the gospel while practicing a mono-ethnic approach to ministry in a multiethnic society? Can a church be faithful to its calling and minister to only one ethnic group in a multiethnic community? Does the church have the prerogative of selecting its target audience for ministry? Are there biblical mandates that speak to the ethnic ramifications of congregationalizing and ministry?

I believe that the multiethnic approach is more consistent with biblical implications than the monethnic approach. While it appears Southern Baptists, for instance, have experienced little difficulty in understanding that the biblical mandate to evangelize the world implied multiethnic evangelism, many churches have stumbled at the implications for congregationalizing.

The social revolutions of the last thirty years in the United States, the rise of Third World nations, and the convicting impact of liberation theology have eloquently and convincingly pointed out the contradiction between ethnic selectivity in church and universal inclusivity in the kingdom of God. The question may ultimately be: Do we really care about people outside our ethnic group? At a deeper level it may be: Is the God we serve ethnically discriminatory? Even further: Do we pervert the Christian witness, and therefore the gospel, by our incarnational style? What are some implications from biblical evidence for congregationalizing in a multiethnic society?

The Great Commission: Matthew 28:19-20

The command to go and make disciples of all nations given by Jesus to the disciples in this passage implies the following for the multiethnic approach to ministry. First, the commission is given to a group of Jews, members of an ethnic group, to go to all nations and make disciples. Clearly, the pattern for the church was to cross ethnic barriers with the proclamation of the gospel. While the church began as a Jewish group, the intention was for this group to go to the other groups. This means that the church is under biblical mandate to be inclusive rather than exclusive in proclamation of the gospel to all nations. So the target groups for the sharing of the gospel in a multiethnic society should be multiethnic as well.

Second, beyond the mandate of proclamation is the command to educate in the things Jesus had commanded. Implicit in the educational phase is the idea of continued relationship which assumes fellowship, dialogue, sharing, and growth. The targets found in congregationalizing are identical to those of the evangelizing. Thus, congregationalizing is to be a natural by-product of evangelizing. Therefore, the church is under a mandate for multiethnic congregationalizing in a multiethnic society.

The Early New Testament Models

Although limited in the beginning in its understanding of the scope of the mission of the church, the church at Jerusalem was multiethnic. The list of countries represented among Jews present on the Day of Pentecost reflects a multiethnic audience of hearers of the gospel at the outpouring of the Holy Spirit. From this group, about three thousand became Christians that day. We may assume this congregation was multiethnic. In fact, in Acts 6, multiethnic conflict had developed within the church as seen in the dispute between the widows of the Grecian Jews and the Palestinian Jews.

Dr. William Hendricks concluded, "There is biblical evidence that there were multiethnic congregations in Jerusalem, Rome, and other early congregations."[5] Dr. Francis DuBose agreed, "The church at Jerusalem was made up of interethnic Jews."[6] This group of Jews had different dialects, nationalities, and cultural experiences. They were clearly multiethnic. While the first church had difficulty in adjusting to the concept of the universality of Christianity as shown in Peter's rooftop experience at the home of Simon, the tanner, in Acts 10, it did from its inception manifest limited multiethnicity.

Multiethnicity in congregationalizing is seen in Acts 13:1, in the church at Antioch of Syria. DuBose pointed out, "In the church in Antioch of Syria, we read of at least two Hellenistic Jews who were from Africa. Therefore, we can assume that the leadership of the church in Antioch was multiethnic, if not multiracial."[7]

The Holy Spirit led Philip to evangelize the Ethiopian eunuch in Acts 8. Implicit in the experience is the biblical model of a Christian being willing to share the gospel across racial/ethnic boundaries. It is inconceivable that congregationalizing would not be consistent with this multiethnicity.

Conclusions from Biblical Evidence

Several conclusions are appropriate from the implications from the Great Commission and early New Testament church models. First, the target groups of evangelism and the resulting congregations should be multiethnic in a multiethnic society. The thrust of the gospel yields inclusiveness rather than exclusiveness. Second, the Bible makes no distinction between the approach to evangelizing and congregationalizing pertaining to ethnic inclusion. After evangelizing, no hint is given of segregation by racial, ethnic, language grouping, or according to an ethnically based homogeneous unit principle. Finally, the only ethnic model that is biblical is the multiethnic approach.

The question arises, Can a monoethnic approach to ministry be

Christian in a multiethnic society? Or, to put it differently, can a segregated church be healthy in a multiethnic society? My position is that it cannot. A segregated church (*de facto* or *de jure*) can grow; it can reach some people with its monoethnic ministry. But at what price? The price is the perverting of the gospel through its "body language," its empirical data which show a portrait of the family of God divided in selective ministry contrary to the spirit of unity desired by the will of God.

Segregation in the church means deprivation, neglect, and perversion. Segregated churches are deprived of the enrichment from multiethnic exposure to resources, gifts, talents, education, and opportunities for ministry. These churches are guilty of neglecting the needs of those not "their kind" and, through the process, their own needs in the area of multiethnicity as well. Worst, segregated churches pervert the image of God's equal love for all people through their incarnational witness.

Multiethnic Ministry: Pathological or Healthy?

Multiethnic approaches to ministry may be pathological or healthy. Because a church may be "integrated" is not guarantee that its attempts at inclusiveness are necessarily Christian. Not only must the quantitative dimensions of multiethnic church growth be explored, but the qualitative as well. It is possible to have a multiethnic church with malignant pathology.

What determines healthiness in a church? The healthiness of a church is determined largely by implications from biblical theology, anthropology, and ecclesiology. When a church deviates in understanding and practice from the biblical teachings in these areas, disease results.

Historically in America, a chief pathology in multiethnic ministry has been racism. Racism in the culture has contributed to the practice of "racial Christianity." Racial Christianity gave rise to an "immoral morality" so well articulated by the late Kyle Haseldon.[8] For example, many monoethnic churches find no contradiction in the practice of evangelizing people from other ethnic groups but not congregationalizing them. For the church embarking upon healthy multiethnic ministry, the pervasive beguilement of racism demands an understanding of the manifestations and ramifications of racism, especially institutional racism.

Racism: The Major Pathology

For centuries, American culture baptized the church in racism. The result has been, in many cases, the imposition of racist values on theology, anthropology, and ecclesiology, as Dr. James Cone so eloquently articulated in his classic work on black theology, *Black Theology and Black Power.*[9]

Racism may be defined in several ways. *Racism* is any attitude, action, or process that results in negative effects on people based on a concept of race; the doctrine or practice of racial supremacy; a strong sense of ethnocentrism based on a concept of race; the practice of distinguishing groups according to a belief in different races. The United States Commission on Civil Rights defined *racism* as "any attitude, action, or institutional structure which subordinates a person or group because of his or their color."[10]

Racism exists in culture through two manifestations: personal racism and institutional racism. Personal racism, sometimes called overt racism,[11] is the expression of racist tendencies through the personal behavior of individuals. Institutional racism, sometimes referred to as institutional subordination, is the intentional or inadvertent practice of institutional behavior which yields negative effects on a group based on a concept of race.[12]

Some distinguishing characteristics of personal racists are: a belief in the validity of defining people according to a concept of "race"; the belief in racial superiority; a denial of the immorality of racism; frequent "scapegoating" of minority groups; sometimes transferral of psychological problems to the racial arena. These characteristics stand in contrast to the antiracist position of Dr. Ashley Montagu, et. al. in *The Concept of Race* in which "ten distinguished scientists attack the concept of race as a biologically unsound, socially invalid and prejudicial means of human classification."[13]

Institutional racism may be intentional or inadvertent. It may be respectable and legal. It may exist in the name of good works; in an integrated situation; without the knowledge of its purveyors.

An interesting factor about institutional racism is that it may be supported and perpetrated by people who personally are not racists. Warning signals for the existence of institutional racism include: little or no minority group representation; programs which have unequal effects on the majority and minority groups; persistent opposition, despite the stated reasons, to programs that improve the status of minorities; a parallel relationship between minority concentration and inequality; a preoccupation with considering people by race; a refusal to implement compensatory programs; no institutional programs to deal with the special needs of minorities; leadership that maintains, "But we have no problems."

Churches without a religious educational curriculum, including a focus on understanding the nature of racism and how it has impact upon contemporary religious bodies, are victims of insensitivity and naiveté. The minister who would thoroughly equip the people for all good works must provide the leadership necessary for not only understanding the nature of racism but for overcoming it as well. American society has conditioned most people to have racist tendencies which are extremely difficult to completely remove. Overcoming racism, then, is the active process of subjugating, controlling, or eliminating racist tendencies on the personal and/or institutional levels.

Overcoming racism usually requires several steps. Steps which are helpful include the following for personal racism: developing an awareness of the racism phenomenon; understanding the nature of racism; developing a commitment to control racist tendencies; employing an educational process on racism; employing therapeutic interracial relationships; and using the therapeutic power of Christ. For dealing with institutional racism, these steps have been helpful: developing awareness of the existence of the phenomenon of institutional racism; developing a commitment to eliminating institutional racism; organizing to eliminate it; identifying specific racist effects of the institution; determining the locus of power and leverage; mobilizing resources at the locus of power; converting or leveraging against the locus of power. These lists of steps are by no means exhaustive, but serve as an approach for a point of reference.

The imperative of healthy multiethnic ministry demands sophistication in understanding and overcoming racism on the part of the minister. To be naive on this matter may mean operating a racist anachronistic church. God forbid!

Some Traits of Healthy Multiethnic Ministry

What are some characteristics of churches striving for healthy multiethnic ministry?

Churches striving for healthy multiethnic ministry have a theological conviction based on the earlier biblical treatment that yields a mandate for multiethnic focus on evangelizing and congregationalizing. "Unto all the world," "to all people," "no respecter of persons," and "whosoever will," are phrases that characterize the conviction that every church should be directly involved with people whom it is possible to reach for the Lord. Anything less than this mandated theological position makes it extremely easy to capitulate to secular social trends which leads to the enculturation of the gospel and the subordination of biblical theology to sociology.

Inclusive congregationalizing is a characteristic of a healthy multiethnic church. This is to say that a church must practice multiethnic inclusiveness rather than exclusiveness. There can be no place for monoethnicity if a church is to be multiethnically healthy. This is not to imply any quota system for ethnic variety or presence, but it does magnify openness to serve people whom God leads a church.

Inclusion of minorities in leadership is a characteristic of healthy multiethnicity. Leadership exclusion is racist and pathologic. A major test of the readiness of a congregation for healthy multiethnic ministry is the willingness to be an equal opportunity fellowship when it comes to leadership. If a church cannot, under any circumstances, conceivably call a pastor who is not of the same ethnic identity as the majority of its members, it is a victim of institutional racism through perversion of theology, anthropology, and ecclesiology. The model of the church at

Antioch of Syria in Acts 13 with men of African descent as leaders is attractive, healthy, and worthy of emulation.

Structural flexibility for multiethnic need meeting is a characteristic of healthiness. In Acts 6, multiethnic conflict led to the selection of the precursors of deacons. In order to meet the needs of its multiethnic consituency, a structural adjustment was made. An implication from this move is that a church should do what is necessary to meet the needs of its various ethnic constituencies. A healthy church may need to add a specialized structure to facilitate multiethnic effectiveness. Where ethnic minority needs have been neglected this may be particularly helpful. A good rule to consider is: Where there has been deprivation there must be compensation before equalization can become a realization.

A healthy multiethnic church is involved in resolving the social problems of its consituency—multiethnic social problem solving. Implicit in Acts 2:45-46 and 11:27-30 is the idea of dealing with the social problems of people. The ministry of the church should be wholistic, not dichotomized. A church cannot really minister to the total needs of people if it neglects their social problems. Healthy churches minister to the social problems of their multiethnic constituents. For example, one common need of minorities in America is in the area of employment. When the general community experiences recession, minority communities usually experience depression. A church could have a ministry in the area of employment.

Cultural appreciation is another characteristic of a healthy multiethnic church. When God sent His only begotten Son into the world, God sent Him as a Jew. Jesus was born into a Jewish family, educated in the Jewish system, reared in the Jewish religion, lived a Jewish life-style, and had a Jewish world view. He was culturally Jewish. The Creator chose to send Him not as the miracle of an acultural being, but as a Jew.

Sometimes multiethnic churches ignore or overlook the principle of cultural appreciation. This cultural chauvinism carried to its logical extreme can result in cultural genocide of minorities. Churches that "treat everybody alike" more than likely reflect cultural insensitivity rather than fairness when they fail to demonstrate multiethnic cultural appreciation. Churches should recognize the positive contributions of cultural diversity and incorporate them into edification of the congregation. God meets people in their culture and uses the good in culture to bring them to the eternal truths of divine reality.

Recognition of the equal value of the different ethnic groups reflected through equal treatment is a trait of the healthy multiethnic church. On the Day of Pentecost the miracle wrought by the Holy Spirit was the enabling of the 120 disciples to communicate in the dialects of the various ethnic groups of Jews present at that time. Part of the symbolism could easily be the idea of equal value reflected through in need meeting of the different ethnic groups. In other words, churches should not show ethnic favoritism. The church at Jerusalem stumbled at this concept initially. In Acts 6 the issue of ethnic favoritism threatened the fellowship of the church and led to administrational corrective action. Imbalance of ethnic concern is a frequent symptom of pathology in multiethnic churches today.

Openness to change for the sake of improvement characterizes healthy multiethnic churches. The first church in Jerusalem had a limited vision regarding the scope of the mission of the gospel. Initially this church assumed that the gospel was for Jews and took it only to them. However, Peter's rooftop experience in Acts 10 convinced the church that the gospel was for everybody. When this church was enlightened, it changed; when it matured, it improved its approach for the sake of the gospel. Churches must be willing to change. The choices for many congregations are adjust or perish.

The foregoing are some traits of healthiness for multiethnic churches. Ethnic humility enables churches to be willing to do what becomes necessary to minister with people from different ethnic backgrounds. Ethnic arrogance alienates.

Traditional Philosophies of Multiethnic Ministry

Three major philosophies of multiethnic ministry have emerged in Baptist life. The issue has rarely been "to minister or not to minister" in multiethnic settings for Baptists. The question has been, How? In attempting to implement biblical mandates, three multiethnic ministry models have emerged: paternalism, proxy, and fraternalism.

Paternalism

Paternalism refers to a multiethnic relationship in which representatives of one group or several groups behave in a superior manner. There is an imbalance of intrinsic worth reflected through power relationships in the paternalistic model. Paternalism insists upon a "parent" role and a "child" role. This pathological phenomenon may exist individually or institutionally.

An evaluation of paternalism reveals several conclusions. First, paternalism can exist only in a pathological setting. Second, the "child" usually ends up disdaining the "parent" when psychological liberation is attained. Third, when the "child" becomes economically and/or politically strong, he will usually disassociate from the "parent," resulting in resegregation. Fourth, this approach is biblically unsound since it violates the doctrine of the equal worth of all people. Finally, this approaches impeaches the credibility of the Christian witness.

Ministry By Proxy

Ministry by proxy is the term which refers to the model in multiethnic ministry in which an ethnic group feels compelled to minister across ethnic lines but prefers not to get involved personally, so a representative is selected to minister to the other group in its behalf. Under this system, churches are not expected to become directly involved with the other ethnic groups.

Ministry by proxy has disadvantages. While it focuses on delivering some well-intentioned kind of ministry, it neglects the fellowship dimension of the faith. A fallacious assumption is that only the "sending" group has something of value to contribute to the relationship. Also, the potential for penetration of any impact is greatly reduced to the scope of the effectiveness of the "program." Moreover, an image of tokenism is promoted. An illusory image of progress is fostered which leads to complacency.

Ministry by proxy is the first cousin to paternalism. While

ministry by proxy is better than nothing, it should never be sub-
stituted for direct responsibility or involvement. If employed, it
should be reviewed as transitional.

Fraternalism

Fraternalism is the practice of people from ethnic groups coming together on an equal basis of respect and individual ability in
an atmosphere of freedom to be used by God in ministry. This
approach is characterized by a commitment of controlling racist
tendencies. Its starting point is: How can we make ourselves available to the Lord and each other in healthy ways to engage in
ministry? It takes its cue from biblical imperatives about how to
relate to people.

Some components of fraternalism include inclusiveness, fairness, equality of service opportunities (equal prioritizing), willingness to change, leadership inclusion, multicultural appreciation,
enthusiastic association, mutual respect, mutual responsibility.
Fraternalism is characterized by total involvement from an interaction point of equality.

The fraternalism model is the healthy approach. It fairly represents the Christian ideal of acceptance and yields a positive witness. Fraternalism should be the goal of multiethnic ministry.

Moving Toward Fraternalism

Toward Preparation for Transition

Although much progress has been made in recent years, most
churches are still probably monoethnic. The social revolution in
civil rights did cause many churches to rethink their approach to
congregationalizing, but many remain frustrated at how to effectively build a multiethnic congregation. The church committed to
multiethnic ministry will have to learn how to implement it. An
understanding of transition is necessary.

Transitional ministry is an extremely difficult area of focus. A
study made by the Home Mission Board of the Southern Baptist
Convention yielded the conclusion that perhaps 10 percent of
Southern Baptist churches face crises because of transitional dy-

namics.[14] Although transition takes different forms (i.e., economic, age, class, industrial,), racial/ethnic transition is the most threatening. The focus for the following discussion will be on racial/ethnic transition.

Pastoral Qualities for Successful Transition Ministry

The minister is usually the key person in determining the response of the church to the challenge of transition. If the pastor is not ready, the church rarely succeeds. What are some of the qualities of pastoral readiness for transitional ministry?

First, the minister should have the theological conviction about the imperative of inclusive ministry for the church. His theology ought to yield the conclusion that the nature of the church's mission is such that it cannot run away from ministering to people and demonstrate Christian behavior. His theology should not be racist: It should have biblical answers for what should happen when ethnic minorities apply for membership and afterwards. The minister should be able to persuasively and convincingly articulate a theology for healthy multiethnic ministry. If the minister stumbles at this point, his leadership ability will be crippled.

Second, the pastor should be an able leader. Effective leadership skills are necessary to lead a church through the often difficult period of transition. The pastor should know how to lead through Bible study, basing transition strategies on biblical foundations. An understanding of the dynamics of church politics will make it easier to avoid mistakes. A strategy for multiethnic church growth should be well defined. The pastor should lead as a magnet for fellowship between people from different groups in the congregation. The minister should be skillful in the art of converting Christians from monoethnicity to multiethnicity.

Third, the minister should have healthy racial attitudes. The shepherd should be the model of the lover of all people. God forbid that the pastor be a bigot! The minister should strive to get rid of all of his racial hangups and should understand the dynamics and consequences of racism so that the congregation can be led to healthy behavior. The pastor should be the local church symbol of what Christ can do in the area of race relations when a Christian yields to Him.

Fourth, the pastor should be knowledgeable about the other ethnic groups in the church community by understanding their history, problems, folkways, mores, culture, and religious systems. Time should be reserved to become familiar with these potential members. There is nothing more powerful than a leader who understands the people.

Finally, the minister needs to prepare for multiethnic ministry. The minister needs to be trained in the area. Denominational (and other) resources should be urgently utilized to prepare the congregation for the challenge of transition. The unwise minister lets the church change by accident rather than design.

Recognizing Problem Areas for Transitional Churches

Attracting a multiethnic constituency does not mean that all problems have been solved in transitional church ministry. It usually means that another set of problems must be dealt with. The following is a list of some traditional problem areas for multiethnic churches.[15]

- A language barrier
- Different concepts of giving
- Inadvertent offending
- Creation of a relaxed atmosphere and environment
- Competing cultural styles in worship, music, or roles
- Cultural chauvinism reflected by unwillingness to share opportunities
- Paternalism
- Ministry by proxy
- Neighborhood instability
- Dominating dynamics from society
- Maintaining satisfactory levels of ethnic involvement
- Maintaining high financial levels of giving
- Personal and institutional racism
- Conflicting values about religious education
- Acceptance of minority ethnic group minister
- Acceptance of possibility of interracial dating

- Interethnic socializing
- Imbalance of representation in ethnically directed ministries
- Cultural ignorance
- Competing denominational loyalties
- Neurotic guilt

Of course, this list is not exhaustive. It does indicate the diversity and complexity of the challenge of healthy multiethnic ministry.

Implications for Multiethnic Ministry

Implications in at least four areas affecting the ministry arise from these observations: leadership preparation, church ministry practice, seminary training, and denominational assistance.

Implications for Leadership Preparation

People preparing for the ministry today need not assume that they will minister in a monoethnic setting. Therefore, they should seek training which equips for multiethnic effectiveness.

Leaders in training should not depend only on a multiethnic training program for the totality of their involvement in this approach to ministry. Joining a multiethnic church will enrich the training experience and facilitate the multiethnic life-style.

Implications for Churches

Churches preparing for or engaging in multiethnic ministry should develop a commitment to change. They must be willing to die to monoethnicity so that multiethnicity may be born.

Churches must deal with theological ramifications of "difficulty" and "struggle." The multiethnic church is not easily built. It costs commitment, pain, struggle, and risk.

Churches must cherish creativity. It is probable that many models of healthy multiethnic churches have not yet been built.

Implications for Seminaries

Seminaries are challenged to embody healthiness in their curriculum, structures, faculties, administrations, staffs, and social ministry to the community and world. A question for seminaries is: How healthy are we in our approach to multiethnicity?

Implications for Denominational Agencies

Denominational agencies need to evaluate services provided in light of criteria for healthy multiethnic ministry. When those services are unhealthy they should be changed.

Denominations should provide resources for churches in need of help in dealing with the dynamics of multiethnicity. Some churches are becoming extinct because of resources too little and too late.

Finally, denominational agencies should reflect healthiness in their ethnic involvement and composition. The denominational agency should be a model worthy of emulation.

Conclusion

A great challenge for churches at the end of the twentieth century is to demonstrate a healthy life-style in human relations. This will not evolve in a vacuum. It demands preparation. It challenges the best in our generation. However difficult it may be, the evidence suggests that it can be done.

Notes

1. William Hendricks, "A Theology for a Healthy Multiethnic Church," September 1980. An article prepared for the Baptist Sunday School Board.

2. *Webster's Ninth New Collegiate Dictionary,* 1986.

3. Wilma Longstreet, *Aspects of Ethnicity* (New York and London: Teachers College Press, 1978), p. 19.

4. Ibid., p. 32.

5. Hendricks.

6. Francis DuBose, *How Churches Grow in an Urban World* (Broadman Press: Nashville, 1978), p. 127.

7. Ibid.

8. Kyle Haselden, *The Racial Problem in Christian Perspective* (New York: Harper & Row, 1959), p. 48.

9. James H. Cone, *Black Theology and Black Power* (New York: Seabury Press, 1969).

10. U.S. Commission on Civil Rights, *Racism in America and How to Combat It* (Washington, D.C.: U.S. Government Printing Office, 1970), p. 5.

11. Ibid., p. 6.

12. Ibid.

13. Ashley Montague, *The Concept of Race* (London: Collier Mac-Millan Limited, 1964), cover statement.

14. Don Mabry, *A Study of Churches in Communities in Crisis in Metropolitan Associations in the Southern Baptist Convention, 1973* (Home Mission Board: Atlanta, 1974), pp. 25-26.

15. Sidney Smith, "An Analysis of the Transitional Process of Selected Multiracial Churches" (Diss. Golden Gate Baptist Theological Seminary, 1973).

8

The Church and Economic Life

W. David Sapp

The gospel is economic. We cannot get around that simple fact. The most frequent subject of Jesus' teaching was the relationship of humanity to the material world. The Bible is shot through with teachings about economics.

Yet when the church speaks on economics, it is usually chided or derided by the culture for intruding into an area beyond the meager abilities of mere churchmen. Witness, for example, the outrage of many business and political leaders when the United States Catholic bishops issued a pastoral letter on economics in 1986.[1] Those who have given us inflation, recession, depression, unemployment, monetary crises, astronomical budget deficits, and trade imbalances feel strangely superior to the church when speaking on economics.

Of course, the role of the church is not to provide technical expertise on the economy.[2] The church's role is to uphold a set of economic values which will keep economic life just and will protect God's children from being victimized by its temptations and abuses. The role of economists is to tell us what makes the economy tick. The role of the church is to tell us why it matters.

The relationship between faith and economics is apparent in at least two ways. First, faith is the means by which people are freed to use economic power ethically. Faith provides us with perspective on the material world. Faith allows us to step far enough beyond the material world to see that it holds no ultimate satisfaction and, therefore, frees us from materialism.

Second, faith and economics are both involved with the definition of values. Economics assigns temporal values; faith assigns

163

eternal values. This would provide a neat separation of faith and economics except for the fact that temporal values and eternal values are related. Sometimes the value assigned by one affects the value assigned by the other. For example, the eternal value of a hungry child gives that child an economic value of the society which must feed him. At other times the value assigned by one wars with the value assigned by the other. Cocaine, assigned a high value by economics, is totally worthless from a faith perspective. The Bible makes abundantly clear the relationship between faith and economics.

Some Biblical Principles Relating to Economics Life

This discussion of the Bible's teaching about economics is divided into two sections. First, three *primary principles* which apply to economics will be discussed. They are the love of God, the love of neighbor, and the goodness of creation. Second, a number of "derivative" principles will be examined from the primary principles. While the primary principles apply generally to economic behavior, the derivative principles tend to apply more specifically.

Primary Principles

The Gospel of Matthew gives us the two most basic principles of Christian behavior: "Thou shalt love the Lord they God with all thy heart, and with all thy soul, and with all thy mind. This is the first and great commandment. And the second is like unto it. Thou shalt love thy neighbour as thyself. On these two commandments hang all the law and the prophets" (Matt. 22:37-40, KJV). This last statement is the most significant ethical insight of all time. All of morality, all of the best in human law and behavior, and the entirety of God's law are based on the love of God and neighbor.

Therefore, *the* primary principle of ethical economic behavior, as of all behavior, is the love of God. When and if an economist ever asks a Christian, "How can we make our economic system more just and fair?" the first answer must be, "Love God!" When the banker asks his pastor, "How can we make ethical decisions about loans, interests rates, and investments?" the first answer must be, "Love God!" Evangelism is always a summons to righteousness.

To love God is *the* basic governing principle of human life. When one is totally committed to the love of God, one's deepest longing becomes to please God. A truly Christian corporate executive, for instance, would care more about pleasing God than about pleasing the stockholders. A truly Christian public officeholder would care more about pleasing God than about pleasing the electorate. And a truly Christian pastor would care more about pleasing God than about impressing the world.

If we applied this principle of the love of God to economic decisions, it would profoundly affect human behavior. For instance, love could never allow a child anywhere in the world to starve while indulging the self in luxury. Love could never cheat Caesar on an income tax return or rob God in an offering envelope. Love could never swindle a customer or extort inflated interest rates from families who are struggling to survive.

The second primary principle is just like the first: Love your neighbor as yourself. This principle is simple, straight forward, and electrifying in its impact on our decisions about the material order. Who can love his neighbor as himself and then devote his life to the accumulation of luxury? Who can love his neighbor as himself and pollute the atmosphere for personal gain? Who can love his neighbor as himself and squander natural resources of the earth?

The love of God and neighbor disciplines our greed. It puts limits on our acquisitive instincts. It summons us to generosity and chastens our addiction to the material. But more than this, it gives up the real security which men and women so often falsely seek in the material world.

A third primary biblical principle which guides economic decision making is the goodness of creation. When God had finished the creation, He "saw every thing that he had made, and, behold, it was very good" (Gen. 1:31a, KJV). This affirmation of the material world checks the tendency of Christian ethics toward both world-rejecting asceticism and world-embracing materialism. Ascetics, such as the hermits of old and the more extreme advocates of the simple life-style movement today, see the material world as inherently evil. This, of course, is a denial of the goodness of creation. Materialists, on the other hand, treat the material world as the ultimate reality. This is a denial of God's creative activity and is exaltation of the material order to a higher place than it rightfully occupies.

The antidote for materialism is not asceticism. It is, rather, the biblical understanding that the material world is truly good because it has been created by God. When creation is properly understood as a very good and costly gift from God, it may be seen as a treasure which must be guarded carefully and shared generously. The ethics surrounding this inheritance apply to man's care of the material world. It is immoral to squander an inheritance; it is immoral to fight for more than one's share; and it is immoral to let the love of the inheritance obscure our love for the benefactor.

Derivative Principles

A number of economic teachings which are derived from these three basic principles permeate the Scriptures. They are the practical applications of the grand ideas discussed previously. The guidance they offer us for both personal and social ethics makes them worth careful examination.

Wealth is a blessing from God.—This idea is clearly espoused in the Bible. "Blessed is the man that feareth the Lord" said the psalmist, "Wealth and riches shall be in his house" (Ps. 112:1,3, KJV). Deuteronomy 8:18 affirms that it is God who gives the power to get wealth. Sometimes the Bible sees wealth as a reward for righteousness, as in the case of Abraham or Job. But even when prosperity fell to the unrighteous, the Old Testament made the point clear that the source of all wealth is God.

Of course, this should never lead us as individuals or as a nation to be self-righteous about our wealth. While it is possible that our wealth is the fruit of our own righteousness, we can never be too sure of that. The ungodly sometimes prosper, and the righteous often suffer. As soon as we begin to believe that we deserve our wealth, we lose the concept of stewardship and appreciation deteriorates into avarice. The proper conclusion to draw from the fact the wealth is the gift of God is the stewardship conclusion: We are responsible to God for its use.

Wealth is highly dangerous.—The Bible warns repeatedly of the intrinsic dangers in wealth. These warnings have been difficult for the church to hear, and they have often been spiritualized away, but they are unescapable. Psalm 49:6-7 reminds us that wealth does not possess the power it appears to have: "They that trust in their wealth, and boast themselves in the multitude of their riches; None of them can by any means redeem his brother, nor give to God a ransom for him" (KJV)

Who can forget those hard words of Jesus, "It is easier for a camel to go through the eye of a needle, than for a rich man to enter the kingdom of God" (Matt. 19:24, KJV). Jesus put plainly the dangers of wealth in a simple phrase, "Ye cannot serve God and mammon" (Matt. 6:24, KJV). Then, in the ensuing section of the Sermon on the Mount, He advised people not to be thinking too much about providing food or clothing for tomorrow. Real security is not to be found in wealth. Jesus also warned of the power of wealth to lure the heart when He said, "For where your treasure is, there will your heart be also" (Matt. 6:21, KJV). And James, to choose one final example, warned in stark language of God's judgment, "Go to now, ye rich men, weep and howl for your miseries that shall come upon you" (Jas. 5:1, KJV). We cannot read the Bible honestly and deny its teaching that wealth is a painful danger to meaningful human existance.

Faithful stewardship is expected.—Of all the derivative principles about economics recorded in Holy Scripture, this one is the most commonly recognized. The responsibility of the tithe was clearly delineated in the Old Testament (Lev. 27:30) and affirmed in the New (Luke 18:12) as one expression of stewardship. Tithing is important not only because it provides the necessary financial support for God's work on the earth but also because it is a discipline by which we remind ourselves that "the earth is the Lord's and the fulness thereof " (Ps. 24:1, KJV). The tenth is given to Yahweh as a token of His power over the other nine tenths.

Tithing is the most effective practical antidote to materialism available.

Tithing, however, is but one part of the larger doctrine and practice of stewardship. The Bible views God as the owner of all and man as His manager. This obviously means that a man is responsible to an authority higher than himself for the use of the material things at his disposal (Matt. 25:14-30).

Christians are not free to pursue selfish ends unchecked or to devote their lives to the acquisition of money for its own sake. Christians are God's managers, charged with spreading the gospel, feeding the hungry, protecting the weak, and healing the sick. To use God's resources in other ways to the neglect of God's purposes is literally to steal from God's treasury (Mal. 3:8). To abuse God's earth is to violate His trust. To waste natural resources is to squander our inheritance from Him. The doctrine of stewardship is profound; it is widely understood; it has the potential to solve most of the problems about which individuals and governments wrestle. But, it is not widely accepted, even by Christians. As long as this is true, the problems of hunger, disease, poverty, and war will plague the earth.

Vocation implies a purpose higher than economic.—A few years ago I heard the chief executive officer of a major American corporation say that the purpose of a corporation is not to make a profit, but to make a product or render a service. He reported a strong adverse reaction to his opinions, but a short time later, Thomas H. Peters and Robert W. Waterman, Jr., wrote a best-selling management book entitled *In Search of Excellence* which echoed his belief. What was their most telling point? Businesses succeed by emphasizing excellence in manufacturing their product or rendering their service. Those who work for profits first are doomed to mediocrity or failure.[3]

Both of these positions are headed in a biblical direction, even if they do not go all the way. Scripture teaches that work is, first of all, service to God. Christians work because God has commanded it (Gen. 3:23; 1 Thess. 4:11; 2 Thess. 3:10), not merely for gain. In fact, the Bible specifically cautions against working primarily for profit (Prov. 23:4, John 6:27).

The Latin root of the word *vocation* means "to call." Martin Luther was the first to articulate clearly that all human work should be viewed as a calling, as a response to the initiative of God.[4]

The Christian can never participate in the workplace, whether as a common laborer or a corporate chieftain, with economics as his or her highest motivation. The purpose of work is to obey God and to give glory to Him.

The right to private property is assumed.—Because the early Christians had all things in common (Acts 4:32), the case has sometimes been made that Christianity opposes the ownership of private property. Yet there is no clear indication anywhere in the Scriptures that private ownership is wrong, and there are many references to people owning property.

Two ideas stand out: (1) The Bible places no great value on whether a person owns property or on how much is owned ("Is not the life more than meat, and the body than raiment" [Matt. 6:25b, KJV]). (2) Ownership is seen as a trust from God. The Bible places great stress on the ethics of ownership, otherwise known as stewardship.

The right to survival is basic.—One of the clearest assertions of the Bible is the right to life. Not only was no murder to be done but also food was to be left in the fields for the hungry to glean (Lev. 19:10). Debts were to be forgiven every seven years (Deut. 15:1-2). Food was to be shared with the poor, not as a matter of choice but in response to the firm commandment of God (v. 11). Amos's fiercest message of condemnation was reserved for those who abused the poor: "Thus saith the Lord; For three transgressions of Israel and for four I will not turn away the punishment thereof; because they sold . . . the poor for a pair of shoes" (Amos 2:6, KJV). In the account of the rich man and Lazarus, the rich man is indicted for turning his back on a beggar at his gates (Luke 16:19-31). James spoke of the Christian responsibility to act and not just to feel goodwill toward the hungry (Jas. 2:15-16).

The Christian's obligation to keep people from starving to death is unconditional. That, of course, is what makes it so hard to accept. Nowhere in the Bible is a distinction made between our responsibility to the deserving poor and our responsibility to the underserving poor. Food is the gift of God to humanity; it is manna from heaven. It does not belong just to the farmer who raised it or the purchaser who buys it. Food belongs to all of God's children, and it is to be shared. Even Paul's admonition that those who would not work should not eat (2 Thess. 3:10) is not to be interpreted to mean that laziness should be punishable by death. Paul believed in withholding food until the person worked, not until he died.

Nevertheless, Paul's instruction to work for our food means that we should never presume our own right to the generosity of others. The needy should feel the responsibility to work above their right to be fed. The well-off, on the other hand, should feel the responsibility to share above their own right to property. This is the Bible's system of values.

These biblical teachings about economics have application to all areas of economic life, both personal and social. Personal economic issues are those issues about which individuals make decisions. Social economic issues are those issues about which society as a whole makes decisions. In the pages which follow, a few illustrative issues at both levels will be considered briefly.

Some Personal Economic Issues

Before economics is social, it is personal. Before social economic questions can be addressed ethically, personal economic issues must be addressed ethically.

Honesty

Honesty, perhaps the most basic virtue of all, is often tested by personal economic decisions. Nearly everyone agrees that "honesty is the best policy" in the big things, but what about the small lie which will help me while doing no real harm to anyone else? The average person would never commit a bank robbery, but what about stealing postage from a billion dollar corporation? The reasoning takes on a strangely immoral flavor: "The corporation will never feel the loss, and besides, I was cheated out of my last raise. I worked overtime last week without getting paid for it. The company takes advantage of its employees. If I steal a few cents in postage, it is no more than I have coming."

The same reasoning is applied frequently to paying taxes: "The government has no right to take so much from my family and me. Washington wastes our money and spends it on things I don't believe in. To avoid paying taxes hurts nothing but a few fat cats, bleeding hearts, and insane government programs." Most of us can steal from institutions with fewer qualms than we can from individuals.

The issue that is overlooked is that the most severely affected victim of dishonesty is its perpetrator. Even if it were true that a company or government would not be harmed by a petty loss or two, the individual suffers internally from participation in what he or she knows to be wrong. To become a thief, even a petty one, colors one's self-image. A new layer of guilt, be it ever so thin, is added to that already lurking in the soul. My resistance to evil is stretched and weakened against stronger onslaughts to come. The real ethical question is not whether dishonesty will hurt its object; it is whether it will hurt me, its subject.

Generally human beings are on guard against blatant forms of dishonesty, but sometimes dishonesty wears cunning disguises. The inflated price seems acceptable when it is the standard price. Can it ever be right for a hospital to turn away a person who cannot afford to pay? Can it ever be right for food or medicine or transportation to cost so much that some people cannot afford to obtain them? To hawk necessary goods and services at oppressive prices is simply the modern-day equivalent of selling the poor for a pair of shoes (Amos 2:6). It is dishonest to tell others these prices are necessary; it is dishonest to tell ourselves that these prices are justified; and it is dishonest to tell God we have done nothing wrong in allowing them. When applied to economic life, honesty is a demanding virtue.

Materialism

Materialism is the root disease of which most economic problems are symptoms. Materialism, simply put, is addiction to the material world. Commonly we say that materialism is the worship of the material world, but secular human beings understand *addiction;* they do not understand *worship.*

Like other addictions, materialism appeals to people who are looking for a missing piece in their lives. Perhaps they lack self-worth, power, or pleasure; the one common denominator is that they all lack security. The material world appears to be an obvious place to turn for security; it seems so very real and stable. Buildings sometimes stand for centuries. Land (with few exceptions) never disappears. (We even call it *real* estate.) People, however, are not ultimately material; we are spiritual. Our security is not to be found in things that can be seen and touched. This is why Jesus said, "Lay not up for yourselves treasures upon earth; where moth and rust doth corrupt, and where thieves break through and steal: But lay up for yourselves treasures in heaven, where neither moth nor rust doth corrupt, and where thieves do not break through nor steal" (Matt. 6:19-20, KJV).

While materialism promises to deliver security, it actually seduces countless human beings into wasting their lives, their substance, and their relationships chasing a phantom. The chief end of persons becomes, not the glory of God, but the acquisition of things. Their personal ethics are reordered according to this goal, and the truth is brought home: "The love of money is the root of all evil" (1 Tim. 6:10).

Sensitive Christians in every age have reacted against materialism. As discussed earlier, the most extreme reaction takes the form of asceticism. Christians must guard against materialism, but they must also be careful lest the overreaction of asceticism tempt them into rejecting God's creation. Gratitude is the proper response to the material world, not hostility or addiction.

Stewardship

The only effective corrective to materialism is the practice of Christian stewardship. To some, stewardship is the gauge the churches uses to extract money from its members. To the perceptive, however, it is the tool God uses to free His people from their enslavement to things. Stewardship is a simple concept: Man owns nothing; God owns everything. Man is under a divine appointment to manage the things that God has placed at his disposal and is ultimately responsible to God for the quality of this management.

Stewardship is a corrective to the seductive illusion of ownership. Ownership convinces the owner he is powerful and tempts the owner to use that power for selfish ends. Gradually possessions assume control and the possessor becomes possessed.

This, however, need never happen to the Christian. The temptations of materialism are checked by the knowledge that God will hold the Christian responsible for the use of such wealth as he has. In a sense, all Christians are asked to take a vow of poverty, to own nothing, and to use all for the glory of God. This is one of the most freeing dimensions of the gospel.

This truth has important implications for personal economic ethics. First, it means that a person cannot in good conscience devote all of his or her time and energy to the acquisition of things. Some time and energy must be reserved to manage and to use those things for the glory of God. Second, it means that tithes and offerings should be given ungrudgingly. This is money which is not ours, and it is being returned to its source and to its proper use.

Third, this truth means that all of the things with which we are entrusted should be used for the glory of God. To use God's money for drug abuse, pornography, excessive luxury, or the support of wanton violence is to violate the trust of God. To waste God's money on frivolity while hungry people suffer and sick people die is a sin. To use the material pleasures of life only for one's self and not to share them is irresponsible and unworthy stewardship.

Debt

Debt is an issue of particular importance in the twentieth century. Debt serves some useful purposes. It enables us to purchase necessities which would otherwise be unaffordable. Most of us could never afford houses or cars or other similar purchases without debt.

Yet debt can be a devastating monster. It chains the poor in poverty. It eats away at the peace of mind and ultimately the health of those caught within its grip. It diverts the energies of Christian stewards from the service of the Master to the service of the lending institution. On a societal level, excessive debt fuels inflation and creates a host of other economic ills.

Debt is not often seen as a moral issue. If it were, perhaps fewer people would be suffering in the world. To allow ourselves to become so overburdened with debt that all our energies are required to service the debt is quite simply a moral evil. On the other hand, debt used in moderation can sometimes free us from worries that would otherwise distract us from kingdom service. In this case, debt actually becomes a moral good.

Absolute moral guidelines about debt cannot be given, but a great percentage of the credit problems in the world would be solved if people at least understood that a decision to take out a loan is a moral decision and not just an economic one. Some key questions might help an individual decide whether to take out the loan in the first place.

- Will it free my mind and energies for other things, or will it burden me?
- Will it help or hurt our national and world economy?
- Will it interfere with my ability to share my belongings with the world's needy?
- Will it be fair to my family?

The work ethic

The work ethic is under attack on two fronts. Recently a friend told me about her Japanese supervisor who had been sent to the United States to manage a plant for a major company. Quickly he became frustrated with the weak work ethic of his American employees. In his view Americans worked neither hard nor well. According to his view, the work ethic is dead in America.

At the same time, Wayne Oates indicated our culture for "workaholism."[5] He contended that many of us are addicted to work and are destroying ourselves and our families by this addiction. In his view, the work ethic has been carried to an extreme in America.

Which observation is correct? Are these contradictory views of American society?

I think they are observations of different segments of our society. The work ethic is dying for the hopeless people. In an earlier day, those who saw no possibility of social advancement and no way out of poverty worked hard anyway because their work had purpose. Now, in the age of the mega corporation, the assembly line, and computer, the purpose of any particular job is increasingly obscure to the worker. Even if the blacksmith were poor, he served an important function in his community and was valued for that function. The assembly line worker or the computer operator, on the other hand, often sees himself or herself as dispensable, easily replaceable, and not valued by the community or the company. In this situation, the worker has little motivation for diligence.

On the other hand, enormous opportunities are open for other persons in our society. Wealth seems there for the taking in many fields of endeavor, particularly in the boom cities and power centers of our nation. But one must compete for this wealth. Workaholism is a problem of the upwardly mobile. As one young friend was told recently by his employer, "Your work is good, but eight hours a day is not enough. You must outwork your peers." Many people are caught in this highly competive pressure at the very time in life when small children need them most and when marriage is nearly crowded out of the schedule.

Both of these problems root in the same moral sickness: the lack of significant purpose in work. The blue-collar worker may have no purpose in work higher than paying the rent. The young professional may have no purpose other than self-advancement or the acquisition of wealth. One responds with indolence and the other with workaholism. Both will lead empty, frustrating lives.

When the purpose of work becomes glorifying God, however, a much different perspective emerges. The problem of indolence is diminished for those as one end of the spectrum because now they have a purpose for their work. The problem of work addiction also is held in check for those at the other end of the spectrum because now their work has a higher purpose which is not well served by work addiction.

Some Social Economic Issues

Far too many economic issues affect society to treat them all here, and each is too complex to address adequately in this space. Therefore, my purpose at this point is only to introduce a few ethical observations about selected issues in the hope that you will be stimulated to undertake more exhaustive reflection.

Economic systems

Two great economic philosophies vie for the allegiance of nations in the modern world. Both philosophies, socialism and capitalism, are built on moral arguments. *Socialism* is built on the ideal of equality. In a pure socialist system, every person has an equal right to the economic benefits of the society. *Capitalism* is built on the ideal of freedom. In a pure capitalist system, every person has an equal opportunity for achievement in the marketplace. Socialists see capitalists as greedy tycoons who trample on the basic rights of other human beings in their quest for wealth. Capitalists see socialists as naive utopians who smother the very initiatives which will in the end solve many of the problems of suffering humanity. Two points which are critical to any ethical examination of the two systems follow.

First, pure socialism and pure capitalism do not exist. They must be evaluated as they exist in practice, not as they are described in theory. Karl Marx's dream of a society without greed is no more a picture of contemporary socialism than Adam Smith's dream of a nation of small entrepreneurs is a picture of contemporary capitalism.

Second, while my personal preference runs strongly to capitalism, it is important to realize that there is no totally Christian economic system. Economic systems are human in origin and temporary in nature. The Bible does not endorse any economic system in its entirety. Rather, the Bible gives us principles by which all economic systems can be judged. The Christian faith must preserve its ability to serve as the moral critic of every economic system. When the faith is identified with a particular system, then Christianity compromises its ability to critize that system and its ability to evangelize those outside that system.

Poverty

Severe poverty is a curse which has fallen on one-fourth of the world's population. Hunger kills at least ten thousand persons a day, the majority of whom are children.[6] In the United States the number of homeless people is currently climbing astronomically.

Some of this poverty may be attributed to lack of initiative on the part of the individual, but the vast majority of the world's poverty must be seen in other terms. Drought, famine, war, lack of natural resources, and politics are just a few of the forces which produce poverty in every corner of the globe.

The existence of such extensive poverty raises a number of questions for the seeking Christian. First, is there a moral obligation for the affluent to work for the elimination of poverty? Of course there is. We have already seen that the Bible is very clear on this point. Some have used Jesus' words, "Ye have always the poor with you" (Matt. 26:11, KJV) to support *not* helping the poor. This is an odd interpretation of the verse since in it Jesus was referring to a passage from Deuteronomy which said, "For the poor shall never cease out of the land: therefore I command thee, saying, Thou shalt open thine hand wide unto thy brother, to thy poor, and to thy needy, in thy land" (Deut. 15:11, KJV).

A second question is what level of poverty is acceptable in our world? How poor is too poor? One reason there is such universal support for antihunger efforts is because it is clearly unacceptable to nearly everyone for people to starve to death. Is it acceptable, then, for individuals to be without adequate affordable medical care? Is this level of poverty any less threatening to human life than hunger? Are adequate housing and clothing basic? What about heat in the winter? These are unresolved questions which cry for Christian attention.

Third is the practical question: How should poverty be fought? This is where the greatest division of opinion among thinking people exists. Should government carry the primary load or can we trust the individuals or private charities to carry the load? Christians will have honest differences on this questions. Yet, surely, we can agree that the church must play a major role. Only the church has the highest motivation for the elimination of human suffering. Only the church cares deeply for the people it seeks to help. Only the church can offer the Bread of Life to the suffering. Only the church can voice the opposition of God to unjust structures which perpetuate poverty. The church is called to carry a heavier part of this load than it has yet carried.

The Role of the Corporation

Another matter which needs increased discussion in our society is the role of the corporation. The framers of capitalism envisioned a multitude of small businesses run by highly motivated entrepreneurs. They could never have conceived of the multinational corporations of today. These huge corporations face unique ethical problems, and they need the help of the church in dealing with them.

The first step in framing a Christian business ethic for the corporation is to redefine the purpose of the corporation. Business has defined its own purpose as profits. This has led to a negative public image for corporations, as well as to misplaced attention on balance sheets rather than quality of goods and services. Ironically the idea that profit is the purpose of business has led to decreased profits. A corporation's purpose is to meet a real and specific need (or desire) of society. The purpose of a car manufacturer, for instance, is not to make a profit; rather it is to manufacture cars. Of course, if the company is going to continue fulfilling its purpose, it *must* make a profit.

Profit is *not* a dirty word, but neither is it the ultimate purpose of a corporation. Profit is simply one means by which a company achieves its purpose. This simple conceptual change frees a corporation to pursue the good of the society rather than just the short-term avarice of its stockholders or managers.

Some other tough questions also need consideration. To whom is a corporation responsible? The standard answer of the past has been that it is responsible to its stockholders, but the truth is that stockholders are investors, not owners. They rarely, if ever, call a corporation to account for anything other than their dividend checks. Government regulates corporations on behalf of the people in some areas, but our system stands on the belief that government control should be limited. Some have tried to make corporations responsible to the marketplace through the use of boycotts, but this is a cumbersome and not very effective means of accountability which is wide open to abuse by any element in society, no matter how extreme. A totally acceptable answer to this question has not yet emerged.

Finally, what is the social responsibility of the corporation? Of course, the first social responsibility of the corporation is to produce its product with quality and integrity; the second is like unto it, to treat its employees with justice and fairness. Beyond that, should a corporation pad its profits so that it can afford to give to worthy causes? Does this not give the corporation too much power over charitable organizations? Or should a corporation refuse to do business in countries with abhorrent moral practices? Absolute answers for every situation are impossible, but this much is clear: Major corporations control too much of our wealth and too many of our lives not to be held accountable for their social responsibility. As a new form of the corporation is emerging, some of the best and brightest must give attention to a new understanding of the corporation's social responsibility.

Taxation

Two basic issues affect the ethics of taxation. The first is the role of government. If government has a large role, broadly defined, a fairly high level of taxation might be considered ethical. If the role of government is defined more narrowly, a proportionately lower level would be acceptable. The second issue is the equitable distribution of the tax burden. How can a government tax rich and poor citizens alike and do it fairly?

The United States has always lived with some tension over the role of government. At one end of the spectrum are Americans who maintain that the sole responsibility of government is defense. At the other end are those who would involve government in every phase of the life of the individual. The former run the risk of a government with on compassion, which ignores human suffering while it has the means to stop it. The latter run the risk of abrogating individual freedom.

The Bible does not address these concerns directly. Certainly Israel's government was to be highly involved in meeting the basic human needs of its citizens, but its theocratic form of government was far different from our democratic form. It is not clear how sharply the parallels should be drawn. In the New Testament Christians were counseled to accept the government as a given and to respect its God-ordained authority. The proper interpretation of Romans 13 is that Christians should be good citizens of the present kingdom in order to remain free to build the coming kingdom.

Perhaps that is all the counsel Christians need. God's people should not become so ensnared in the system that they lose their freedom to work for the system which God is establishing. Therefore, whatever level of taxation is established, taxes should be paid ungrudgingly ("Render therefore to all their dues: tribute to whom tribute is due; custom to whom custom" Rom. 13:7, KJV). Only when the level of taxation becomes the instrument of real oppression to others does it become a matter of concern to kingdom citizens.

The equitable distribution of the tax burden is in some ways a more difficult problem. One the one hand, our income tax (and perhaps some other taxes) is structured regressively. That is, the rich pay a higher percentage of their income than the poor. On the other hand, the sales tax, for instance, is an essentially level tax, theoretically affecting rich and poor alike. In reality, such taxes fall most heavily on the poor.

The argument for the regressive tax is based on this inequality in "level" taxes. To pay 20 percent (for example) of a poverty level income is a far great burden than to pay 20 percent of an affluent income. To place a heavier tax burden on the backs of the working poor than on the backs of the rich is a disincentive to work. Regressive taxes are built on the conviction that those who benefit most from a society owe the most to that society. Regressive tax plans are really secular applications of Jesus' words: "For unto whomsoever much is given, of him much shall be required" (Luke 12:48, KJV).

The argument for various "level" taxes (used here to refer to any tax which does not change with income levels) is that they provide incentive for individuals to advance economically since the tax burden shrinks as the income rises. The economic advancement of individuals, in turn, strengthens the overall economy and provides jobs for the poor. There is enough truth in this argument to justify some such taxes. From a Christian perspective, however, the "incentive to wealth" argument is weak. Those who have heard and understood Jesus' words that it is easier for a camel to pass through the eye of a needle than for a rich man to get into the Kingdom of heaven (Matt. 19:24) cannot seriously think it is important to provide an incentive to create rich men. Only to the extent that level taxes do, in fact, strengthen the economy can they be justified from a Christian ethical perspective, and then they must be carefully applied so as not to do more harm than good. A further problem with the argument that government should provide incentives to wealth is that most human beings do not seem to lack this incentive. People may lack the opportunity or understanding of how to seize their opportunity; but the incentive to acquire things does not need to be fed in very many human beings.

What we have in the American tax system is two views of taxation held in tension. The values in each tend to check the dangers in the other, and the result is a reasonably equitable system which needs ethical monitoring and adjustment from time to time.

There is a great need for creative Christian reflection on a number of other economic issues. The list of issues which have been discussed here, both personal and social, is not exhaustive. It is illustrative. In no way is this discussion a final word; it is rather a first word which needs to be completed by serious members of the community of faith. But this chapter would not be complete without some examination of the role of the church in the application of the gospel to economic life.

The Role of the Church

The church has two primary responsibilities relative to economic ethics. Both are extraordinarily important.

The first responsibility of the church in the realm of economics is to proclaim the truth. Many Christians have never understood that the gospel has a bearing on economic life. They have never realized how much Jesus had to say about materialism. Without marrying an economic system or a political perspective, the church must help its adherents know what the Bible says about economics and how to apply these teachings. If the Church fails to do this, it is guilty of cutting pages out of the Bible and failing to offer proper guidance for Christian living.

At times the church must speak to the culture about economic ethics. No one needs the church intruding into every technical economic decision, but "when the poor are being sold for a pair of shoes," the church cannot be silent. When justice is being eroded, the voice of God's prophets must be raised.

Secondly, the church must provide a community of alternative values. The world values wealth and measures a person's worth by it. The Book of James makes a clear case that this is not to happen in the church (2:1-9). The church must provide for Christians a community whose values are different, a context in which the pressures of the world can be resisted, and a place where the richness of a higher reality can be experienced. This demands education for church leaders, as well as constant vigilance by the family of faith.

The role of the church in economic ethics needs much more exploration than has been accomplished in these pages. My purpose has been to establish that the church does have such a role. This fact has dawned on too few Christians and has been resisted by too many. Faith is not one dimension of life; it is a way of life. When it becomes a way of economic life for Christians, then we will be much nearer an answer to Jesus' prayer: "Thy kingdom come. Thy will be done, in earth, as it is in heaven" (Matt. 6:10). Meanwhile, we would do well to join His prayer while we work for righteousness.

Notes

1. See, for example, Michael Goldberg, "Two Letters on the Economy: Two Sides of the Same Coin?" *The Christian Century,* 10 April 1985, pp. 347-350.

2. T.B. Maston, *Christianity and World Issues* (New York: The Macmillan Company, 1957), p.122.

3. Thomas H. Peters and Robert H. Waterman, Jr., *In Search of Excellence* (New York: Warner Books, 1984), p.103.

4. Roland Bainton, *Here I Stand* (New York: Mentor Books, 1964), p.156.

5. Wayne Oates, *Confessions of a Workaholic* (Waco: Word Books, 1972).

6. James P. Grant, "Hunger and Malnutrition and the World's Poorest Billion," from the unpublished proceedings of the 1978 Southern Baptist Convocation on World Hunger, p.7.

9
Sexuality: Reflecting Who We Are

Libby Potts

Introduction

A sexual revolution has been evolving in the world for years. Some believe the revolution is actually over, that commitment and intimacy are on their way back "in." Still, writing on the subject of sexuality is a risk because it is, indeed, a very precious and delicate issue and, therefore, potentially volatile and turbulent. However, I hope this chapter will add understanding where there usually has been confusion.

The thesis of this chapter is that sexuality and identity are so linked that they cannot be separated. Our identity is best found in the love of God, self, and others. Therefore, our sexuality is a reflection of who we are.

Many times we want to minimize or even negate our sexuality. We are created in the image of God; God viewed His creation as very good. Thus, we should perceive our sexuality as good.

Definitions of Sexuality

This chapter will use a definition of sexuality that is more inclusive than a sexual act. A distinction is made between *sex* and *sexuality.*

One dictionary definition considers *sex* to be either the character of being male or female or anything connected with sexual gratification and reproduction. *Sexuality* is said to be that state or quality of being sexual.[1]

The distinction between sex and sexuality is important and useful. However, this distinction is difficult to maintain with clarity and consistency. Sexuality is who we are as "body-selves" who experience the emotional, cognitive, physical, and spiritual need for intimate communion—both human and divine.[2]

Sexuality is a much more comprehensive term than *sex*. While including sex, sexuality goes beyond sex acts. To be sure, sexuality is not the whole of our personhood, but it is a very basic dimension. While sexuality does not determine all of our feelings, thoughts, and actions, in ways both obvious and concealed, it permeates and affects them all.

Sexuality includes our attitudes and understanding as male and female and affectional orientation toward those of the opposite or same sex. Sexuality is a sign, a symbol, and a means to communion and to communication. The mystery of our sexuality is the mystery of our need to reach out and embrace others, both physically and spiritually.

Sexuality expresses God's intention that we find our authentic humanness in relationship. But such relationship cannot occur in the human dimension alone. Sexuality is also intrinsic to our relationship with God because it is a part of who we are, our identity.

Sexuality and Identity

Sexuality involves much more than sexual anatomy or sex-role attitudes. It involves self-image and self-esteem. Sexuality, more than anything else, has to do with our capacity for relationship and connectedness in transcending our separateness. Sexuality involves our ability as human beings to open our minds and hearts to one another and to give and receive emotional intimacy. Thus, sexuality is the external manifestation of the internal process of human identity.

An example of how we do not understand this idea can be seen in how we discuss sexuality with the youth in our churches. We talk about the do's and don'ts in their sexual behavior. We stress behavior as extremely important, but we often forget about identity and self-esteem as a probable root cause to behavior.

In the process of communicating about sexuality, we must help our audience understand that the creation of our identity comes from our relationship to God. Many times individuals will try to fill the void in their lives by connectedness exclusively with other persons. But, the void can only be filled by God.

Thus, healthy sexuality moves from a personal relationship with God to the human relationship. The response we have in relationship to others is a reflection of who we are in relationship to God.

Old Testament Perspectives on Sexuality

Much of our biblical understanding of sexuality comes from the Old Testament. The root meaning of sexuality and a person's identity is found in the account of the creation and the relational dimension of humankind.

The Image of God

We are created in the image of God. Drawing on an analogy in the human context, a child bears the image of his or her parents. There is a resemblance physically and emotionally. Humankind in much the same way bears resemblance to the Heavenly Father. By our choices and actions, we often try to deny this relationship, but we cannot remove ourselves from the fact that we are created in His image.

Thus the biblical teaching concerning humanity is not that we are only a collection of chemical elements; rather, the emphasis is that we are made in the image of God. Even our maleness and femaleness is a part of being created in God's image. None of this implies that we are a miniature deity, but that we have a capacity for relationship and fellowship with God and with other persons. To the extent we show His divine image, we have potential for living responsibly with one another.

Man Needs Community

Genesis 2:18-25 introduces a profound theme found throughout the remainder of the Old Testament and into the New Testament. The focus of the passage is the importance of intimacy and the basic human need we all have for interaction and community with one another. None of the animals provided the sense of community for Adam, so God created woman from Adam.

In Genesis 2:4-25, we see woman as the concluding event in the narrative and the fulfillment of humanity occurs. The human mutuality in this scene is fundamental to community.

Throughout the Old Testament, we can observe the movement of civilization toward the building of cities. The Hebrews developed the concept of the corporate personality. Humankind was not created to be solitary.

The other thing that is brought out in the need for intimacy and a sense of community is the need for commitment. Man and woman have the opportunity to enter into a covenant relationship with one another as Adam and Eve did. God created us with a need for community which leads to a need for commitment in various forms (i.e., business, church, friendships), and this oftentimes leads us to a need for a covenant relationship in marriage.

The Fall of Man

Genesis 3 portrays humankind's relationship with God and with each other being severely damaged by sin. We can recognize manifestations of this fall in our sexuality in a variety of ways. Rather than having mutuality and equity in relationships as God seems to have intended, humankind's sexuality became a source for attempting to manipulate and to control others.

The distortion of the image of God and the resulting impact on identity of man and woman was immediate. This distortion caused their eyes to be opened to themselves and to change their view of their own self-image. They made clothes to cover their nakedness in a feeble attempt to restore the loss of relationship to God and its associated sense of inward identity. In essence, man and woman manufactured an identity on their own that was less than they were created to be.

Sin not only resulted in alienating humankind from God but also resulted in man and woman holding on to each other closely for the sake of survival. Sin created an unhealthy dependence of man and woman upon each other. Sin provided the illusion that all of a human's need could be met through another human being.

In their plight resulting from God's judgment, man and woman unfortunately limited themselves to reaching for identity within human relationship rather than the divine/human relationship found within God's creation intent. When this distortion of relationship is played to its fullest conclusion, the external development of human sexuality becomes the vehicle in which man and woman attempt to create wholeness without God. David sinned as he sought fulfillment in Bathsheba which set off a chain reaction of sinful acts. Samson lost the strength God had given as he yielded to the temptation of assuming all of his strength was his and not God's.

New Testament Perspectives on Sexuality

The New Testament perspectives on sexuality are represented by a blend of Old Testament themes on sexuality and new meanings or teachings that Jesus gave in the Gospels. The remainder of the New Testament, especially in the writings of Paul, reflects the teachings of Jesus.

Jesus' Perspectives

Jesus reflected and focused the emphases the Old Testament makes about our sexuality. That is, the focus of all relationship is in direct conjunction with God. Thus, Jesus said that all Scripture can be summarized in the two Commandments related to love (Matt. 22:37-40). Such love both liberates and disciplines. Love freely gives and yet requires the whole of oneself for God, neighbor, and self.

The emphasis is upon loving God and neighbor as well as self. Self-love when limited to itself becomes depravity. When self-love is intertwined with godly love, the essence is unmerited or unselfish *agape* love.

If we truly love God, our motives and desires are pleasing to Him. Love of God is the key to love of self and others. Only when we love God and feel loved by God can we share with others the true essence of love.

What is the relationship between love and our sexual identity? Jesus demonstrated that love and sexuality are interdependent.

One's identity and sexuality are inseparable. God created human-kind as sexual beings. Therefore, how one relates to another is from one sexual being to another. How we feel about ourselves (our identity and sexuality) is reflected in how we relate to others.

While Jesus did not have sexual relationships with women, the Gospels make it plain that Jesus related closely and lovingly to women. The basis of His relationship was His role as the servant of God. He did not use women sexually, but related to them as persons of worth.

John 11 is a beautiful passage of friends hurting together and supporting one another. The tender exchange among Mary, Martha, and Jesus is exemplary for us. Throughout the Gospel accounts, Jesus talked to, healed, and loved women just as He did men. Jesus gave us the perfect model for our sexuality in loving and relating to others.

Jesus' ethic serves as a starting point for all sexual relationships for His followers. If our sexual relationships are not based on the kind of selfless love that Jesus exhibited, then in a very real sense, these relationships are less than God intended.

Many times we ask questions concerning relationship to the opposite sex. According to the Gospels, Jesus related fearlessly and openly to women. He blessed the prostitute who anointed His feet in the Pharisee's home; He healed the widow's son; He spoke intimately with Mary and with the Samaritan woman; and He sought the woman who had the flow of blood.

These incidents are especially significant because they represent violations of first-century Jewish piety. In offering help and close friendship to women, Jesus risked the wrath of Jewish authorities and eventually His life. Yet, the value of relationships for Jesus, even to the opposite sex, was a higher ideal from which to exemplify a way of life.

We should not be surprised to find women figuring prominently in Jesus' ministry. Mary Magdalene, Joanna, and others provided for Jesus and the disciples "out of their means" (Luke 8:1-3, RSV). Women were among the major figures attending to Jesus at His burial, and women were the first to believe that Jesus had risen from the dead.

Paul's Perspective

Paul said more directly concerning sexuality and sexual behavior than anyone else in the New Testament. In 1 Corinthians, Colossians, Ephesians, and Galatians, Paul talked about sexual behavior and immorality. Many times the reader's first impressions of Paul's writings concerning sexual behavior can be very negative. Further study shows his writing in a more positive view. Paul's letters addressed specific needs and situations of particular people. Therefore, he applied the principles set out in the Old Testament and by Jesus to specific people in very difficult and immoral cultural situations.

Paul's emphasis was that everyday Christian living requires an unending appropriation of God's grace through obedient faith. Paul set forth a proper understanding of sexual conduct in 1 Corinthians 6:12-20. Since the body is the outward expression of a person, what a person does to his body, he does to his personality or self. Sexual immorality damages the personalities or selves of those who engage in it.

The interrelatedness of sexual misconduct and one's personhood is drawn out in Paul's letters. The theme is grace and obedience in relating to God, others, and self.

Another positive aspect in the area of identity and love of God, self, and others is that Paul was very much the "community man." A common theme throughout his letters is the sense of community among the church. He emphasized the support and love needed among individuals. He called for Christlike responses to such needs.

Distortions of the Biblical Norm

People cover themselves with a great many distorted expressions of sexuality or "clothes" in an endeavor to mend their fragmentation. These internal distortions are frantic attempts to placate the anguish of separation from God through sexual perversions. To fill the void of God's role or identity in one's life is a misguided effort.

One of these distortions is promiscuity. Promiscuity is essentially infidelity. Many people, whether married or single, in their search for intimacy and fulfillment will mistake the sexual act for intimacy. When humankind breaks fidelity, it breaks relationship with God, neighbor, and self. It is a sin that causes harm to the identity of those involved and, therefore, is sin against God's very creation, as well as the Creator.

Another distortion is pornography, which is a gross misuse and abuse of sex. Again, people wanting to fill intimate needs and desires mistake the use of pornographic materials as fulfilling that need, when, in fact, pornography creates more of a void and a problem. Pornography causes one to believe in illusion and fantasy. It brings about lust and evil sexual desire.

Homosexuality, another distortion, is condemned in the Bible (Lev. 18:22; 20:13; 1 Cor. 6:19; Rom. 1:26-32). A homosexual is one who prefers and establishes erotic feeling toward another person of the same sex. Biblical references to homosexuality are apparently to homosexual behavior and not to homosexual "orientation."[3] Romans 1:24-27 is the most devastating passage for practicing homosexuals. The concern is the sin against the body as God created humankind. As many tend to be repulsed and judgmental toward homosexuals, we should apply the gospel full of grace to those who have this distorted view of their sexuality/ identity.

Other distortions are bestiality (Lev. 19:19; 20:15-16), rape, and incest (Lev. 20:11-12, 17, 19-21). All of these are perversions of one's own identity manifested in distortions of sexuality. Each seeks identity by using another of God's creation.

Questions! Questions! What is happening in our society with this prominent sexual revolution? What has happened to our Christian morals and values? What is happening with the young people, college students, single and married adults? What about sexual addictions? Where does the church stand? Why do we tend to avoid talking to our children about sex or providing sex education from a Christian perspective in our churches? Are we being seduced into a sexual wilderness or beckoned toward a sexual freedom?

Sexual Identity Through Relationship in Family

The Single Adult Phenomenon

The Christian community all too often views singleness as a transitory condition which, with God's help, can be healed through marriage. Many well-intentioned people will say casually to a single adult, "Why hasn't someone grabbed you up yet?" As well-intended as that comment is, it very clearly implies a view of singleness that is predominant in our Christian community: (1) that singles are waiting to be married and (2) that there must be a lack of fulfillment without a spouse. These viewpoints not only distort the single person's identity as being a whole person within his or her relationship with God but also view singleness as less than whole, diminishing the role of God in the single person's view of calling and direction in life.

Because a person's wholeness is derived from his or her relationship with God, the single life can have meaning and fullness in and of itself. Consequently, for some singles, there is no need to live under the fallacy which states that a person will not find true happiness until he or she is "joined in matrimony." A single person's sexuality is not diminished in the least. This is not to say that singles do not need intimacy. For all human beings, there is a need for intimacy, love, support, and a connectedness with others.

Single Adults and Sexual Intimacy

A word needs to be set forth about the single life and sexual intimacy. Physical touch is of critical importance to every human being. Statistics have shown that infants who have been denied the gift of touch have developed at a slower pace than their peers who have been blessed with hugs and kisses. Many times single adults are denied this physical touch because of fears and reservations toward an expression of feelings and affection.

The single adult is no different in the need for touch. Should intimacy between single adults include sexual intercourse? Obviously the answer is no. Sexual intercourse is more than just the pinnacle of physical contact between a man and a woman. Sexual intercourse in an ideal relationship is the culmination of two individuals united in marriage, with a sense of completeness found in identity, and expressed through the persons' sexuality freely given and tenderly received. Tragic is the person whose identity is defined only by sexual contact.

Single Adults and Service

Throughout the Scriptures, we read about single adults who contributed to other's lives through service and love for one another and God. Paul is an excellent example of the wholeness that can be found in singleness (1 Cor. 7:7-8; 26-35). Singleness apparently did not alter Paul's effectiveness. If anything, it appears to have enhanced his ministry and time dedicated to God and his fellowman. Paul appreciated the single life-style because of more availability for serving God and others.

Paul's singleness did not deter him from expressing his sexuality. Even a superficial glance at the life and teachings of Paul found in the New Testament reveals a man of deep love and intimacy in relationships. He showed genuine concern, a grieving spirit for those in turmoil, and a boldness in the face of opposition. Aware of his own need for love, working from guilt to forgiveness, Paul had a sense of purpose and mission in life. Through Paul's service, he was able to communicate love to others because of his strong identity and sexuality.

In 1 Corinthians 7:17, Paul responded to the Corinthian church's question of singleness and marriage. "Only, let every one lead the life which the Lord has assigned to him, and in which God has called him" (RSV). It would be wise for the Christian community today to heed Paul's words and celebrate with those whom God has called to live out their wholeness in singleness—whether temporarily or permanently.

Marriage—Two Becoming One

The unity candle is often used in weddings. Both the bride and groom have lighted candles. During the ceremony, they light a single candle in unison. In some cases, the individual candles are blown out to symbolize that the two become one. In other cases, the individual candles remain lighted to symbolize the couple's need to be separate but interwoven in love. Which is the correct symbolism? Either is appropriate.

In Matthew 19:4-6 and Mark 10:6-8, Jesus talked about the two becoming one flesh. Each person's individual heritage and identity contribute to a lifetime covenant relationship within marriage. Jesus did not mean that individuality is lost in marriage any more than it is lost in redemption as a disciple is made one with Christ. Christ was quoting from the passage in Genesis 2:24.

It is interesting and pertinent to note the meaning of the word *flesh*. The Genesis reference to flesh is referring to kindred or blood relative. The one flesh, therefore, refers to relational interaction rather than the merging of two individuals into a single being. God created woman from man in order to establish relational compatibility. They were two people in kindred relationship.

In Genesis 2:24, the term "one flesh" has a definite sexual connotation, but relational intimacy is also a key factor. Getting to a level of relational intimacy in a marriage that is referred to as one flesh involves a great deal of work. It does not occur automatically with marriage. It involves becoming transparent with one another and emphasizing communication and trust, which oftentimes can be difficult. This is an aspect of the one-flesh relationship that is frequently overlooked.

Marriage Related to Wholeness

Marriage is not the completion of an individual. Rather, it is the enhancement and fulfillment of the desire for the whole person to interact intimately with another whole person. This intimate relationship of two people can certainly enhance each individual's personality and sexuality, but the relationship cannot create wholeness found in either dimension.

A sad commentary on our present-day distortion of what marriage can provide can be seen in our accelerated divorce rate. People are asking for wholeness to be created by their partners when wholeness was never present to give to the other partner. Wholeness can only be shared. This concept encourages us to continue to become people in the image of God, to have a strong foundation in our sexuality prior to becoming married. The purpose for marriage can be distorted in the sense of one trying to complete "the whole." In our search for filling a void in our lives that only God can fill, we attempt to become fulfilled through marriage.

Marriage and Intimacy

Becoming one flesh is a continual process. It is not living parallel lives, but two lives becoming intertwined. Each person's perspective changes to include the other. It is mutually opening one's life in love and allowing another to see one's vulnerability. It is allowing another into the inner chambers of one's life.

Relating and communicating are crucial to becoming one flesh. Communication involves revealing who we are and how we feel. We cannot know one another without trusting and allowing our identity and sexuality to be known intimately.

How may the marriage of one man and one woman be the best God meant for it to be? Marriage is much more than reciting vows. It is devotion and commitment. Companionship is the operative word. Companionship of two personalities, each developing to his and her fullest, giving and receiving the utmost both can share. When marriage does not have mutuality, it fails to reach its highest potential.

In 1 Corinthians 7:3-6, Paul gave beautiful advice to husbands and wives about this mutuality involving sex and sexuality. Not only did Paul advocate marriage but also counseled husbands and wives to be sensitive to one another's sexual needs. Marriage is a partnership. The husband or wife must never regard the other simply as a means of self-gratification. Each must regard the whole marriage relationship, both in its physical and spiritual aspects, as a relationship in which each finds gratification and the highest satisfaction of all desires.

Sexual intercourse is intended exclusively for marriage partners. Sexual intercourse is only a small portion of one's marriage, but it is also a culmination of all other aspects of the marriage, including emotional, physical, spiritual, and cognitive. Even our terminology of sexual intercourse, "making love," distorts the beauty of the event. Love is not made through sexual intercourse. Love is sometimes expressed through sexual intercourse.

The intended purpose of marriage is quite a beautiful relationship. The one-flesh relationship in its sexual, emotional, and spiritual manifestations can be a rewarding lifelong relationship. But, like anything worthwhile, it comes as a result of work and sacrifice. It is similar to the role model Christ lived out for us in the fidelity of God's love.

Divorce

We often joke about divorce. Many times humor relieves some of our anxiety. A punch line to a joke is, "My wife just ran off with my best friend and I sure do miss him." But divorce is not a joke. It is not an event that can be put in an emotional isolation tank. Everyone loses something. Some lose more, some less; but, definitely, loss is an ultimate repercussion of divorce.

Divorce affects everyone involved: the individual, the couple, the children, the parents/grandparents, brothers and sisters, friends, professional peers, and church friends. The emotional effect upon the immediate family includes the brokenness, the guilt of perceived failure, resentment, grief, physically dividing up the household belongings, loss of financial security and status, and low production in work. The children are tremendously affected and feel torn and disillusioned many times; occasionally, some are relieved. Children feel their very foundation, good or bad, shifting. The custody of children is an extremely difficult issue. The grandparents fear not getting to see the grandchildren, as well as having to see their children grieve. If the couple has been active in church, which one stays in the church membership?

Ironically, there are cases where the divorced person and/or children immediately manifest signs of wholeness. Such manifestations can be seen where people were relieved that a horrible relationship was finally over. Both sides of the pendulum reflect the tragically imbalanced relationship that deteriorated to the point of divorce. The point we need to keep in mind is the attack through divorce on identity. We need to relate compassionately at that point as image bearers of God and lovers of our neighbors.

Divorce is a direct attack on identity, and as discussed throughout this chapter, identity influences the entirety of one's whole life. Divorce can fragment any dimension of personality or identity. This fragmentation can be manifested in low self-esteem and insecurity.

Parenting

In Luke 1:46-55, Mary expressed her feelings of Jesus' mission even before He was born. In Jesus' first sermon (Luke 4:18-19), He used the same words and impressions that Mary had used. She parented by freeing and encouraging Him in His mission in "freeing the captives."

Mary could have very easily been overprotective of Jesus. Because she knew of the prophecies from the prophets, she knew what the fulfillment of those prophecies included. Can you imagine the mixed emotions that Mary had as a mother in knowing the Christ child's mission? But Mary was a tremendous role model of obedience and service to God.

Children should not be viewed as burdens. Parents too often see their role in light of responsibility rather than relationship. Therefore, it constricts the true meaning of parent-child relationships.

A child learns and observes from everything going on around him, especially in the early months and years when a child's personality is formed. We learn more through modeling than being told. It is vitally important for parents to be the role models that God would want them to be, letting love for God and for one another be exhibited through their life-style.

"Train up a child in the way he should go, and when he is old, he will not depart from it" (Prov. 22:6, RSV). How do we train up a child in our society with negative media influence, drugs, materialism, and sex distortions?

We attempt to be role models and facilitators of the better way. Through our own lives, in our weaknesses and strengths, we show how the fulfillment, acceptance, and peace comes from no other source like it comes from God. We exhibit the unconditional love that God shows us. We show our own vulnerability and need for acceptance as well as discipline.

The attempt to create a child's identity in the parents' own image is a mistake. Along the same lines, the attempt to have the child fulfill the parents' unfulfilled dreams indicates the fragmentation of the parents' identity. Only God can bring wholeness of personhood into the parents' life which, in turn, frees the child to seek his or her own identity. Children are human beings who should be seen as gifts from God and a privilege to parent.

We should follow God's example. He cares for His children. We are made in His image. He cares for us as a facilitator, not a dictator.

A child needs guidelines, help, and discipline, but many times that is the only way we see our role as parents. Parents should be facilitators who give direction, rather than dictatorial commands. Parents do not need to create or dictate, but facilitate. They should help lead their children to a deeper understanding of who they are in light of being created by God in His image. To be accepted is one of the biggest needs children and adolescents have. Parents need to be facilitators in helping a child discover who he or she is and move from understanding to acceptance in love.

When we view our role in parenting as in relationship, not responsibility, as facilitator and not creator, parenting becomes easier in some ways.

Relationships with children change as the children grow older, coming to a time referred to as "the empty nest." The adolescent years prior to this time can be tumultuous. If parenting is viewed as relationship, many times communication and self-esteem can be better than if parenting is viewed as total responsibility. The transition from child to the empty nest will not be as difficult.

The following is a portion of a letter from an adult daughter to her father who was obviously a role model and facilitator.

> Through your discipline to me as a child, which I thought was many times unfair, I learned about the combination of justice and compassion. Through hugs and being rocked to sleep with an earache many a night, I learned about forgiveness and not growing weary in loving. Through crawling in bed with you or your responding to that whisper, "Daddy, will you come sleep with me?"

I understood a little more about God's comfort during times of fear and the refuge and strength of those Everlasting arms.

Through your work, I learned about discipline and service. Through our church, I learned about the body of Christ and Christianity. Through your laughter, I learned to enjoy life. Through your tears in times of crisis, I learned that it's okay to be sad and hurt. Through your commitment to one another and family, I learned something of the fidelity and consistency of God.

Through your *love,* I've seen something of the very essence of the soul of our Lord. Through Mother's death to this life, I've experienced even more fully God's grace through the resurrection. Through the ache of missing her so deeply words can't express the void that's felt, I understand a little more about God's sacrifice of His Son.

For now we see through a glass dimly . . . but then face to face. Thank you for helping me see, understand and experience even dimly a little bit more about God.

Conclusion

We have many questions, anxieties, and new thoughts about the sexual revolution occurring in the world. However, we can say for sure that we were created sexual beings. God pronounced our maleness and femaleness "very good." We were created in God's image as whole persons regardless of marital status. Our feelings, desires, and drives are not evil in and of themselves, but it is how we handle them and what we do with them that matters.

Sexuality is a reflection of who we are. It involves our ability as human beings to open our minds and hearts to one another and to give and to receive in emotional intimacy.

Notes

1. Nelson, James B., *Embodiment* (Minneapolis: Augsburg Publishing, 1978), p. 15.

2. *Webster's New Collegiate Dictionary* (Springfield, Mass.: Merriam, 1974), pp. 1062-1063.

3. Maston, T. B. with William M. Tillman, Jr. *The Bible and Family Relations* (Nashville: Broadman Press, 1983), p. 192.

4. Gesenius, William, *Hebrew and Chaldee Lexicon of the Old Testament,* trans. Samuel Prideaux Tregelles (Grand Rapids, MI: William B. Eerdmans, 1949), p. 147.

Suggested Reading

Foster, Richard J., *Money, Sex, and Power: The Challenge of a Disciplined Life* (Harper & Row, 1985).

Pinson, William M., Jr., *Families with Purpose* (Nashville: Broadman Press, 1978).

Smedes, Lewis B., *Sex for Christians* (Grand Rapids: Eerdmans Publishers, 1976).

The Concordia Sex Education Series (The Lutheran Church, Missouri Synod, 1982).

10
World Peace

Ronald D. Sisk

"Peace I leave with you; my peace I give to you; not as the world gives do I give to you" (John 14:27, RSV).

Few issues in Christian ethics have created as much difficulty for the church, for individual Christians, and for the political leadership of the Christian world as the question of what Jesus meant to teach us about peace. What is the Christian attitude toward war? Toward military service? Toward nuclear weapons? Was Jesus talking about politics or spiritual values or both? How do you reconcile the teachings of Christ with the events of the Old Testament? With Paul's instructions on loyalty to government? With Revelation's condemnation of the same Roman Empire Paul praised? Obviously each Christian has a responsibility to answer these questions for himself or herself. This chapter is not intended to argue for or against any particular position on specific issues. Rather, as a way of beginning to search for answers, this chapter looks at biblical, historical, theological, and practical aspects of Christian ethics and world peace.

Biblical Foundations

John Macquarrie said, "Peace is in Biblical teaching, both eschatological and primordial."[1] Peace was a reality in the beginning. Peace will be a reality in the end. The problem for modern Christians, though, is what to do about peace now. Getting a handle on biblical teachings concerning actions in the present is more difficult than invoking either memory or promise.

The Old Testament

The primary Old Testament conception of peace is bound up in the meaning of the Hebrew word *shalom*. *Shalom* means much more than the absence of war. It means wholeness, completeness, fullness, health, happiness, prosperity, political and spiritual well-being. *Shalom,* in other words, is life in the present lived as it is meant to be lived in the fullness God intends human life to have. It is both religious and secular, both individual and communal, both the promise of God to those who are righteous (Isa. 32:17) and the result of human actions (Deut. 2:26).[2] The depth of feeling evoked by the concept of *shalom* in Hebrew culture is shown by the fact that even today *shalom* is the primary word both of greeting and of farewell. The hope of the Hebrew was to live life in God's *shalom* and to experience *shalom* as the content of salvation (Isa. 52:7).

The Old Testament begins, of course, in the peace of Adam and Eve's relationship with God in the garden. From the time of the Fall onward, human political and spiritual history is the story of the attempt to return to something akin to the peace in which we began. From the beginning, however, attainment of that peace depended upon the initiative of God. God's covenant with Abraham (Gen. 12:1-3) was a gift of peace through Abraham and his descendants to the nations of the world. The Mosaic law was intended to show the children of Israel how to experience the benefits of God's blessings. They would keep His law. In return God would bring them into the Promised Land, giving them the benefits of their peace with him (Gen. 23:20 to 24:9).

As Israel wandered from her commitment to God, the warning of the prophets again and again was that peace, *shalom,* depended on her faithfulness to the convenant relationship. In Jeremiah, chapter 7, is a classic warning to Judah to return to genuine faithfulness as the condition of peace:

> Thus says the Lord of hosts, the God of Israel, Amend your ways and your doings and I will let you dwell in this place. Do not trust in these deceptive words: "This is the temple of the Lord, the temple of the Lord, the temple of the Lord." For if you truly amend

your ways and your doings, if you truly execute justice with one
another, if you do not oppress the alien, the fatherless, or the
widow, or shed innocent blood in this place, and if you do not go
after other gods to your own hurt, then I will let you dwell in this
place, in the land that I gave of old to your fathers for ever (vv.
3-7, RSV).

Isaiah believed correct ritual, the Temple cult alone, was not a
sufficient guarantee of God's blessings on the nation. Heartfelt
personal and corporate adherence to convenant ethics was God's
prerequisite for national peace.

As Israel consistently failed to respond to this kind of warning,
the prophets began to speak both of God's impending punishment
for unfaithfulness and of a new divine initiative which would bring
the promised *shalom*. Long before Jeremiah's warning, Isaiah
wrote in this vein.

> For the palace will be forsaken,
>   the populous city deserted;
> the hill and the watchtower
>   will become dens for ever,
> a joy of wild asses,
>   a pasture of flocks;
> until the Spirit is poured upon us
>   from on high,
>   and the wilderness becomes a fruit-
>   ful field,
> and the fruitful field is deemed a forest.
> Then justice will dwell in the wil-
>   derness.
>   and righteousness abide in the fruitful
>   field.
> And the effect of righteousness
>   will be peace,
> and the result of righteousness,
>   quietness and trust for ever (32:14-17, RSV).

Sooner or later God would bring His promised peace by His own
initiative whether Israel responded in faithfulness.

Perhaps the most difficult aspect of Old Testament teaching

regarding peace from the perspective of modern Christians is God's apparent sanction of violence by the nation of Israel against her neighbors (e.g., Ex. 23:27-28; Josh. 6:15-16). Interpreters have never satisfactorily harmonized these events with the apparent nonviolent thrust of the New Testament. The second-century heretic Marcion went so far as to reject the God of the Old Testament totally, arguing a God of such violence had to be a different deity from the loving God and Father of Jesus Christ.

The New Testament

As in the Old Testament, peace is a central concern in the New. Unlike Old Testament interpretation, traditional New Testament interpretation since Constantine has tended to spiritualize (read "make impractical, make exclusively religious") New Testament teachings concerning peace, divorcing them from the political life of the individual and the nation. The advent of the nuclear era and the Vietnam War have led to serious reevaluation of this approach. We begin, however, with a look at the teachings themselves.

The primary New Testament term for peace is the Greek word *eirene*. In classical Greek, *eirene* meant primarily the absence of war. In the New Testament era, however, *eirene* was used in the Septuagint to translate the Hebrew *shalom*. As a result, in Judeo-Christian thought *eirene* took on much of the depth and breadth of the more inclusive Hebrew term.

Basically, *eirene* in the New Testament follows three meanings. It may mean the absence of war or conflict, either in a political or a personal and domestic sense (Luke 14:32; 1 Cor. 7:15; Rom. 14:19). It may mean right relationship with God, as in Romans 5:1, "peace with God through our Lord Jesus Christ" (RSV). Or it may mean peace of mind, the confidence and assurance which come to a Christian through his or her relationship with Christ.

> Have no anxiety about anything, but in everything by prayer and supplication with thanksgiving let your requests be made known to God. And the peace of God, which passes all understanding, will keep your hearts and your minds in Christ Jesus (Phil. 4:6-7, RSV).

Nonetheless, all these specific usages are informed and deepened by the heritage of *shalom*.[3] As a result, the ethical content of New Testament peace differs little from that of the Old.

In the New Testament, God's initiative toward peace with and for humankind comes in the form of the life and ministry of Jesus Christ. That Jesus Himself taught peace in all its depths of meaning as a primary value for His followers goes without saying. From the angels' announcement of His birth to his greeting of the disciples after the resurrection (John 20:26), both by precept and example He made peace a central aspect of the faith.

In the first instance, Jesus called Israel to peace with God through repentance of sin and a return to genuine personal righteousness. He inaugurated His ministry in Nazareth by identifying Himself with the redeemer figure in Isaiah (Luke 4:18-19). The ethical content of the Isaiah passage is the restoration of peace by the correction of specific abuses and sufferings which are peace destroying.

Those who would follow Him, Jesus made it clear, must join Him in this *shalom*-making revival. The Sermon on the Mount, particularly, focuses on the Christian's responsibility to be a peacemaker (Matt. 5:9), to take the initiative in actions which make peace possible. Jesus' specific teachings concerning love of enemies and nonviolent response to violence are elaborations of that principle. To "love your enemies and pray for those who persecute you" (v. 44, RSV), to "not resist one who is evil. But if any one strikes you on the right cheek, turn to him the other also" (v. 40, RSV) is to take what Glen Stassen called a surprising "transforming initiative."[4] It is to create the possibility for peace by taking specific action designed to defuse hostility. As with God's own surprising transforming initiative in sending His Son, the Christian's initiative puts evil off balance by meeting it with good.

Problems for New Testament interpreters arise from those scattered events in which Jesus appears to have taken a different perspective. The Synoptics (e.g., Matt. 21:12-13) make the forcible cleansing of the Temple the precipitating event for the passion and the crucifixion. Luke 22:36, "Let him who has no sword sell his mantle and buy one" (RSV), is sometimes taken as a proof text for the occasional necessity of violence.

Problems also arise as we attempt to understand Pauline and Johannine interpretations of the proper relationship of Christians to government. Romans 13 is normally taken as justification for the service of Christians in the police force and the military. Along with Jesus' "Render therefore to Caesar the things that are Caesar's" (Matt. 22:21, RSV), Paul's "Let every person be subject to the governing authorities" (v. 1, RSV) undergirds a powerful argument for Christian service in the military as well as for the legitimacy of the use of political and military force.

The Pauline perspective is brought under criticism, however, both by Jesus' dominant nonviolence and by John's antipathy to imperial Rome. Revelation's apocalyptic "War of the Lamb" may be interpreted in either political or spiritual terms. I lean to a perspective which views the beasts in Revelation 13 as the twin evils of the oppressive political and religious machines of the Roman Empire of John's day. The result is that Paul's acceptance of the authority of Rome is balanced by John's healthy skepticism of all human institutions.

However one interprets specific passages, the most consistent Christian perspective is that the New Testament is the story of the continuation of God's initiative for peace with and among humankind. God's initiative began with the Old Covenant and was completed with the New. It was brought into reality with the life, death, and resurrection of Jesus Christ and involves the Christian in work toward the fulfillment of God's promise.[5]

War in Christian History

When Jesus said, "You will hear of wars and rumors of wars" (Matt. 24:6, RSV), He was describing the fact as has been known through all of recorded history. According to the Baptist writer J. T. Ford, from 1496 BC to AD 1861 there were 3,130 years of war and 227 years of peace.[6] Nor have we done appreciably better in the century and a quarter since Ford's count ended.

Outside biblical culture, the ancient world was as ambivalent concerning peace and war as was biblical culture. The *Iliad* and the *Odyssey* are basically war poems. They both glorify the strength and achievements of warriors and unpack the devastating cycle of violence, vengeance, and escalation which war brings.[7] The great Greek playwrights Aeschylus, Sophocles, and Euripides showed in their works the senseless futility of war. Aristophanes's classic comedy *Lysistrata* told the story of what happened when the women decided war had gone on long enough. For their part, the Romans chose to try to prevent war by conquering all their enemies and enforcing the *pax Romana,* their own brand of peace.[8]

Within specifically biblical and Christian history, interpreters have delineated three basic approaches to the questions of war and peace. Each has been present in some measure throughout, though they have alternated in their dominance of Judeo-Christian thought. We shall describe each approach, saving most evaluation for the theological section to follow.

Holy War

The concept of the crusade or holy war, the war undertaken for the purposes of God under His direction and control, finds its origins in the Old Testament conquest of the Promised Land and in the intertestamental Maccabean revolt. In Deuteronomy 7:1-2 are specific instructions from Moses to the children of Israel on the war strategy they were to adopt:

> When the Lord your God brings you into the land which you are entering to take possession of it, and clears away many nations before you, the Hittites, the Girgashites, the Amorites, the Canaanites, the Perizzites, the Hivites, and the Jebusites, seven nations greater and mightier than yourselves, and when the Lord your God gives them over to you and you defeat them; then you must utterly destroy them; you shall make no covenant with them, and show no mercy to them (RSV).

God's people, fighting with God's help, are to defeat and destroy God's enemies.

The same concept, of course, informed the medieval attempts

to retake the Holy Land from the Muhammadans. When the popes issued repeated calls to the faithful to take up arms against the infidel, Christians believed they were fighting God's war.

Again, at the time of the Reformation, Catholic fought Protestant, and vice versa, believing themselves to be defending the very cause of the Almighty. With the end of the age of faith, however, we find the crusade idea only occasionally evident. It is a different thing for the modern nation-state to determine its policies then claim "God is on our side" than it was for the Israelites or the knights of medieval Europe to go into battle believing "we are on God's side."

Perhaps the only genuine twentieth-century example of the crusade is found outside the Christian tradition altogether, with the *jihad* or holy war of Islamic fundamentalism. Only there do we find the absolute conviction of God's command necessary to meet the criteria for authentic holy war.

Pacifism

Only a germ of the idea of pacifism, that God calls those who follow Him to refuse to participate in war, is present in Old Testament times. Bainton argued, "The thought of the Hebrews was so deeply religious that human devices for achieving peace were seldom proposed. Peace is a gift of God."[9] He did, however, point to what might be called the "redemptive pacifism" of the Suffering Servant passages in Isaiah. Peace was always considered to be dependent upon trust in God rather than military victory. Indeed the Hebrews were sometimes defeated because they refused to fight on the sabbath.

For the first two hundred years of the Christian era, the church appears to have been almost exclusively pacifist. Tertullian in *On Idolatry* argued, "For albeit soldiers had come into John, and had received the formula of their rule; albeit likewise, a centurion had believed; *still* the Lord afterward, in disarming Peter, unbelted every soldier."[10] In *Against Celsus,* Origen declared, "He nowhere teaches that it is right for His own disciples to offer violence to any one, however wicked."[11] Interestingly, while both held war to be unacceptable for Christians, both admitted the occasional justice of wars fought by others.

The first mention of Christians in the military comes in the year 173. After that, the incidence of Christian involvement rises gradually until the conversion of Constantine and the subsequent wholesale "Christianization" of the empire in the fourth century. The institutionalization of the Catholic Church and the identification of its fortunes with those of Rome led leaders such as Augustine to reject pacifism as the only position for Christians. In a letter to Count Boniface in AD 418, Augustine observed, "Do not think that it is impossible for anyone to please God while engaged in military service."[12] Augustine, thus, became one of the authors of the just war theory to be discussed following.

Pacifism as an ideal survived through the Middle Ages primarily in certain sectarian groups and in the exemption of the clergy from military service. Beginning in the tenth century, however, attempts were made to put certain limits on violence in the name of the faith. These were called the "peace of God." They amounted to a set of limits, such as the sacredness of Christian lives and the immunity of noncombatants, which were later incorporated into just war theory. The Lateran Council of 1139 went so far as to institute the "Truce of God," forbidding fighting altogether for Christians from Wednesday sunset to Monday sunrise and during Advent.[13]

With the Reformation came the development of several small groups specifically devoted to pacifism. The historic peace churches, the Quakers, the Mennonites, and the Brethren, trace their roots for the most part to the sixteenth-century Anabaptists who formed the left wing of the Reformation. These groups, thus, share a similar spiritual ancestry with Baptists, though Baptists never went as far as pacifism in any significant degree. The Mennonites, for example, developed a two-kingdom theology which demanded a radical separation of church and state. Unlike Baptists, however, their stance was so radical church members were forbidden to serve in the military.

The rise of the Social Gospel and the American political movement known as Progressivism gave pacifism perhaps its greatest general popularity in the early years of the twentieth century. War was seen as one of those social evils which the evolutionary attainment of Christ's kingdom would end. The organization of the League of Nations and the visionary Kellogg-Briand Pact "outlawing" war gave impetus to the belief that war could be legislated out of existence.

With the coming of World War II, however, pacifism quickly returned to its traditional status as a minority protest movement within Christendom. In the latter half of the century, the debate within Christian circles has largely centered around the question whether the advent of nuclear weapons makes at least "nuclear pacifism" the position of necessity for Christians. Also particularly important during the Vietnam era, was the question of the propriety of individual conscientious objection to military service on Christian grounds.

Just War

In many ways just war theory represents a historical middle way between the two Judeo-Christian extremes of pacifism and the crusade. The idea that some wars are just and others are not is an attempt to reconcile Christian idealism with the realities of existence in a broken and sinful world.

Many of the concepts used in just war theory are not, however, Christian in origin at all. They come rather from classical antiquity. The Greeks believed mediation was preferable to violence, that peace should be the object even when fighting became unavoidable, and that violence should be limited only to that which was necessary. Still Greek ideas of justice left much to be desired. The Greek concept, Bainton argued, "was conceived in terms of a static society resting on the basis of social inequality. That was why Aristotle could apply the term, a 'just war'—and he first coined the expression—to a war whose object was to enslave those designed by nature for servitude."[14] A consistent problem with just war theory from the beginning has been the ease with which nations have been able to convince themselves their own particular goals are just, no matter what the facts.

Christian just war theory was developed in the late fourth and early fifth centuries as the Christian Roman Empire came face to face with the prospect of barbarian invasion. Ambrose and Augustine took Greek and Roman concepts and Christianized them, developing a list of criteria under which a Christian war could be considered just. Extended and codified by Thomas Aquinas and others in the Middle Ages, just war theory became a rough restraint on the worst excesses of combat.

Glen Stassen of The Southern Baptist Theological Seminary in Louisville, Kentucky summarized the classic just war provisions, requiring that a just war meet all the following criteria:

1. The war must have a reasonable chance of success. The objective sought must be capable of achievement.
2. The war must be fought for a just cause. A just cause is defined as the removal of a serious and continuing injustice. The desire for conquest of territory, increase of power, etc., do not constitute just cause.
3. The war must be a last resort after all peaceful options for resolution of the conflict have been exhausted and it becomes absolutely intolerable to permit the injustice to continue. Mediation and arbitration must be used if at all possible.
4. The war must be fought under legitimate authority. Those conducting the hostilities should be the properly chosen representatives of those called upon to do the fighting.
5. Combatants should use just means. Noncombatants should be protected. Cruel and inhuman techniques such as torture, biological warfare, etc., cannot be used.
6. As much as possible, the war's costs should be proportional to the goal to be achieved. A nuclear conflict over the Falkland Islands, for example, would hardly be proportional. The risk of losing must not be greater than can be born.
7. The war must be just in its intent. That is, its intent should be to restore peace and to correct intolerable injustice.
8. The intention to conduct war should be duly announced. In effect this announcement constitutes an ultimatum to the opponent, a warning to noncombatants and a final opportunity for capitulation before hostilities begin.[15]

The student will find it particularly informative to use the just war criteria set forth above as a diagnostic tool in evaluating twentieth-century conflicts in particular. The Allied involvement in World War II, for example, is found to meet all the just war criteria, at least until the saturation bombing of Germany and the introduction of nuclear weapons. Supporters of those policies generally argue that by the time they were introduced all Germans and all Japanese could legitimately be considered combatants and, therefore, targets.

In the nuclear era, many have begun to argue that the nature and extent of devastation caused by nuclear weapons makes just war theory no longer applicable. Paul Ramsey's *War and Christian Conscience* argues for the need to retain just war theory as a guide. Michael Walzer's *Just and Unjust Wars* is an excellent post-Vietnam application of just war theory.

Theological Reconstruction

The believer who seeks to develop his or her own coherent Christian response to the problem of world peace finds that response must necessarily flow from and be an expression of his or her theology. In this section we shall look briefly at the impact on a concept of world peace of specific understandings of God, the ministry of Jesus Christ, and the calling of the Christian. I will complete the section by a summary of the ways Southern Baptists have responded to America's wars in the 142 years since the formation of the Convention.

God

As has been suggested earlier, one of the most serious issues for Christians who would develop a consistent ethical stance regarding war is the apparent discrepancy in the understandings of God in the Old Testament and the New.

Any number of interpretations have been offered to answer this dilemma. The concept of progressive revelation suggests that the early Hebrews basically misunderstood God's intention; they interpreted their God as the leader in battle, just as did the pagan tribes around them.

Spiritualization is often used to argue that the "accounts of war and the use of force are understood in terms of spiritual action."[16]

In other words, the important thing about the Old Testament accounts is not the wars themselves, but what God is doing with His people through them.

Interpreters have also attempted to say that the problem with the Old Testament description of God as a warrior is linguistic. Human language can never fully describe or explain God. Rather we use images which make sense to us in terms of our culture and limitations. Vernard Eller made one of the most colorful attempts in recent literature to use this ideas as a springboard for a comprehensive interpretation.

In his breezy work *King Jesus' Manual of Arms for the Armless,* Eller suggested, "The Bible as a whole presents a unified argument regarding peace and war. By 'unified argument' we do not mean to suggest that a person would find the Bible saying the same thing about peace and war no matter where he happened to dip in."[17] Eller argued that "to fight is in the image of God."[18] From the beginning Scripture presents God as fighting against chaos to bring the order and beauty of creation. He invites humankind to join Him in the fight to subdue the earth and bring it to fulfillment. We went wrong when we saw ourselves as needing to fight one another in order to reach our goals. God's battle from the Fall has been "to get men to switch from fighting their wars to join Yahweh in fighting his war."[19] For Eller, the New Testament, of course, makes it plain that God's new way of fighting is Jesus.

Any such interpretation as Eller's still faces the difficulty of God's apparent approval of war in the texts. It has the advantage, however, of both taking the texts quite seriously and encouraging us to take one step back from them in order to look for a comprehensive pattern.

The Ministry of Jesus

Perhaps the central question the Christian must answer in attempting to take from Jesus a model for an approach to questions of war and peace is, What, precisely, was Jesus trying to do? Did He intend to state a comprehensive social and political ethic, or were His efforts primarily spiritual? Certainly Jesus lived in a day and a political climate in which war was very much a part of life.

The Roman yoke sat uneasy on the Jewish neck. Some of Jesus' own followers were Zealots, revolutionaries committed to the violent overthrow of Rome. The accusation of subversion contributed to His own crucifixion. The Jews, moreover, were expecting a political Messiah, a new David, a national hero who would throw off the Roman yoke and restore the glory of the Jewish state. His own disciples' constant question was, "Will you now restore the kingdom?" In other words, is it time for the revolt?

Against that backdrop, Jesus' teachings about peace, peacemaking, and nonviolence must be seen as both personal and social, both spiritual and practical. In effect, He suggested a strategy for God's army in a world already at war. His strategy is nonviolence, nonretaliation, and positive initiatives toward reconciliation. Simmons argued, "Jesus' own decision to suffer and die rather than foment a religious war was the supreme example of suffering love for the sake of the other."[20]

Perhaps the most persuasive argument for this perspective on Jesus' ministry is found in the Mennonite professor John Howard Yoder's work *The Politics of Jesus.* Calling the Christian to Jesus' model of suffering servanthood, Yoder argued that Christians are not called to be effective in preventing evil in God's world but rather to be obedient to the teachings of Christ, "The relationship between the obedience of God's people and the triumph of God's cause is not a relationship of cause and effect, but one of cross and resurrection."[21] Christian victory depends not on the success of the Christian military but on the war of the Lamb that was slain. It is already assured in the resurrection of Jesus Christ.

The Calling of the Christian

If the previous section seems to suggest that the Christian must necessarily be pacifist, it should be remembered that there exists a considerable body of Christian opinion to the contrary. At least from the time of Augustine's letter to Count Boniface in AD 418, Christians have believed it possible to "please God while engaged in military service." Augustine stated the case perhaps as well as anyone. "Peace should be the object of your desire; war should be waged only as a necessity, and waged only that God may by it deliver men from the necessity and preserve them in peace."[22] In this sense, the Christian's calling is seen as peacemaking when possible and peacekeeping when necessary.

During and after World War II, Reinhold Niebuhr argued persuasively that the Christian's role in the specifics of history must compromise Jesus' ideals with the world's necessities. Love, Niebuhr argued, is an impossible possibility. In the sinfulness of human life, justice is often the best that can be hoped for. The Christian obligation is, therefore, to resist evil, to accept military power as a tool with which to resist evil, and to keep efforts toward justice under the constant critique of the ideal of love.[23]

Similarly, the Presbyterian theologian Paul Ramsey argued that pacifism is an unrealistic approach for Christians in a dangerous world. Ramsey reaffirmed just war theory, declaring that the most loving thing a Christian can do for neighbors in an evil world is to defend them from oppression. He argued particularly, for example, that American Christian participation in the counterinsurgency war in Vietnam fell within the definition of just war. In effect, he stated, the only way to fight guerillas, who have themselves set the terms by choosing the means of attack, is to fight them and their support system, the apparent noncombatants among whom they hide.[24]

Ramsey and Niebuhr argued that Christ's calling and the calling of the Christian are different in activity if not in kind. In a sinful world the Christian resists evil with the means available, counting on the sufficiency of Christ's grace.

Southern Baptist Positions

As an organization existing primarily for the purposes of evangelism and missions, the Southern Baptist Convention has made relatively little effort to develop a cohesive social and political theology. Rather, that theology has emerged as Southern Baptists have reacted in their churches and seminaries and on the Convention floor to specific issues and controversies. The dominant Baptist ethic is still that the individual determines his or her position on issues by personal interpretation of Scripture under the guid-

ance of the Holy Spirit. Within that framework, however, a
majority Baptist approach may be discerned.

The only general Southern Baptist statement on the issue of
world peace beyond Convention resolutions is paragraph sixteen
of *The Baptist Faith and Message* statement of 1963. It reads:

> It is the duty of Christians to seek peace with all men on princi-
> ples of righteousness. In accordance with the spirit and teachings
> of Christ they should do all in their power to put an end to war.
>
> The true remedy for the war spirit is the gospel of our Lord. The
> supreme need of the world is the acceptance of His teachings in all
> the affairs of men and nations, and the practical application of His
> law of love.

Clearly the statement, while establishing a Christian obligation
and preference to work for peace, offers no specific guidance for
how individual Christians are to act.

Throughout Baptist history specific positions have been taken,
primarily as Baptists have been confronted by particular conflicts.
Generally speaking, with the exception of the Civil War during
which Southern Baptists defended the Confederacy, they have
supported the United States in every conflict in which it has been
involved during the history of the Convention. They have done so
by means of a conceptual framework compatible with just war
theory. The ideal of peace has been upheld throughout. The meaning of justice has been adjusted in tune with the tenor of the
times.[25]

Since Vietnam, Convention attention has focused primarily on
the nuclear issue, supporting the continued maintenance of a
strong military establishment while calling for negotiations toward the reduction and elimination of nuclear weapons. The 1978
resolution on Multilateral Arms Control calls in its last paragraph
for shifting spending priorities away from the arms buildup toward meeting human needs. The 1982 resolution "On Peace with
Justice" is perhaps one of the best of such resolution's for reflecting the middle ground of Southern Baptist thinking:

> WHEREAS, Our national security interests require both a strong
> defense and a responsible limitation of nuclear weapons.

THEREFORE, be it RESOLVED, That we affirm our historic Baptist commitment to peace with justice as a goal in personal, social, and international relationships.

Be it further RESOLVED, That we encourage Southern Baptists to work actively in the pursuit of peace with justice not only through preaching, teaching, and praying in our homes and churches, but also through involving ourselves in the political process, doing the things which make for peace as an expression of our ultimate loyalty to Jesus Christ as Lord.

Be it further RESOLVED, That we support a program of mutually verifiable disarmament, including nuclear disarmament; and, we assure the United Nations' Special Session on Disarmament of our prayers and hopes for progress toward peace.[26]

In a context of substantial political and theological diversity, Southern Baptists have, thus, hammered out a compromise position which places them well within the mainstream of traditional Christian thought on world peace.

Current Issues

While I have confined this chapter's discussion within relatively narrow limits, it must be recognized that problems of world peace in the last years of the twentieth century go far beyond the question of whether to fight wars to their origins in the human condition. Basic human rights, such as the rights to physical safety and economic and political justice, must be addressed if there is to be any progress in eliminating war. Richard Barnet's illuminating works, including *The Roots of War,* deal with the ways in which the very structure of international economic and political society contributes to war in our day. In order to help focus how Christians approach particular problems, I shall conclude this chapter by raising two current issues in world peace.

The Growth of Militarism

Before World War II, the basic military posture of most nations, including the United States, involved the maintenance of minimum peacetime military establishments. The near victory of the Nazis in that conflict resulted in a profound change in the direction of constant military preparedness. The dominant philosophy became the need to maintain a military establishment at least as large as that of the most likely enemy. As a result, at the close of World War II the military-industrial complex, continued to expand rather than to cut back to prewar levels. With the advent of the nuclear arms race, that expansion has taken on terrifying dimensions.

In terms of the United States and the Soviet Union, this has meant that huge segments of the most powerful economics in the world are focused on the production and maintenance of materiel the only use of which is military. Each M-1 tank, for example, costs $2.7 million to build, and the prototype was already being redesigned before its initial production run was completed. Military spending, by its very nature, is extremely capital intensive. Representative Les Aspin of Wisconsin has estimated, for example, that $1 billion would pay about 48,000 defense workers or about 100,000 teachers.[27]

While this kind of spending is difficult for the United States and the Soviet Union, it becomes quickly disastrous for Third World nations which attempt to build their own conventional (nonnuclear) arsenals by purchasing weapons from arms producers. Worldwide military expenditures exceed 940 billion dollars per year.[28]

The problem, of course, is that the only way to finance such military expansion is to take money which could meet some other need. In his farewell address to the nation, President Eisenhower warned, "Every gun that is made, every warship launched, every rocket fired, signifies, in the final sense, a theft from those who hunger and are not fed, those who are cold and are not clothed."

For Christians, President Eisenhower's warning is disturbingly reminiscent of Isaiah 31:1 "Woe to those who go down to Egypt for help and rely on horses, who trust in chariots because they are many and in horsemen because they are very strong" (RSV). It suggests the condition of Israel at the time of the prophet Amos when the wealthy and powerful purchased ease at the expense of the needy and brought upon themselves the judgment of God.

Clearly the issue for Christians is the question of balance. By biblical standards righteousness before the Lord, justice for the poor, are considered more effective guarantees of a nation's safety than military power. Still, in a world of power realities, many Christians agree military preparedness is necessary. How much "theft from those who hunger and are not fed" can be justified in their political defense? How does the nation establish its priorities given the finite character of its resources?

Nuclear Weapons

Since the United States let the nuclear genie out of the bottle at Hiroshima and Nagasaki over forty years ago, no issue has more engaged world attention than the question of what to do about nuclear weapons. No issue has been less successfully dealt with.

In the late 1980s, the combined nuclear arsenals of the United States and the Soviet Union totaled the equivalent of more than sixteen trillion tons of TNT or more than 3.5 tons of explosive power for every man, woman, and child on the planet. Tensions were high. The United States began to go beyond the limits established by the never-ratified SALT II(Strategic Arms Limitation Talks) treaty. The American government claimed many Soviet SALT violations. The two powers also appeared unable to agree on a current interpretation of the ABM (antiballistic missile) treaty. At the same time, both powers publicly proclaimed eagerness to find workable formulas for possible agreements.

Nuclear control was also hindered by the increasing number of nations which already either possessed nuclear weapons themselves or were technologically advanced enough to build them. There was a very real and increasing possibility that nuclear weapons could fall into the hands of terrorists. There were also scientific predictions that even a "limited" nuclear exchange, defined as the firing of perhaps only one thousand of the more than twenty thousand weapons possessed by the two major powers, could result in a climatological disaster called a "nuclear winter."[29]

In the face of such an unprecedented threat, Christian ethics necessarily falls back on basic principles such as: the biblical ideal of *shalom,* the stewardship of creation, the reality of sin, and Christ's injunctions to be peacemakers.[30] Within the context of those principles, there is, of course, room for widespread disagreement regarding specific policies.

Some Christians have argued that the destructive power of nuclear weapons, the inability to limit their use to combatants, renders just war theory obsolete and compels Christians to become nuclear pacifists. Others maintain that the evil of the Soviet threat is greater than any likely nuclear conflict.

Conclusion

What appears clear is that Christians must approach issues of war and peace in the late twentieth century with an awareness that for the first time in human history, we have gained to our sorrow the fulfillment of the serpent's promise in the garden. We have the knowledge of life and death. We have the ability to frustrate for ourselves and our planet the creative purposes of God.

No easy solution is at hand. Neither naive idealism nor bitter cynicism is satisfactory from a Christian point of view. Rather Christians must gain all possible knowledge on the facts of political situations from differing perspectives; support all good-faith negotiations toward arms limitation, reduction, and elimination, while maintaining a healthy respect for the reality of human evil on all sides; oppose any policies which tend toward arms proliferation or adventurism; support efforts toward greater human understanding between peoples (many Baptists in the United States have been astounded to learn there are more Baptists in the Soviet Union than in any other nation outside our own); support political candidates committed to solving the nuclear problem, as well as the myriad outstanding nonnuclear issues we face; and pray for the working of the Spirit of God in the midst of our incredibly dangerous and terrifyingly fragile human situation.

Notes

1. John Macquarrie, *The Concept of Peace* (New York, Harper and Row, Publishers, 1973), p. 19

2. E. M. Good, "Peace in the OT," *Interpreter's Dictionary of the Bible*, III, pp. 704-706.

3. C. L. Mitton, "Peace in the NT, *Interpreter's Dictionary of the Bible*, III, p. 706.

4. Glen Stassen, "A Theological Rationale for Peacemaking," *Review and Expositor*, LXXIX, Fall, 1982, p. 632.

5. See Paul D. Simmons, "The New Testament Basis of Peacemaking," *Review and Expositor*, LXXIX, Fall, 1982, pp. 597-605.

6. J.T. Ford, *The Truth About War* (Nashville: Broadman Press, 1970), p. 36.

7. William Klassen, *Love of Enemies: The Way to Peace*, (Philadelphia, Fortress Press, 1984), pp. 12-13.

8. For a detailed discussion, see Roland H. Bainton, *Christian Attitudes Toward War and Peace* (Nashville, Abingdon Press, 1960).

9. Ibid., p. 30

10. Arthur F. Holmes, ed., *War and Christian Ethics* (Baker Book House, Grand Rapids, 1975), p. 39.

11. Ibid., p. 48.

12. Ibid., p. 61

13. Ibid., p. 87.

14. Bainton, pp. 33-39.

15. This summary of the provisions of just war theory is given by Glen Stassen in his Introduction to Christian ethics classes at The Southern Baptist Theological Seminary.

16. Marvin E. Tate, "War and Peacemaking in the Old Testament," *Review and Expositor*, LXXIX, Fall, 1982, p. 589. Tate provides an excellent brief discussion of the major lines of Old Testament interpretation.

17. Vernard Eller, *King Jesus' Manual of Arms for the Armless*, (Nashville, Abingdon Press, 1973), p. 11.

18. Ibid., p. 18.

19. Ibid., p. 40.

20. Simmons, p. 598. See also Ronald J. Sider, *Christ and Violence*, (Scottdale, PA: Herald Press, 1979).

21. John Howard Yoder, *The Politics of Jesus* (Grand Rapids, MI: William B. Eerdmans, Publishers, 1972), p. 238.

22. Holmes, op. cit., p. 61-63.

23. See especially, *Love and Justice: Selections from the Shorter Writings of Reinhold Niebuhr,* D.B. Robertson, ed. (Gloucester, Mass., Peter Smith Publishers, 1976); *An Interpretation of Christian Ethics,* chapter 4, "The Relevance of an Impossible Ideal, and *Christianity and Power Politics,* chapter 1, "Why the Christian Church Is not Pacifist."

24. Paul Ramsey, "Is Vietnam a Just War?" *The Just War: Force and Political Responsibility,* (New York, Charles Scribner's Sons, 1968). See also, *War and the Christian Conscience.*

25. See the *Annual of the Southern Baptist Convention,* for the years 1861, 1863, 1917, 1932, 1939, 1941, and 1959 for a study of the progression of Baptist attitudes.

26. *Annual of the Southern Baptist Convention,* 1982, p. 79

27. These figures are matters of public record. I discuss them somewhat more thoroughly in *Peace with Justice* (Christian Life Commission of the Southern Baptist Convention, 1983).

28. *World Military Expenditures and Arms Transfers, 1985.* U.S. Arms Control and Disarmament Agency, p. 3.

29. For a good discussion of the dangers, see *What About the Russians and Nuclear War?* (New York: Pocket Books, 1983).

30. Dale Aukerman, *Darkening Valley: A Biblical Perspective on Nuclear War* (New York, The Seabury Press, 1981).

Suggested Readings

Aukerman, Dale. *Darkening Valley: A Biblical Perspective on Nuclear War.* New York: The Seabury Press, 1981.

Bainton, Roland. *Christian Attitudes toward War and Peace.* Nashville: Abingdon Press, 1960.

Eller, Vernard. *King Jesus' Manual of Arms for the 'Armless.* Nashville: Abingdon Prss, 1973

Ground Zero. *What About the Russians and Nuclear War?* New York: Pocket Books, 1983.

Holmes, Arthur F., ed. *War and Christian Ethics.* Grand Rapids: Baker Book House, 1975.

"Peacemaking and the Church," *Review and Expositor.* LXXIX, Fall, 1982.

Ramsey, Paul. *War and Christian Conscience.* Durham, NC: Duke University Press, 1961.

Robertson, D.B., ed. *Love and Justice: Selections from the Shorter Writings of Reinhold Niebuhr.* Gloucester, MA: Peter Smith, 1976.

Sider, Ronald J. *Christ and Violence.* Scottdale, PA: Herald Press, 1979.

Walzer, Michael. *Just and Unjust Wars.* New York: Basic Books, Inc., 1977

Yoder, John Howard. *The Politics of Jesus.* Grand Rapids: William B. Eerdmans Publishing Company, 1972.

11
Issues of Life and Death

Daniel B. McGee

Introduction

The questions and dilemmas within the issues of life and death are many and complex. The rapid advances in medicine seem to create new ethical problems each year before the dilemmas of the last year are solved. New definitions of death and life are posed. Efforts to radically reshape the gene pool or control human behavior are underway. The ethical dilemmas baffle and frighten us. To chart our way through these dilemmas, let us examine four basic theoretical questions that are present in all life and death problems. These four questions are: Shall we play God? How do we define human life? What is our attitude toward technology? Who should decide? After considering answers to these questions, attention will be given to four areas of concern: controlling birth, controlling death, controlling behavior, and abortion.

Shall We Play God?

Throughout history, human beings have asked, Shall we play God? How far should we go in attempting to control the reproductive or the dying process? The excitement of new advances in medical technology encourage us to exercise more and more control over our lives. The uncertainty, and sometimes fear, of such control cautions us to be less assertive. The more adventurous spirits say, "God helps those who help themselves." The more cautious say, "God will provide."

Defenders of these two views turn to the Bible and find support for their competing positions. Those of us who call for caution are attracted to the Tower of Babel account of human sinfulness. There, sin was expressed in the human effort to be equal with God. When this story informs my view of things, I am suspicious of human wisdom. Other Bible verses like Proverbs 16:18 jump out at me: "Pride goes before destruction,/and a haughty spirit before a fall" (RSV).

This perspective helps me see more clearly the examples in medicine where mistakes have been made because we reached ahead of our knowledge. Risks that failed frighten me, and I am ready to take the lower road of caution. Trust in God means not trusting in human ingenuity.

One theological formulation of this cautious approach is called "God of the gaps theology." In this perspective, human experience is divided into two spheres. In one sphere humans have a high level of understanding and control. There, human wisdom is well tested, and we are confident in what we are doing. In the other sphere, everything is beyond our control. We do not know what causes things to happen or if we do know, we cannot predict or control events. Within these gaps of human understanding God operates. This perspective is reflected in our legal tradition where an event that cannot be attributed to any human act is called "an act of God."

If I approach life from the perspective of the "God of the gaps theology," I am inclined not to invade what I understand to be God's territory. When I consider doing anything that has previously been beyond my control, and therefore within God's realm, it appears that I am "playing God" or running God out of business. The kind of radically new procedures to control life and death in modern medicine appear to be haughty and an affront to God.

There is an alternative view that promotes human creativity and initiative. In the biblical creation account, God asked Adam to name the animals. To the Hebrew mind, nothing was complete until it had been named. Therefore, in Genesis 2:19 God asked Adam to be co-creator by naming the animals, thus completing their creation. Also, in Genesis 1:26-28, there is the dominion passage where God explicitly charged humans to subdue and control all of creation. In both of these passages, the same impression is given—God calls humans to be active in history, joining Him as a partner. It is not the picture of an envious God who is afraid to share power and responsibility with humans.

Those of us who are influenced by this perspective are likely to feel obligation to discover, create, and act. When there is a problem, I will feel responsibility to use my talents and skills to solve the problem. Indeed, the New Testament teachings on stewardship and talents encourage me to venture out. Jesus' parable of the talents is a call to action (Matt. 25:14-30). In Christ's parable, the cautious servant, who protected his talent by burying it, is called "wicked and slothful." From this perspective, numerous opportunities available in modern medicine are interpreted as invitations from God to advance. Here, God is seen as working through human effort to reduce suffering and to heal.

An exaggerated expression of this activist stance contends that everything that can be done should be done. The Christian faith guards against any kind of blind worship of progress for progress' sake. The New Testament image is that of a steward who recognizes that gifts and talents are not his or her own creation. They come from God and are to serve God's purpose.

How Do We Define Human Life?

The Christian does not value human life because of qualities that humans possess. Human beings are valued simply because we are objects of God's love. Beginning at this point precludes the use of a definition of human life to determine who is more or less valuable. Rather, the purpose here is to identify the essential aspects of the human experience that we should seek to protect and enhance. If we love human lives as God does, what are the qualities or aspects of those lives that we are to guard and strengthen?

At the heart of any biblical view of human life must be the affirmation that our physical existence is an essential part of our being. Dualism makes a radical distinction between physical and spiritual aspects of human life. Dualism claims that the essence of any human life is some kind of nonphysical reality called soul or spirit.

The biblical perspective is very different and is usually called a holistic view. This outlook is reflected in Genesis 2:7 where God created a body from the ground, breathed life into the body, and it became a living soul or being. The human soul or being incorporates the living body. There is no radical division between body and spirit. The human is more than body.

A second essential element of human life is autonomy. A special feature of our existence that sets human life apart from the rest of creation is God's gift of *His own* image (Gen. 1:27). God gives human beings the ability to will and to decide, to say no even to God. In Christian history this capacity has often been referred to as freedom of the will.

Modern medicine imposes many powerful controls upon lives. The strength and frequency of these controls threaten the autonomy or freedom of everyone. At every turn, we seem threatened with the loss of personal control over our lives. Those who take seriously the Christian view that autonomy is a God-given capacity in every human life will protect that gift within this environment of control.

The biblical story of humanity not only points to human autonomy but also to human sociality. We are communal beings, created by God in such a way that each of us does not realize his or her full humanity except in fellowship with others. We become fully human only through the communities that nurture and enrich our individual lives. This sense of the communal nature of humanity is seen in the creation account in Genesis 2:21-25. By himself, Adam was incomplete. By nature, we are social and possess a need for community. If I say that I love human life, I will be committed to promoting that which unites people.

American culture tends to deny this communal nature of humanity. A philosophy of radical individualism promotes the notion of the "self-made man." Our cultural heroes are the strong, silent types who depend on no one but themselves. This philosophy teaches us that autonomy and sociality are polar opposites and that we must choose one or the other. The biblical view sees these two human characteristics as complements. The unique differences that each of us possesses make it both possible and necessary for us to be joined to each other in communal relationships. In the tough decisions about controlling life and death, this fabric of the human community, its diversity and unity, must be protected.

What Are Our Attitudes Toward Technology?

In the twentieth century medicine has become a science. It is no longer viewed primarily as an art. The white lab coats of the medical team are the uniforms of the scientist. We should not be surprised, then, that a person's basic attitude toward science and technology will affect greatly that person's attitude toward advances in medical science.

Protechnology

In our modern, industrialized society, the dominant attitude toward technology is very positive. Indeed, one of the prominent themes of our culture—as reflected in our myths and literature—is the story of how we, through the use of technology, have conquered some of our traditional enemies. Nature is viewed as the enemy to be conquered, or at least an inadequate or uncertain ally of humanity.

The basic assumption in this protechnology apology is that technology enhances or expands the natural gifts and potentials of humanity. Technology is not alien to the human spirit, but is its complement. The internal combustion engine expanded the power of human muscle. More recently, the human mind's capacity to calculate has been extended by the computer.

Expanding technology has increased human options and the human community through increased travel and communication. Humanity is no longer bound to one spot on earth. The God-given quality of autonomy is increased by the options made available by this new access and mobility. The communal nature of humanity is blessed as well by the expanded fellowship that is now available.

Antitechnology

A different evaluation of technology sees it as a threat to human life and its most precious values. The Frankenstein story reflects an anxiety that technology is really our enemy. The monster, created in the scientist's laboratory, became a power that its creator could no longer control. What initially was greeted as a grand experiment in improving human life became a menace. Those who voice this fear today point to the greatest scientific discovery of the modern age, splitting the atom, as the source of power that may very well destroy the human race.

Some contend that high-tech machines of the medical arena have taken on a life of their own that cannot be controlled adequately. Once in place, no one can pull the plug. The patient is captured—unable to die, unable to live meaningfully, unable to escape. The machine is the master rather than the servant of human life.

Technology's critics also claim that it destroys orderly community. Rapid advances in technology blur traditional mores and values. New techniques of controlling life and death make traditional standards, such as our definition of death, obsolete.

There is also the fear that modern technology is destroying human freedom and diversity. The machines of the assembly line grind out thousands of exact, monotonous duplicates. We become captivated by the mass media and succumb to every fad. The result is a homogeneous culture in which diversity and spontaneity are discouraged.

The purpose here is not to arbitrate this debate between the "pros" and the "antis"; however, the Christian faith does provide two perspectives that may be helpful. First, we are warned against the prevalent sin of idolatry. This is the most subtle of sins because it takes that which is good and treats it as if it were God. Either technology or nature can be turned into such an idol. Indeed, a very good case can be made that both the "naturecrats" and the "technocrats" of our day have fallen victim to this sin. They have taken a good gift from God and treated the gift as if it were God.

The second Christian teaching that is relevant to this issue is the traditional understanding of stewardship. Technology is a good gift with the potential to bless human life. Our task is to be good stewards and insist that technology be used to bless the members of the human household within which it is distributed.

Who Should Decide?

One of the most persistent puzzles and struggles in modern medicine is finding an answer to the question, Who should decide? Who should decide about pulling the plug or about behavior control? As our options increase, more decisions must be made. As more people become involved, more claims are made about who should decide. Should it be the patient, the family, the physician, the nurse, the hospital administrator, the clergy, the legislature, or the insurance company? Each of these parties can make a case that it has an important interest in what is done and a certain wisdom about what should be done.

The earlier discussion of defining human life contains a clue to answering the question about who should decide. If we live in an interdependent community, the decisions we make must reflect the various segments of that community. No one part of the community can make the decisions in isolation from the other parts. We should devise communal decision-making procedures that tap the insights and experiences of all sectors of the community. The apostle Paul's description of the human community as analogous to the human body with diverse parts captures this sense of interdependence: "The eye cannot say to the hand, 'I have no need of you,' nor again the head to the feet, 'I have no need of you' " (1 Cor. 12:21, RSV).

In matters of controlling life and death, each of the interest groups mentioned has an important contribution to make, yet the wisdom of no single person or group is sufficient. To be sure, there are times when the special insights of a particular group make it the appropriate *leader* in decision making. No one suggests that a group which is representative of the broader community should vote on where the surgeon makes the incision. However, personal, social, and economic factors beyond the expertise of the surgeon impinge on the question of whether surgery should take place at all. Yet each group has its contribution to make. Each group has a limited perspective. That is why we have become dependent upon each other.

In the earlier part of the twentieth century, a German social philosopher, Ferdinand Toenneis, made a distinction between two kinds of communities. A *Gemeinschaft* community is made up of people who have similar experiences and interests. This community is held together by commonality. A *Gesellschaft* community is made up of diverse people, like parts of the body in Paul's analogy. They have differing interests and abilities. This community is held together by mutuality. The people are bound to each other by the fact that they need each other. As specialists, no one of them can do the job. It takes all of them, complementing each other. Toenneis argued that modern communities have become increasingly of the *Gesellschaft* type. If he and Paul are correct, the various groups that are involved in health-care decisions must find ways to learn from each other. The decision-making process must incorporate the wisdom of all.

A final consideration indicates the appropriateness of collective decision making. In the history of American government, the necessity of maintaining a balance of power has been recognized. Some historians have argued that the Founding Fathers were influenced by the traditional Christian doctrine of human sin. Since all people are sinful, no one group should be allowed to gain absolute power. If one group gains absolute power, the result will be that they will misuse it. Thus, a balance of power is the safest way to save all of us from our own sinfulness. This need for maintaining a balance of power exists not only in governmental affairs but also in all areas of human life. In the health-care field, this balance is achieved best by guaranteeing that the decision-making process is genuinely communal.

Controlling Birth

The process of human reproduction is loaded with the most sensitive and deeply felt human emotions. Prospects of creating another human life are both exhilarating and frightening. There is mystery, danger, and hope. As at death, there is a special awareness of the nearness of God. Deeply felt and long-established traditions and values are associated with birth. Recent changes in human reproduction made possible through new medical technologies and procedures have produced shock waves of both expectancy and fear.

Advances in genetic research, such as genetic screening and prenatal diagnosis, open possibilities for reducing the frequency of genetic diseases and malformed children. Artificial insemination and "sperm banking" can help couples overcome infertility. In vitro fertilization holds out hope for childless couples, but they also present new legal and social tangles that are difficult to unravel.

Traditionally we have spoken of "having" a baby, but today references to "making" babies are increasing. The term *having* suggests that birth is something that happens to the couple. They wait and receive the child, with little sense of controlling the process. The term *making* suggests a far more active role of the parents as they control and design. Thus, the emphasis shifts. Analyzing the significance of this shift is helpful. Is any significant dimension of responsible parenthood diminished or increased by the shift from *having* to *making* babies? There are four suggested changes.

Parental Responsibility

To *make* babies can heighten the parental sense of responsibility as co-creators with God. The new medical procedures require a great deal of planning and effort by all involved. There can seldom be the claim that this pregnancy was an "accident." This means that the child has the clear advantage of being wanted from the very beginning. Making babies reduces the likelihood that a child is reluctantly or belatedly accepted. Its place is firmly established in the family earlier, rather than later, in pregnancy—or even after birth.

A number of parents who have gone through extensive prenatal diagnosis and planning have said that they had an early identification with the child. In prenatal diagnosis, doctors and parents usually know the gender, general health, and other characteristics of the fetus. All of this can contribute to a sense of parental responsibility and an early bonding between parent and child.

Managing Children

The second consideration is that making babies may encourage parents to establish a management relationship with their child. The child whose birth is carefully planned, and to some extent designed, is more likely to be exposed to the wish-fulfillment syndrome of the parents. Of course, this possessive or domineering tendency has always been present in parents. Children have always been both blessed and cursed by parental dreams and expectations. The difference now is that the newfound parental powers to design expose the child to a more potent form of paternalism.

Furthermore, this parental instinct to dominate is fostered earlier in the parent-child relationship. From the beginning, the parents' expectations are established. When the parents had to wait and "receive" the child, they were at least psychologically conditioned to accept the child on his or her own terms. The parents who go to the trouble of designing their child are the ones who are most likely to institute a rigorous program of fulfilling that design. On the other hand, parents who are prepared to "have" a child are likely to be more open to be surprised by what their child becomes.

Valuing Children

A third consideration is that making babies may encourage parents to value their child in terms of how close the child approximates the parents' design. Even in the "good old days" of having children, parental disappointment was an emotion with which all responsible parents struggled. The only difference is that, when the child does not live up to the parental dream after much planning, effort, expense, and promised success from medical science, the depth of disappointment may be much greater.

Parents who carefully avoid a specific genetic disease may not find it easy to accept some other totally unexpected health problem. The child who arrives on its own terms may be more readily accepted. We must find ways to protect stability and unconditional commitments that characterize redemptive family life.

The Danger of Our Mistakes

The fourth consideration is that in making babies we expose ourselves and our children to the dangers of our designs. Historically, most designs of the ideal person or the ideal child have been amazingly provincial and shortsighted. A very concrete example of this shortsighted wisdom is seen in the surveys of gender preference by parents. If parents could exercise that choice today, approximately 70 percent of the next generation would be male. We tend to be fickle and faddish, even in the dreams we have for our children. The tendency is to strive for homogeneity, but the beauty and strength of the human race is its diversity. Great care must be exercised in designing our children, for our long-term vision of what is good for them can be very faulty.

The conclusion from this analysis need not be that all efforts at exercising parental designs and plans for our children should be abandoned. Indeed, the new technologies tend to increase our sense of responsibility. In the exercise of these new parental choices, what we must avoid are the dangers that are present in them. There should be no fear of seeking to save our children from destructive diseases and conditions. There should be a healthy suspicion of grand dreams that we may have about making ideal children and then establishing parent-child relationships upon those dreams.

Controlling Death

No aspect of the human experience may be more provocative and compelling than death: It is inevitable, intimate, and mysterious. It forces us to deal with the most basic religious and ethical issues of the human experience.

Recent developments in controlling the end of life are forcing a reassessment of our attitudes and practices regarding death. Modern medicine has decreased the frequency of death from infectious diseases and, consequently, increased the frequency with which we die from senility and degenerative diseases. The result is that dying is increasingly a prolonged and torturous experience. As our capacity to control has increased, so has the necessity for assessment and reevaluation.

General Assessment of Death

In contemporary American culture, two attitudes toward death are held. One attitude essentially views death as the denial of life and all the values associated with human life. Death is the ultimate enemy of human life—to be avoided at all cost. From this perspective, nothing is worse than death: It is to be feared and prevented if at all possible.

In recent years people have reacted against this denial of death. Led by the writings of Elizabeth Kübler-Ross, an alternative view of death has become popular. Here, death is viewed as a natural event in the life cycle. Death is not to be greatly feared or shunned, but is to be accepted. Supportive of this sentiment is the life-after-life movement that seeks to prove scientifically that there is a meaningful existence beyond death.

Although dimensions of a Christian view of death may be found in both of these views, neither is on target in portraying a Christian view of death as seen from the resurrection. The Christian understanding of death involves both the cross and the resurrection. The cross affirms that death is cruel and shattering. It is not a masquerade that just appears to be tragic. The Christian answer to this destructive power of death is not denial, but resurrection. The resurrection event does not disguise or belittle death. It overcomes death. The Christian gospel claims that death is not unreal, but that God's loving power overcomes even the disaster of death. When seen from this perspective, death is not merely a "bump in life's road"; neither is it an ultimate calamity beyond which all is lost. Rather, it is seen as tragedy that is overcome through God's loving sovereignty.

Euthanasia

Traditionally the term *euthanasia* has been used in reference to the question of controlling death. Euthanasia means "easy death" and points to the choice between extended suffering and death.

Even though much progress has been made in controlling pain, people frequently face prolonged and intractable pain. Those who would choose death argue that suffering is at least useless and more commonly destructive of human life and values. Suffering robs its victims of joy and affirmation and turns life into an endurance race that cannot be won.

The alternative perspective contends that death is the only enemy. Suffering is a part of life and must be accepted. Indeed, suffering can be a source of meaning and strength, if the sufferer will have faith and will endure. The sufferer's character can be strengthened, and he can be an example of faith and hope to others.

Though the choice between death and suffering has a long history, new medical technologies have multiplied the options. Many times today suffering is not the issue; the issue is the choice between death and a demeaning or useless existence.

In the Karen Ann Quinlan case, the accounts often focused on a shriveled body drawn into a fetal position, hardly recognizable as the young woman of just a few months earlier. Alzheimer cases present a body and mind that have been ravaged by a disease that turns the patient into a shell of his or her former self. While the victim may not experience great pain, this condition is an affront to the memory of the formerly active and vital person. Many claim such continued existence repudiates human life. In such cases it is argued that the value of human life is better served by choosing death over demeaning existence.

These appeals are variations on the "quality-of-life" argument. In every case the central question is whether losing a certain quality of life justifies choosing death. Is existence, per se, worth having without those qualities?

Two Value Traditions

When choosing between death and one of these conditions of life, two competing value traditions influence us. One tradition very prominent in American culture places the highest value on the autonomy and freedom of individuals. To deprive someone of her right of self-control is to deprive that individual of the most precious of human possessions. The final expression of this freedom is the right to choose death if life is no longer tolerable or meaningful.

The other value tradition focuses not on the value of freedom, but on the value of life (i.e., the very condition of existence). Sometimes this position is supported by the theological claim that no one owns her own life. God owns each of us, and God alone decides when each should die. The emphasis is not on human freedom, but on the value of life and a power beyond us that affirms life. Thus, a life is to be preserved no matter what qualities may have been lost and no matter what the individual may personally desire. No one should choose against life.

Active and Passive Euthanasia

In most discussions about the choice between life and death, a distinction has been made between active and passive euthanasia. Active euthanasia, sometimes called mercy killing, is an active attempt to cause the death. Passive euthanasia is not causing death, but allowing death to occur. This involves withholding some commonly used treatment that, if applied, would probably extend the patient's life.

Some contend that there is no moral difference between active and passive euthanasia because the intent and result in both cases are the same. Nevertheless, on the American scene a clear precedent has been set in distinguishing between active and passive euthanasia. There is widespread, though not unanimous, support for passive euthanasia in certain cases. Those who have maintained the distinction typically argue that passive euthanasia can be justified in some cases but that active euthanasia can never be justified. Several factors make the difference.

For one thing, passive euthanasia guards against an incorrect diagnosis. If there is a mistake in diagnosing a person as terminal, then the policy of passive euthanasia will allow that one to live, while active euthanasia will have unnecessarily and tragically taken a life. Also, passive euthanasia is much easier to regulate. A system of laws that allowed active euthanasia would require widespread and vigorous control procedures. Finally, a basic ethical distinction is made between allowing and causing a result. Allowing a person to die when there is good reason to do so is cooperating with God and nature.

Controlling Behavior

Human life is more than a beginning (birth) and end (death). Throughout our lives, we confront efforts to regulate or control our behavior. Indeed, today's drug scene reflects one very popular technique used by people to affect the way they feel and act. Behavior control efforts are a major part of the work of physicians, psychologists, and educators today.

Increases in Control

Concern about behavior control has increased in recent years for three major reasons. First, technological advances put many new tools, and thus the power, into the hands of controllers. These advances include a wide array of psychoactive drugs, new surgical techniques, communication technologies, and new surgical procedures.

Second, more sophisticated theories of control have been put forth. Many traditional theories about changing or shaping behavior (as in old wives' tales about child rearing) now have been scientifically tested, systematically organized, and, finally, shaped into finely tuned programs of behavior control. What once was done rather haphazardly is now systematically organized and methodically executed.

Third, more controllers exist today. The role of "total institutions" has increased in our society. A total institution is one that has an all-embracing control over the individuals within its domain. Such institutions include the military, prisons, hospitals, schools, and child-care facilities. Sometimes other institutions, such as business corporations and social service agencies, take on many of the characteristics of these total institutions.

Techniques of Control

The techniques of control can be conveniently divided into three types. One category of control techniques involves the direct physical modification of the brain. The most common procedure here is psychosurgery, but there is also electrical stimulation, freezing, searing, or the direct application of chemicals to the brain.

The second technique of control involves changing the bio-chemistry of persons through the introduction of drugs, either orally or intravenously. The alteration of the body chemistry, in turn, modifies the function of a variety of organs. The end results are changes in mood and/or behavior.

The third category of control techniques does not focus on any direct change of the person. Rather, it seeks to change the environment or the controllee's interpretation or interaction with the environment. These are the techniques we generally associate with psychologists, psychiatrists, and counselors.

Although we can distinguish among these three techniques of control in our discussion, in real life they are usually combined by most professionals who are involved in behavior control.

Purposes of Control

What are the moral, legitimate purposes or goals of behavior control? How far do we go in serving the needs of society, rather than just the explicit therapeutic needs of the client or patient? Certainly, if humans are communal beings, as we discussed earlier, it is appropriate to remove those barriers to meaningful community. From this perspective, everything from disciplining children to prisoner rehabilitation would seem to be legitimate. The problem emerges when an emphasis on orderliness alone turns into a kind of tyranny.

If diversity is as important as orderliness in human community, an essential element of behavior control should be the assisting of persons to develop their unique and diverse potential. If homogeneity is the standard, both individuals and society lose. Individuals lose their freedom and autonomy, and society loses the richness inherent in the variety of the human race. It is especially important to protect the weaker persons in our society who cannot defend themselves easily. Strong institutions tend to disfranchise weak individuals by using techniques of behavior control to homogenize and standardize.

Who Should Control?

Another important issue centers around the question of who should be allowed to modify the behavior of others. The truth is that at different times, all of us act as controllers just as at other times, all of us are controllees. However, we do place more controlling power in the hands of certain people and groups, and we need to consider who is most likely to use that power responsibly and therapeutically.

If anyone can be expected to have your best interest at heart, that person would be you. Generally, self-interest can be assumed. There are exceptions, but an important rule is to give the controllee as much power as possible in the process of behavior control. This means procedures structured to assure that consent is acquired whenever possible. To be sure, in some circumstances a person is incompetent to understand or to act in his own best interests. Then we look for others who are most likely to act in the controllee's best interest. A helpful guideline is to consider who is going to be in a position to accept the responsibility for the end product of the control effort. For example, the family has the kind of natural relationship with its members that makes it more responsible than other institutions might be. Where there is little inherent responsibility, great care must be exercised to build in protection or to limit the power of the controllers.

As noted earlier, the potential controllers increase each day. What we must establish are therapeutic traditions and systems of checks and balances that will increase the likelihood that these new and powerful control techniques will be in the hands of those who are the most responsible and the most caring.

What Means of Control?

Some persons contend that certain methods of control are inherently more ethical than others. They suggest that the human brain is inviolate, and to physically manipulate it is to assault the "seat" of the human personality. Others contend that no procedure is inherently unethical but that we can make ethical judgments about different procedures.

Irreversible procedures present some very difficult problems. A lobotomy on the brain cannot be reversed if the desired results are not achieved. Generally, the more responsible avenue of control is to try reversible procedures first and turn to irreversible procedures as a last resort. They should be used only in the most severe cases and when there is nearly universal agreement that the irreversible results are both certain and desirable.

Some methods are unproven or unpredictable. Many claim that psychotherapy is unscientific and unpredictable. Others claim that psychosurgery is not based upon proven knowledge of how the brain functions. In our haste to alleviate psychic suffering, we need to distinguish between what is experimental and what is proven. The experimental should be used with the greatest caution and care.

The final consideration relates to those procedures that bypass the patient's consciousness. For example, some techniques involve subliminal influences or even deception. The value of human autonomy suggests that, if everything else were equal, methods that involve the conscious participation of the patient should be preferred. When this is not possible, stringent procedures need to be taken to protect patients when they cannot protect themselves. Those who exercise the power of control (parents, counselors, physicians, educators, and other authority figures) should exercise great self-restraint. In addition, rigorous professional and societal regulations need to be established to protect those being controlled. The shaping of a human life is too serious a matter to be done carelessly or irresponsibly.

Abortion

Through the centuries the practice of abortion has been controversial, but in recent years the intensity of the dispute has increased. Currently the debate revolves around three issues.

Status of the Fetus

The first issue is the status of the fetus. The focus of attention here is on when human life, as personhood, begins. Traditionally answers have ranged all the way from conception to birth. Answers which lie between these extremes have included implantation, beginning of heartbeat or brain waves, "quickening," or viability. It is important to note what evidence is used to determine the point of life's beginning. Although some determinations depend upon evidence from only one source, positions most often are defended with data from sociology, biology, theology, and/or biblical studies. Currently many who argue that life begins at conception point to biblical passages (Jer. 1:5; Ps. 51:5) which refer to God's knowing a person before or while he was in the womb. Others counter that the creation account in Genesis 2:7 indicates that life begins with the first breath, or at birth. The emphasis on biological data has shifted in recent years. Neonatal care has improved to the point that viability is progressively earlier in pregnancy. All of this points to the dilemma of seeking to establish a fixed moment in time when life begins.

This issue of the status of the fetus is important and contributes to a person's attitude toward abortion. It is a mistake, however, to assume that one's conclusion on this issue determines his final judgment on the abortion question. Some people who conclude that life begins at conception believe that abortion can be justified on some occasions. Other people who believe that life begins at viability, or birth, are against abortion out of their concern for the defenseless fetal life that has the potential to become a person.

Competing Rights and Interests

This brings us to the second major issue of the abortion debate: the various competing rights and interests. The three most obvious parties with important interests are the fetus, the pregnant woman, and society. The debate centers on which party should have exclusive, or at least dominant, rights.

Some contend that the fetus' interests should be paramount, either because it is fully human or because it is defenseless and deserves special protection. This position has been supported recently by what can be called the increasing visibility or presence of the fetus. Medical advances including sonograms, photographs of the fetus, and prenatal diagnosis have contributed to an increase in our understanding of and identification with the fetus. Usually this emphasis on the rights of the fetus leads to an essentially antiabortion position. At times, however, abortion is argued for because it would be in the best interest of the fetus to save it from some unfortunate future.

The pro-choice sentiment of today is generally based on the contention that the pregnant woman's interest and rights should be dominant. They should be so because both biology and society have given the woman the primary responsibility in pregnancy and child care. With this responsibility, it is said, goes the right to decide. Occasionally this argument is reversed by those who contend that a woman's best interests are served by the fulfilling of her "God-given" maternal role.

Finally, there is society's interests and rights. Historically, society has sought to either increase or decrease the birth rate. Currently the most dominant view is that the "population explosion" requires that the birth rate be reduced: if necessary, by the extreme measure of abortion. If the society, through its government, is to protect the welfare of future generations, it should have the right to limit a population growth that threatens the future. Usually an emphasis on society's rights has led to a conclusion favoring the option of abortion, but—as in the preceding cases—this argument can be turned in the opposite direction. Some contend that the long-term best interest of society is served by prohibiting abortion and, thus, preserving a pro-life sentiment and tradition that protects everyone.

Matching Morality with Legality

A third area of dispute within the larger abortion debate is the issue of matching morality with legality. To what extent should the practice of abortion be regulated by law? If a group of Christians agrees on what the mind of Christ indicates for Christian behavior, how far do they go in enforcing this conclusion, through the power of the state, upon a pluralistic society? Both basic church-state issues and practical considerations affect the church's conclusion on how far it goes in seeking to implement, through public law, its moral convictions on abortion. Today the positions range from something close to a theocracy to an essentially hands-off policy.

The theocratic view is that public law should enforce God's will, thus, both establishing God's kingdom on earth and educating the public in the ways of righteousness. The major theological theme is the sovereignty of God over all of history.

The tradition of church-state separation sees the purpose of the state as limited to enforcing only those convictions that are broadly held within the society. There is also an emphasis on promoting religious liberty so that minority views, based upon deeply felt religious and moral traditions are carefully protected. The emphasis is on the radical nature of the Christian ethic and the folly of expecting such an ethic to be obeyed by a nonredeemed public.

Conclusion

The life-and-death dilemmas of modern medicine are many and complex, but the resources of the Christian faith are adequate for our task of moral decision making. As stewards of both the resources of modern medicine and the resources of the Christian tradition, we can discover solutions to these dilemmas. Our task is to accept the challenge of these dilemmas without being intimidated and to be faithful to the vision of a loving God revealed to us in Jesus Christ. If we are faithful to both the newfound healing power and our vision of Christ, we can hope to hear: "Well done, good and faithful servant; you have been faithful over a little, I will set you over much; enter into the joy of your master" (Matt. 25:21, RSV).

Suggested Reading

Barbour, Ian G. *Technology, Environment, and Human Values.* New York: Praeger Publishers, 1980.

Barnette, henlee H. *Exploring Medical Ethics.* Macon, Ga.: Mercer University Press, 1982.

Beauchamp, Tom L. and Walters, Leroy, eds. *Contemporary Issues in Bioethics.* 2nd ed. Belmont, Calif.: Wadsworth Publishing Co., 1982.

Hollis, Harry, ed. *A Matter of Life and Death: Christian Perspectives.* Nashville: Broadman Press, 1977.

May, William. *The Physician's Covenant.* Philadelphia: The Westminster Press, 1983.

Winslade, William, Jr., and Ross, Judith Wilson. *Choosing Life or Death.* New York: The Free Press, 1986.

12
Special Concerns in a Contemporary World

Dick Rader

Introduction

Some ethical concerns do not fit neatly into well-established categories, and others could be discussed under more than one heading. The issues considered in this chapter are also related to such matters as economics, the family, human relations, and the Christian and the world. Some of these special concerns encompass traditional "don't" issues, such as alcohol and gambling, while others explore contemporary problems related to pornography, the media, and the changing status of women in society and the church.

Each ethical concern will be examined in its cultural context. The extent of the problem may vary with time but the causes and effects will remain basically constant. A second section on each problem will treat biblical principles, as well as specific biblical commandments and examples. Each concern will be considered in how it challenges the churches to action.

Alcohol and Drug Abuse

The Nature of the Problem

In the last half of the twentieth century drugs and alcohol have become major social and personal problems. All areas of society have been greatly harmed by practices as old as Noah (Gen. 9:20-24, NASB).

Doctors, understandably, prescribe some drugs to help people who are sick, but the societal problems are related to the gross

249

abuse of drugs for nonmedical purposes. Drugs that people abuse are grouped into four categories: Depressants, which slow down the function of the brain or central nervous system; Stimulants, which speed up the body; Hallucinogens, which distort reality; and Narcotics, highly addictive drugs which produce a "high."

The abuse of drugs causes devastating physical problems; perhaps the worst is dependency or addiction. Physical and emotional addiction can lead to an ever-increasing craving. Studies show that one out of every ten persons who drinks alcohol becomes an alcoholic.

Ours may well be called an alcohol/drug culture. In such a social environment, drug and alcohol abuse is passed from generation to generation. Children of parents who regularly drink alcohol are much more likely to drink than children of nondrinking parents.[1] Parents have a difficult task teaching a child that the use of alcohol and tobacco or the abuse other drugs is harmful if the parents do not practice what they teach. The availability of alcohol and/or drugs in the home can serve as a strong temptation for children.

Young executives eager for promotions often feel the pressure of peers and superiors to "be sociable" and have a drink. School-age children, mothers in social clubs, and workers on the job may fall into the trap of the social acceptability of drinking. Both in advertising, which promotes drinking for acceptance, fun, and popularity, and programming, where drinking is pictured as common in our society, the media peddles products and promotes practices harmful to people.

The drug and alcohol menace is having disastrous effects on our society by causing the death of scores of people each year and destroying the health of others. Homes are broken, children and spouses are abused, and individual lives are endangered by drug and alcohol abusers. Businesses and industries are affected by those who miss work or are unable to function properly because of their "problem."[2]

The Bible Speaks to the Issue

Wine and other fermented drinks were part of the cultural context of the Bible. Wine was used both as a beverage, primarily with meals (possibly diluted with water), and as medication. While there are some biblical references to certain drugs being used as medicine (Gen. 30:14-16; Num. 5:11-31; Mark 15:22-23), there is no parallel to today's drug usage except for references to drunkenness.

One question which surfaces repeatedly on this subject is whether the wine mentioned in the Bible was fermented or unfermented. Some have sought to prove that the wine used could have been unfermented. Others contend that the wine was an intoxicating beverage because grape juice ferments under normal conditions. Some references do talk about wine and its obvious effects of intoxication. Since the same biblical terms can refer to either wine or unfermented grape juice, the linguistic argument is inconclusive.

The Bible does issue strong warnings against drunkenness. Wine and strong drink are called a mocker and a brawler (Prov. 20:1). In Proverbs 23:29-35, the drunkard is described as a person of woe. Drunkenness is listed in the New Testament as a sin which brings eternal punishment as well as troubles in this life (Rom. 13:13; 1 Cor. 6:9-10; Gal. 5:19-21; Eph. 5:18). Church leaders are not to be drunkards nor addicted to wine (1 Tim. 3:3,8; Titus 1:7).

In supporting a position of moderation in the use of alcohol, some church leaders cite the biblical use of wine as a background for their position. The liquor industry uses the phrase *responsible drinking* in their advertising. This stance assumes people will drink, but encourages control.

On the other hand, a case for total abstinence from wine or any kind of intoxicating drink or drug is affirmed by biblical examples. The Nazarites were people dedicated to God by a vow which forbade them to drink wine or strong drink. In fact, they were not to eat anything produced by the grapevine (Num. 6:1-4). Samson was a Nazarite (Judg. 13:3-7) and, from the description in Luke 1:13-15, John the Baptist was under a similar vow. Daniel had not taken the vow of a Nazarite, but he chose to refuse the wine and rich food from the Babylonian king's table in order to "not defile himself" (Dan. 1:8, NASB). These examples show the value of total abstinence as an ideal, even in a society where wine and strong drink were common.

While there may be some difficulties in establishing a strong case for total abstinence on the basis of specific biblical references, such a position can be undergirded by firm biblical principles. Some of these principles for Christians are: (1) A Christian is responsible to care for the body God has created and given to him or her (Gen. 1:27). Paul said our bodies are temples of the Holy Spirit (1 Cor. 6:19) and they are to be presented as holy sacrifices unto God (Rom. 12:1-2). The effects of alcohol and other drugs, even in small amounts, can be harmful. The brain does not function properly and actions and thoughts can be impaired when drugs or alcohol are ingested. Certain organs deteriorate or become diseased from continual use of specific drugs. No person can be sure he or she will escape the clutches of alcoholism or drug addiction when taking a first drink or pill (1 Cor. 6:12). Addiction or even the occasional use of drugs and alcohol can cause a person to lose control of his or her mind and body and keep one from being sober and alert to the direction of God (1 Thess. 5:6; 1 Pet. 1:13; 4:7; 5:8).

(2) A Christian is responsible for the welfare of others. Because all of us exert influence on others, Christians should not practice something that may eventually destroy another person. A father may say he is in control of his drinking, but his son may be the one in ten who becomes addicted. We are not to be "stumbling blocks" to others by what we do (Rom. 14:13, also see v. 21, NASB).

(3) A Christian should strive for God's ideal as seen in such persons as the Nazarites, Daniel and John the Baptist.

The Challenge to the Church

What can the church do in the midst of this social and personal problem? The church must challenge each Christian to live a holy life which respects the body and other people. Christians must choose to honor their bodies and, thus, protect all those whom they touch. Pastors and teachers must educate church members about this problem and boldly raise the ideal of God's standard of purity toward which all His people should strive.

Congregations must be alert to those who are suffering because of drug and alcohol abuse. Programs which demonstrate true compassion and competent counseling need to be made available to those who are alcoholics and drug abusers and their families. Supporting those without families could also encourage many to avoid the pitfalls of drug abuse. Churches can support organizations like Alcoholics Anonymous and drug education programs for all age groups.

Gambling

The Nature of the Problem

Some have called gambling America's largest industry. Official estimates are not possible because much gambling is illegal, but one expert suggests that Americans bet $500 billion per year. Gambling in its many forms—bingo, racetrack betting, betting on sports events, office pools, casinos, jai alai, and state-run lotteries and others—has become an integral, respected part of the American scene.

The growth of materialism and America's insatiable appetite for entertainment have fueled interest in games and programs that offer a monetary reward. As people desire more wealth, the glitter of gambling becomes more alluring. Others prey on the greed of their fellowmen to make an easy profit and so establish new gambling enterprises. As opportunities for gambling increase more people gamble.

Poor economic conditions also seem to foster interest in gambling schemes. Many individuals who are without jobs are easy prey for get-rich-quick plans. Those who can least afford to gamble are the ones who spend the most on gambling.[3] Even state legislatures struggling to fund programs without raising taxes are enticed by gambling interests to adopt state-run lotteries and to legalize pari-mutuel betting and casino gambling. These programs are praised as quick-fix solutions for sagging state budgets and are called "voluntary taxation" programs.

There is an apparent link between organized crime and gambling. One organized crime defector said, "Organized crime can live on its gambling and loansharking, if it has to give up prostitution and narcotics."[4] The link with organized crime increases the incidence of gambling-related corruption among public officials. This inevitably causes the breakdown of public trust in officials.

Business professionals usually are the ones who lead in battles against legalized gambling and state-run lotteries because they know that an increase in gambling quickly leads to a decrease in the amount of money available for food, clothing, and other essential items. Bills go unpaid, bad checks abound, bankruptcies increase, crime rates soar, and employee absenteeism increases when gambling is readily available and legal.

Lives are wrecked by those who become entangled with gambling. Gambling appeals to a person's covetous nature and causes him or her to become reckless and irresponsible, perhaps even criminal, in pursuit of another thrill. People become addicted to gambling while going deeper into debt.[5] Not only is the gambler hurt by this habit but family members may suffer poverty and abuse. Financial problems create tensions which can result in child or spouse abuse and divorce.[6]

The Bible Speaks to the Issue

The Bible contains numerous principles which point us away from gambling. The Commandments warn against covetousness and theft (Ex. 20:15, 17; Matt. 6:24-34), which are both related to the gambling problem. Those who operate gambling schemes are actually stealing from people by failing to give something for the money spent by the losers. Those who gamble covet something which they want but cannot afford.

Gambling is based on chance while the Bible emphasizes the sovereignty of God over human events (Matt. 10:29-31; Jas. 4:13-15). God created man and gave him the task of working creatively and being a good steward (Eph. 4:28).

Jesus taught His disciples to love their neighbor just as they love

God and as they love themselves (Matt. 22:37-40). Gambling promotes selfishness and greed. Progambling forces support an ethic which says the end (revenue) justifies the means (gambling) without regard for persons.

Another aspect of biblical teaching is emphasis on the treatment of the poor. The Old Testament prophets make a strong case for compassion toward the poor. The prophets reminded the people of Israel that God was not pleased with their ill-treatment of the poor (i.e., Amos 2:6-7). The law told the people to care for the poor, just as God had cared for Israel (Deut. 15:4-11). Jesus had compassion on the poor, the early church cared for the poor, Paul took up offerings for the poor, and James championed the cause of the poor. The great separation at the judgment will be largely determined by the way we have treated the poor (Matt. 25:31-46). Offering opportunities to gamble does not show compassion toward the poor.

The Challenge to the Church

Because gambling has become such an accepted part of the American culture, the church needs to sound a clear message which challenges Christians to a more noble life-style that stretches toward God's ideal. While some forms of gambling may seem innocent, the Christian must remember that his or her involvement can lead to other forms of gambling, as well as influence others to gamble.

Churches have a responsibility to teach people the facts about gambling, as well as biblical principles which emphasize that Christians live under the sovereignty of God and that man was created to work for his livelihood. Compassion for others, especially the poor, must be followed by actions which minister to the needy (Jas. 2:14-26).

Christians need to become politically active in an effort to prevent state and national governments from legalizing gambling and becoming involved in government-operated lotteries. Christian citizens need to oppose such measures because of the harm done to society: (1) gambling is regressive, preying on desperate people, (2) legalized gambling does not control organized crime, (3) legalized gambling contributes to the increase of compulsive gamblers, and (4) legalized gambling will not do for a state's economy what is promised.[7]

The Media

The Nature of the Problem

Television, including cable networks and TV videos, is our most popular form of media. Most Americans own at least one TV set and spend more time watching TV than in any activity other than sleeping and working. While television does have positive aspects, the negative impact is causing problems which are rotting the very fabric of social morality. So-called "free TV" is based on the use of commercial advertising designed to entice people to buy products, and many programs themselves are designed to influence the audience. While not all programs have a hidden agenda, television does influence its viewers.

An area of great concern is the impact of violence portrayed on television. While some argue that such an influence is minimal, evidence is increasing that TV violence is a contributing factor in acts of aggression. As one writer said, "People who package violence and call it entertainment are guilty of contributing to the saturation of our society with violence."[8] A constant diet of aggressive behavior on TV can decrease emotional sensitivity to pain and suffering. Repeated viewing of scenes depicting agony and death can cause viewers to develop uncaring attitudes toward those who actually suffer and die. Children may even confuse the make-believe world of TV and the world of reality.

Some TV heroes and heroines break the law and never have to answer for their deeds. At times the law is ridiculed and law enforcement is belittled, thus causing people to lose respect for the law and those who enforce it. Violence is sometimes glorified and lawlessness is shown as expedient, while justice is often perverted by the heroes and heroines.

Another area of concern is the way television perverts human sexuality and family relations. Television programs often glorify, or at least treat as normal and appropriate, premarital sex, adultery, and homosexuality. Programs which distort the picture of love relationships and commercials which exploit women as sex objects contribute to the lowering of morals and the destruction of marriages.

Television advertising also contributes to the materialistic idolatry running rampant in America. Commercials seek to sell items to people regardless of their need for them or their ability to purchase them. False pictures of success are transmitted simply to sell a product. Some ads are misleading and manipulative, especially those directed at vulnerable children. Some programs which depict as normal beautifully decorated homes, sports cars, and extravagant wardrobes increase the hunger for this life-style.

While television producers insist that they are simply showing life as it is in America in their soaps, prime-time situation comedies, and other programs, a careful scrutiny of such programming reveals that their characters represent only some segments of American life. Surveys indicate that a majority of Americans are influenced by some form of organized religion, most believe in God, and many read the Bible and pray.[9] However, life which is enacted on TV is either void of references to religious practice, or if God, the Bible, or church is mentioned it is usually in a negative context.

The devastating impact of television has been felt most by the family. The fact that television can enter our homes so easily makes it a formidable foe. Christian values are constantly assaulted by violence, sexual exploitation and perversion, materialism, profanity, and a host of other vices which seek to erode family life. George Gerbner said, "Television has profoundly affected the way in which members of the human race learn to become human beings."[10]

The Bible Speaks to the Issue

Television and the other media make it necessary for Christians to practice discernment. The apostle Paul warned that many evil forces in our world seek to destroy us. In seeking to know our enemy, we must not succumb to that enemy. Paul encouraged

Christians to equip themselves to withstand the evil foe (Eph. 5:10-17).

Truth is necessary in TV programming and advertising because of its powerful influence on society. Throughout the Bible God is revealed as a God of truth and righteousness. Because God is righteous and the source of truth, His people are to bear the truth (Ex. 20:16). Lewis Smedes said the Ninth Commandment not only requires truth telling but also truth living and truth seeking in order to maintain trust in the community.[11]

The Bible calls those who love violence wicked and evil (Prov. 4:14-17, Ps. 11:5), and James indicates that violence comes from lusts and selfishness (Jas. 4:1-4). The Bible condemns lawlessness by saying that God has ordained government for our good and Christians are to support those who enforce the law (Rom. 13:1-7; 1 Pet. 2:13-17). Paul said that those who are sexually immoral will not inherit the kingdom of God (1 Cor. 6:9-10) and Christians must flee from immoral practices (vv. 18-20).

Another biblical principle which can guide us is the command to seek what is good and pure (Phil. 4:8). Our thoughts are formed by what we see and hear. Therefore, it is necessary for us to assimilate those sights and sounds which will yield pure thoughts (Matt. 6:19-21; Prov. 23:7).

The Challenge to the Church

The challenge goes far beyond the words we utter or write. God calls us to practice our ethic in our homes and community. Parents must demonstrate discernment and tell children why certain programs are better than others. Filth, violence, and sexual perversion are not appropriate for adults any more than they are for children. If children see such a double standard, they will be tempted more than ever to "sneek a peek" while they are young and become avid, or even addicted, viewers of filth when they are older.

Christian families are exercising several different options regarding television and other media. Some parents have chosen to live without television and other media that can have a corrupting influence. This stance, while it does curb the detrimental influence of the media, gives no opportunity for parents to teach discernment to their children and offers no positive values which some programs provide.

Other Christians monitor the programming offered and watch those which are positive. This option gives the family an opportunity to practice Christian decision making, and it also allows for the pursuit of other activities when no good programs are available.

Another course of action is the boycott of certain program sponsors. Letters to companies explaining objections may be very helpful, as well as letters to local stations and networks. Some channels have been influenced to remove certain programs because of letters, economic boycotts, and pickets by concerned citizens. Christians should demand the pure and good from the media producers and sponsors, for the benefit of all people.

Pornography

The Nature of the Problem

Pornography is one of the most profitable businesses in America. Material created and distributed to arouse sexual desires is a multibillion dollar a year venture. Accurate estimates of its volume are impossible because of the industry's link with organized crime and various illegal activities.

Pornography is disseminated in a variety of forms. Men, women, and children are exploited in these materials where all kinds of sexual behavior are shown or described. Pornography is sold in bookstores, theaters, convenience stores, drugstores, newsstands, and through the mail.

Pornography has become prolific for several reasons. Dealers make large profits from their investments, and this spurs more people to become involved in the sale of pornography. Dealers spend heavily to send pornographic materials through the mail, especially to curious children. An estimated one million school children receive brochures and catalogs through the mail each year. Dealers make as much as 200 percent profit from these mailings.

The popularity of pornography provides a constant demand for more material. The curiosity of some young people about sexuality causes them to purchase pornography in order to learn what their parents have not told them. Young adults often consider pornography a symbol of sexual freedom. They see sexual prowess as a sign of masculinity and success. Because people can easily become addicted to pornography, luring the young into the pornography habit secures long-time buyers. This addiction, like alcoholism and drug addiction, also calls for more severe and exotic kinds of sexual adventures to satisfy the craving.

A third reason pornography is so rampant is because good people are passive regarding the problem. Passive citizens, including many Christians, who are either unaware of the problem or unwilling to get involved in curbing the problem are allowing this menace to thrive. Some seem to feel that it is just part of our sex-saturated society, while others believe that everyone has a right to purchase whatever they want. These people may cry "censorship" when any effort is made to limit what can be seen or heard. There are also those who know about the severity of the problem but doubt that they can do anything about it. Some believe the laws are on the side of the offenders.

The laws regulating pornography are not always understood and often are not enforced. The Supreme Court has long held that obscenity (pornography which is so morally debased as to be unlawful) is not protected by the free-speech clause of the First Amendment to the Constitution. The 1957 *Roth v. United States* decision defined the test for determining obscenity as "whether to the average person, applying contemporary community standards, the dominant theme of the material taken as a whole appeals to prurient interest." In 1966 the Court ruled in three cases that hard-core obscenity for profit is illegal. Again in 1973, in the *Miller v. California* case, Chief Justice Warren Burger wrote, "This much has been categorically settled by the court, that obscene material is unprotected by the First Amendment." In this case the Court also limited the scope of obscenity to very graphic depiction and gave examples of what this includes.[12] However, most citizens and some public officials are apparently unaware of these rulings.

Another problem in fighting pornography has been the lack of evidence which demonstrates that there is a link between pornography and criminal acts, particularly sexual offenses. However, a 1986 panel has found convincing evidence that substantiates the many horror stories linking deviant sexual behavior and pornography. Their findings include evidence concerning: (1) the addictive nature of pornographic material, especially on children, (2) the claim that pornography victimizes women by desensitizing men toward violence and making them trivialize rape, (3) the charge that pornography promotes and glamorizes adult/child sex, even in primarily adult publications, and (4) the concept that people who have committed sexual killings have received visual sexual stimuli in developing rape fantasies before they killed their victims.[13]

Not only is there increasing evidence of pornography's link with criminal activity but the case is strong against pornography's effect on women, children, and marriages. Women are treated as objects of pleasure for men to dominate and even mutilate or hurt in some way. Children are also treated as throwaways and playthings for the satisfaction of others. Family life is disrupted because attitudes toward sex are perverted. Wife abuse often results from efforts to reenact masochism depicted in pornography or as punishment because the wife cannot fulfill the fantasy fostered by pornography. Pornography may either replace normal sexual relations or it may pomote unreal expectations in sexual relations that can even leading to divorce. Using pornography can also lead to sexual addiction.

The Bible Speaks to the Issue

The philosophy behind pornography is that morality and ethics are relative. This translates into allowing any activity that is mutually pleasurable between consenting persons. In other words, everyone does what is right in his own eyes (Deut. 12:18). Christian theology teaches us that our ethic must be consistent with the God we worship and with whom we claim a relationship, thus our ethic is not relative (Eph. 4:1-6; 1 Cor. 6:13-20; Heb. 13:4-9).

God teaches us that persons should neither be treated as things, nor used for personal gratification or gain (Lev. 19:18). The intimacy of sexual relations demands privacy and is intended for enjoyment and companionship within the marriage relationship (Gen. 2:18-25). That which exploits sex and glorifies the satisfaction of base human desires is degrading to men and women and abhorrent to God (1 Cor. 6:12-20). Pornography appeals to man's animal instinct and not to his higher nature (Gal. 5:16-21). The marriage relationship is sacred and honored by God (Heb. 13:4), and anything that destroys it is forbidden by God (Matt. 19:6).

A further principle that the Bible holds forth is that we are to maintain pure thoughts (Phil. 4:8). Jesus said that to look on a woman with lust is tantamount to adultery (Matt. 5:27-28). James pointed out that sin begins with our desires and entices us to want what we cannot have, which is sin (Jas. 1:14). Christians are admonished to resist evil and seek good (1 Pet. 5:8-9).

Not only are Christians to keep their thoughts pure but also their lives should conform to the image of Christ. Peter warned his readers to refrain from living like those in the world (1 Pet. 4:3) and not to be conformed to the passions of their former ignorance (1 Pet. 1:14). Paul also warned about being squeezed into the mold of the world (Rom. 12:2). Jesus admonished His followers to live in the world without belonging to the world (John 17:14-16).

Pornography is effectively described in 1 John 2:15-17, as "the cravings of sinful man, the lust of his eyes . . ." (NIV), and we are told not to love these things of the world but to do the will of the Father. Paul reminded Christians to walk according to the leadership of the Spirit so we will not gratify the lusts of the flesh (Gal. 5:16). Christians are to strive for moral purity so they can be holy in all they do (1 Pet. 1:15).

The Challenge to the Church

Christian parents may need help to be able to teach their children a Christian concept of sex. Churches can provide literature containing Christian ideals for sexual relationships as well as provide classes or seminars in which biblical principles of sexuality are taught to parents and youth.

Churches must educate not only members but also the community about the dangers of pornography. Christians must be informed about the availability of pornographic materials in their local area and encouraged to rid their community of it (Eph. 5:8-14). Concerned Christian citizens need to know the obscenity laws and the Supreme Court's interpretations of them.

Because the laws governing pornography are based on local community standards of morality, local citizens can and must be the ones to fight this form of crime. Working with local officials can help citizens make their voices for moral decency heard. Public officials cannot do the job alone, they need the support of concerned citizens and vice versa. The church should foster such support among its membership.

The Changing Role of Women

The Nature of the Problem

Traditionally women have been childbearers and homemakers, however, in our ever-changing society women have entered the job market in large numbers. Some social scientists are predicting that soon women will comprise over one half of the total labor force in the United States.

Women have gained recognition for their abilities in these newfound roles. Sex discrimination battles have been fought on several fronts, and women are now able to compete favorably for most jobs. Although not all problems have been completely solved, just as all racial discrimination has not been eliminated, government regulations have helped women gain equality in society.

As women move into new roles in the work force, either out of economic necessity or the desire for a career, they also face new roles in the home. Traditional male dominance is being challenged. Questions of responsibility for decision making, housekeeping chores, and the care of children have surfaced in many homes. Many women no longer feel total economic dependence on their husbands, which may be one factor in the increased incidence of divorce.

Changes for women have been confined primarily to areas of society outside the church. Though women usually outnumber men in churches, relatively few have a voice in determining church programs and policies. Although women are active in the life of most churches and hold vital positions, few women serve as pastors and relatively few are on church staffs or serve as ordained deacons.

Some churches have ordained women. The issue is too divisive for most churches, however, because there are strong emotional views on both sides. Some Southern Baptist associations have withdrawn fellowship from churches which have approved the practice of ordaining women.

The Bible Speaks to the Issue

Much has been written about the meaning of the biblical material concerning the role of women in the church. Some churches have been resistant to changing the role of women in the church because of a belief that the Bible teaches that women should not speak or teach in the church; that they are to be submissive to men, both in the home and in the church (1 Cor. 14:34-35; 1 Tim. 2:11-12); and that ordination for both pastors and deacons is reserved for men (1 Tim. 3:2; Titus 1:6, "the husband of one wife,"NASB). These passages, and others of a similar nature, are understood to be adequate evidence that women should retain their subordinate role in the church. According to this interpretation women are not considered inferior to men but their position has been established by God primarily because of the woman's sin in the garden of Eden (Gen. 3:6, 16; 1 Tim. 2:13-14).

Interpretations which show the biblical material to be more culturally conditioned find greater freedom for women to exercise their changing roles in the church. For instance, some insist that 1 Corinthians 11 and 14 should be seen as answering specific questions concerning some problems in the Corinthian church. Paul K. Jewett suggested that Paul's remarks reflect the rabbinic tradition which governed worship in Jewish synagogues.[14]

Proponents for the ordination of women point to several passages of Scripture which indicate equality for men and women in a redeemed relationship. Paul's words in Galatians 3:28, are often quoted as showing this equality in Christ. The fact that several women followed Jesus and supported His ministry (Luke 8:2-3) and numerous women are mentioned in the Gospel accounts further indicates the importance of women in ministry roles. Paul's mention of Phoebe as "a deaconess of the church at Cenchreae" (Rom. 16:1, RSV) is also cited, but the interpretation of the word for *deaconess* is debated. Also mentioned is the use of the term "wives" in 1 Timothy 3:11 (KJV), which is translated by some as "women" and may refer to women deacons instead of the wives of deacons. There are also examples of prophetesses in the Old and New Testaments (Ex. 15:20, Judg. 4:4; 2 Kings 22:14, Neh. 6:14; Acts 2:17-18; 21:8-9).

One of the crucial questions in this debate centers around the practice of ordination. New Testament ordination seems to have been a very simple ceremony of dedication for those who had been called by God for specific ministry (Acts 6:6; 13:3). The more elaborate ordination service which is used in many churches seems to reflect the tradition of Roman Catholic theology which bestows power and authority upon those being ordained. Perhaps the suggestion of T.B. Maston is worthy of consideration: "If this simple type of ordination were followed, then the only concern of a church should be whether God has called the individual to some phase of specialized ministry."[15]

The Challenge to the Church

While the body of Christ must not follow every whim of cultural change, the church must be sensitive to its culture and be prepared to respond to change. The events in the Book of Acts, for example, show how the church responded to changes as it moved to the Gentiles in Samaria, Asia Minor, and Europe. Historically, however, those churches which have compromised their theology and allowed syncretism to move them to the fringe of Christendom or beyond have gone too far in their efforts to accommodate culture. Some believe that to allow the ordination of women would violate basic theological principles and lead to syn-cretism, while others see the issue as the church's response to change.

Therefore, a major question seems to be whether the issue of ordination is a vital part of Christian theology. Those who refuse to change their traditional position of opposition to the ordination of women hold that this matter is important enough to cause a breach of fellowship between churches. They contend that the issue raises a question of biblical interpretation and that they cannot cooperate with a church which ordains women.

Those who are open to the ordination of women believe the question should be decided by each congregation, and local church autonomy is viewed as a more important theological issue. Churches of this persuasion are more inclined to maintain fellow-ship with congregations who differ on ordaining women.

Decisions about ordination need to be confronted and thoroughly researched. An investigation of ordination and the role of women which allows the Bible to speak above preconceived ideas is appropriate for the church. Exegesis with a clear biblical hermeneutic which goes beyond mere proof-texting may lead to a change in one's position or it may strengthen the previously held belief.[16] If there is disunity in the church over this issue, the matter needs to be handled in love with respect for one another.

The changing role of women in society demands that the church recognize the need for more ministry opportunities for women in the church. This does not necessitate the ordination of women, but it might mean some practices in the church need to be reviewed. Churches should recognize the sovereignty of God's call to people, even if it means struggling with traditional roles and functions. We must be open to recognizing the Holy Spirit's gifts in any of God's children and help them find ways to exercise legitimately those gifts to build up the body of Christ and glorify God.

Conclusion

While each of these special concerns relates to other areas of discussion, they are linked together in several ways. Lack of per-sonal self-control is evident in the abuse of drugs and alcohol, gambling, television viewing, and pornography. This failure to control appetites often leads people into the clutches of addiction in any of these areas. Exploitation of persons is another trait common to these concerns. Anyone may be abused by those who profit from gambling, drugs, and alcohol, or even some media programming. Obviously human personhood is under attack when persons become secondary to revenue, pleasure, or tradition.

Responding to these special concerns requires a sound biblical hermeneutic which will not just reply to the external symptoms but will meet the needs of persons. Human worth and dignity call for aggressive action against those things which deprive individuals of their value or infringe upon their freedom. The church cannot afford to be passive or hesitate to become involved in society's problems. Jesus calls us to minister to the world which God loves and for which Christ died.

Notes

1. Statistics show that 82 percent of drinking parents raise children who also drink, while 72 percent of nondrinking families have children who do not drink. *Abstracts and Review in Alcohol and Driving,* April, 1981, p. 1, quoted in Ron Sisk, *Alcohol Awareness* (Nashville: Christian Life Commission, 1983).

2. America's 100 million drinkers are involved in 69 percent of the nation's drownings, 83 percent of the accidental fire fatalities, 10 million job accidents annually, and 25,000 traffic deaths each year. The consequences of alcohol problems, including treatment, accidents, welfare, lost productivity, and crime, cost this nation $49.4 billion a year, according to a study by the National Institute of Alcohol Abuse and Alcoholism. Allan Luks, *Will America Sober Up?* (Boston: Beacon Press, 1983), pp. 1-2.

3. Larry Braidfoot, *Gambling: A Deadly Game,* (Nashville: Broadman, 1985) pp. 39-40.

4. "Issues and Answers: Gambling," pamphlet published by the Christian Life Commission, SBC.

5. The American Psychiatric Association classifies compulsive gambling as a mental disorder.

6. *Braidfoot,* Chapter 7.

7. Ibid., pp. 199-200.

8. Harry Hollis, "Will the Medium Get the Message?" *The Baptist Program,* September 1977.

9. The Princeton Religion Research Center reports that eight of ten Americans say they are Christians. "Emerging Trends," Princeton Religion Research Center, March, 1986.

10. *Newsweek,* 21 February 1977, p. 63.

11. Lewis Smedes, *Mere Morality* (Grand Rapids: Eerdmans, 1983), pp. 215-218.

12. Tom Minnery, "Pornography: The Human Tragedy," *Christianity Today,* 7 March 1986, p. 18.

13. Ibid., p. 20.

14. Paul K. Jewett, *Man as Male and Female* (Grand Rapids: Eerdmans, 1975), p. 114.

15. T.B. Maston, with William M. Tillman Jr., *The Bible and Family Relations* (Nashville: Broadman, 1983), p. 82.

16. Charles J. Scalise, "The Priority of Scripture: Biblical Hermeneutics and Baptist Women in Ministry," *Folio,* Winter 1986, p. 1.

Suggested Readings

Braidfoot, Larry. *Gambling: A Deadly Game.* Nashville: Broadman Press, 1985.

Drakeford, John. *Pornography, the Sexual Mirage.* Nashville: Thomas Nelson, 1973.

Hewitt, T. *A Biblical Perspective on the Use and Abuse of Alcohol and Other Drugs.* North Carolina Department of Human Resources, May 1980.

McBeth, Leon. *Women in Baptist Life.* Nashville: Broadman Press, 1979.

Pinson, William. *The Word Topical Bible of Issues and Answers.* Waco: Word Books, 1981.

Sisk, Ron. *Cop Out, Conform, or Commit.* Nashville: Convention, 1985.

13
Christian Ethics:
A View From the Pew

David R. Wilkinson

Where do we go from here? In the preceding chapters, you have read the experts. Now, for some reason, the editor felt it would be instructive for this final chapter to offer the perspective of a layperson—a view from the pew, if you will.

That is precisely what I offer: *one* view on Christian ethics from *one* layperson. In fact, as a layperson, I am doubly qualified. First, I am a layman rather than an ordained clergyman. Second, I am a layman in the field of ethics. I am not an ethicist in terms of academic training or vocation. I have maintained an active interest in the field, especially during six years as a journalist on the staff of the Christian Life Commission, the national ethics agency of the Southern Baptist Convention, but I am neither an expert nor a specialist. As a layman who has only dabbled in an area that challenges the sharpest of minds and bravest of souls, my only hope for the pages which follow is that they will make some modest contribution to your understanding of and appreciation for Christian ethics.

Introductory qualifiers aside, I am impressed that the editor chose to include the viewpoint of a layperson. The truth is that without the laity, Christian ethics, like every other dimension of the Christian life, would have little meaning. Through laypersons serving in real churches, living in real families, and working in the real marketplace theoretical ethics gets translated into applied Christianity.

This is by no means to denigrate the contributions of "professional" ethicists. (Some of my best friends, as they say, are ethicists.) Nor is it to dismiss the validity of Christian ethics as an academic pursuit. It is simply to say that the credibility of Christian ethics—indeed, Christianity as a whole—is never fully established until it finds expression in everyday life. Southern Baptist ethicist and layman T. B. Maston has observed that ultimately Christian ethics "is not a theory of life but a way of living."[1]

With that definition in mind, this view from the pew attempts to look as objectively as possible at "the big picture." Its orientation is not toward what Christian ethics asks of laypersons but rather what laypersons—who may not have studied the textbooks, read the pronouncements, or heard the classroom lectures of the trained ethicists—are looking for in Christian ethics. Stated differently—and more ambitiously—the question is: What ought Christian ethics to be, viewed from the vantage point of the pew?

The Body of Christian Ethics

Life is not always neatly divided into chapters. Persons seldom fit into simple categories. Similarly, a comprehensive understanding of Christian ethics involves much more than totaling the sum of its parts. Christian ethics needs first to be viewed as a whole.

This seems obvious. Yet Christian ethics often suffers from two damaging approaches: It is either cut to pieces through compartmentalization or cut off through isolation. Both approaches diminish the potential contribution of ethics to the Christian faith.

Compartmentalization of Christian ethics is a problem that sneaks in easily and subtly. When a person thinks of ethics, he or she often thinks immediately of issues. Indeed, we are often nudged along in this mental association by the ethicists themselves. In the classrooms and in the textbooks, Christian ethics is considered in terms of subject areas: family, race relations, economics, war and peace, citizenship, alcohol and other drugs, world hunger, and so forth. While useful, this categorization sometimes tends to reduce ethics to little more than a catalog of moral concerns rather than a more systematic study of the Christian faith and its application to daily life. The unfortunate result is that Christian ethics is treated piecemeal, and the proverbial forest gets lost in the preoccupation with the trees. (Parenthetically, this should not be interpreted as an appeal for more laborious and often obtuse dissertations on philosophical ethics or ethics methodology which seem never to move to the practical application to life. It is simply to say that ethics involves more than issues.)

The problem of piecemeal ethics has often been exacerbated by "true believers" within a particular category who imply in their zealousness that "their" issue is "the" issue for Christians. The resulting exclusiveness robs the adherents of constructive dialogue across issue lines and drains vitality from Christian ethics as a whole.

In American Christianity, this tendancy was demonstrated vividly in the late 1970s and the 1980s by the "pro-life" issue. Off in one corner, antiabortion pro-lifers spoke out against a callous attitude toward human life demonstrated most blatantly by abortion on demand as a means of birth control. In a different corner, nuclear disarmament pro-lifers challenged the sanity of the superpowers' nuclear arms race. And in yet another corner, antihunger pro-lifers appealed for worldwide support for the basic right to food. Meanwhile, the tunnel vision inherent in single-issue mentality blinded many of these committed persons to the common themes as well as the troubling inconsistencies within the larger pro-life movement.

Finally, Cardinal Joseph Bernadin, chairman of the United States Catholic Conference of Bishops' pro-life activities committee, articulated the "seamless garment" view, setting forth a consistent and biblical ethic of life which effectively brought together various segments of the pro-life question. Bernadin was joined by a few other leaders in the evangelical community who championed a consistent ethic of life that was pro-life on abortion, on arms control, and on issues of poverty and hunger. Their primary emphasis was on the common theological theme of the sanctity of human life, but they also stressed similar biblical rationales and political strategies toward affecting social change. Said Bernadin:

> It is not necessary for every person to engage in each issue, but it is both possible and necessary for the church as a whole to cultivate a conscious explicit connection among the several issues. And it is

very necessary for preserving a systemic vision that individuals and
groups who seek to witness to life at one point of the spectrum of
life not be seen as insensitive to or even opposed to other moral
claims on the overall spectrum of life . . . No one is called to do
everything, but each of us can do something. And we can strive not
to stand against each other when the protection and the promotion
of life are at stake.[2]

Bernadin and others also stressed that this respect for the viewpoints of others does not have to come at the expense of the
singleness of purpose which is necessary to affect lasting social
change. Conversely, singleness of purpose need not result in single-issue narrow-mindedness.[3]

During those same years, the absence of Bernadin's "systemic
vision" hampered Christian efforts on another social issue—pornography. Many Christians had relegated the battle against pornography to conservative and fundamentalist groups. "There are
many people who will applaud us when we condemn the arms race
or apartheid or economic injustice," said Bernadin "but they often
prefer that we look the other way when the issue is pornography."[4]
This attitude, of course, was perpetuated by single-issue en-
thusiasts who picketed against convenience stores which sold pornographic magazines and boycotted commercial sponsors of
unacceptable television programs. While their intentions were
generally commendable, their rhetoric was often exaggerated, and
their comprehension of the issues involved was sometimes limited
and simplistic.

In 1986 a broad coalition of religious groups formed the Religious Alliance Against Pornography (RAAP). Recognizing the
bigger picture, RAAP organizers called attention to some basic
attitudes about the sacredness of life and the fundamental evil of
violent and degrading pornography in its most extreme forms,
particularly child pornography. In this case, RAAP decided to
narrow the focus to "illegal obscenity"—pornographic materials
which lay outside the broad-sweeping protection of the First
Amendment—in order to broaden the coalition's base of support
and bolster its influence. Among other things, RAAP supporters

found they could be for the enforcement of obscenity laws while also standing solidly against censorship.

Cardinal Bernadin was a principal leader in this effort as well. In the alliance's first conference, he cautioned against an approach which treated pornography as an isolated phenomenon rather than one that is linked to many other social issues. He called for a consistent ethic, built upon a solid theological base of the sacredness of human life created in God's image. (Indirectly, Bernadin put his finger on another problem that has frequently plagued Christian ethics. Too often, social action is undertaken before adequate theological reflection has taken place, a tendency that will be addressed below.) Bernadin pointed out that recognition of the "linkage" between the issues of pornography, prostitution, sexism, and racism would give greater credibility to efforts to combat pornography. Indeed, the resulting coalition immediately carried much more weight than the previously sincere but fragmented and anemic efforts.[5]

Christian ethics, then, should resist being divided and subdivided prematurely or unnecessarily into specific issues. In contrast to the problem of compartmentalization, Christian ethics needs a healthy and holistic emphasis on the linkage between and interconnectedness among the various moral issues. The real stuff of ethics in the material which precedes, undergirds, and informs the examination of the issues themselves.

Secondly, and just as importantly, Christian ethics should not be unduly isolated from the other dimensions of the Christian life. To achieve a balanced perspective, Christian ethics should be viewed within the larger context of the whole Christian life and the entire Christian gospel. Without an emphasis on ethics, the Christian landscape would be incomplete. At the same time, the other elements of the Christian life should complement and contribute to ethics.

This point was illustrated during my seminary experience. I remember students complaining that an introductory course in Christian ethics was required for the basic theology degree. Some considered ethics an unnecessary detour on the road to graduation and an unfortunate distraction from the real heart of ministry preparation. What does ethics, they implied, have to do with theology or preaching or pastoral care or Christian education? The answer, I would argue, is everything!

In the academic setting of Christian colleges and seminaries, the study of ethics should be incorporated into an interdisciplinary approach. In particular, ethics should relate to theology. "Theology," according to Maston, "provides the foundation; ethics builds the superstructure on the foundation. Both are essential for the completion of the building."[6] To change the analogy, without proper theological moorings, ethics easily strays off course. How one understands God and how one interprets what the Bible has to say about the nature of God and His relationship to humanity informs profoundly how one understands and how one "does" Christian ethics.

In addition to theology, Christian ethics should be integrated with biblical studies, preaching, philosophy, church history, humanities, the social sciences, and other fields of study. Ethics should never hesitate to seek insights and correction from other disciplines. The cross-pollinization of ideas through interdisciplinary dialogue contributes to a well-rounded education and a comprehensive approach to preparation for Christian ministry.

Outside the traditional realm of religious studies, many colleges and universities are now offering courses in medical and biomedical ethics, business ethics, legal ethics, and other areas. By and large, this reflects a healthy trend, although in some cases ethics is treated with a shallowness bordering on flippancy. When respected as a full partner, ethics can bring helpful reflection and penetrating insight to any discipline.

Likewise, in the setting of the local church, ethics should be taught and preached within the total context of the complete Christian life. Ethics should be integrated into the various ministries and programs of the church—worship, preaching, Bible study, and Christian education. In the local church as well as the larger Christian community, ethics and evangelism should be friends rather than suspicious foreigners. Social action and social ministry should be complementary partners. To repeat a theme that has been preached better than it has been practiced in American Protestantism, and in Southern Baptist life in particular, there is room in the classroom, the church, and the individual life for ethics and evangelism, social action and social ministry, political activism and personal devotion. Stated negatively, there can be no excuse for celebrating one dimension of the Christian faith while denigrating the importance of another. Each one plays its part in contributing to the whole gospel and to the whole body of Christ.

Once the dangers of compartmentalization and isolation have been recognized, it is possible to focus more specifically on the nature of Christian ethics from a lay perspective. To borrow from the inspired New Testament analogy of the church as the body of Christ, and without ignoring my own warning about piecemeal ethics, I believe the whole body of Christian ethics should include the following parts.

Ethics with a Face

The Christian life stands in need of both personal ethics and ethics of persons. The first category, personal ethics (as opposed to social ethics), traditionally has been a strength of American conservative Protestantism, in general, and Southern Baptist history, in particular, with their emphasis on the individual. Yet personal ethics has received renewed attention in recent years. National newsmagazines have featured cover stories about the ethics crisis in American life, triggered by a deluge of scandal, sleaze, and corruption within every social institution—from the corner grocery to Wall Street, from city hall to the Capitol, and from the county seat church to the televangelist's empire.

In the wake of what church historian Martin E. Marty has called a "widespread sense of moral disarray,"[7] some signs of hope are emerging. With the crisis has come a welcomed reemphasis on such categories of ethics as character, integrity, virtue, and values. Once again ethicists are pointing out that good people make good choices. The perils of values-poor public education have been exposed, and the critical importance of teaching basic Christian values in the home has been reemphasized. In 1986 a nationwide poll conducted by a national newsmagazine found that more than 90 percent of the persons surveyed agreed that moral supports have crumbled in America because parents have reneged on the responsibility to imbue their children with decent moral standards.[8]

The outcome of this renewed interest in personal ethics remains to be seen. For Christians, however, the clear biblical truth about personal ethics has been present all along. The biblical message, stated Foy Valentine, is that "Christians ought individually to be Christ's persons from head to foot, in every area and in every relationship of life. To walk personally and daily in the light of the gospel of God in Christ is not optional for the people of God. It is mandatory."[9]

Ethics needs a face in another way as well. One of the basic principles of journalism is that people relate best to other people. They respond to stories that feature "human interest." They relate better to models than to theories.

The same is true for ethics. A picture, a model, a person, is worth a thousand words about moral oughtness and ethical decisions. Like the preschooler's reaction to the concept of a transcendent God, we need ethics "with a face on." Expert analyses of weighty issues is important, but that alone will not suffice. Christian ethics involves principles and rules, but it is far more than that.

G. K. Chesterton once noted that "nothing is real until it is local."[10] To be real Christian ethics needs to be "up close and personal." It must find concrete expression and validation through human lives. Stated in theological terms, "Christian ethics is characteristically incarnational,"[11] drawing from the unique model of the incarnation when the God of the universe miraculously and lovingly took on a human face. The Christian faith and an unbelieving world stand forever in need of courageous prophets who challenge society's moral status quo, of creative pioneers who forge new paths in social action, of bold champions of social justice who tear down racial and economic barriers. The Christian faith also needs more of those quiet persons of biblical righteousness who live consistent lives of integrity within their families, their businesses, and their churches.

The Holy Scriptures offer an excellent example of this emphasis on ethics with a face. The Bible is the inspired written record of God's revelation to and relationship with humanity. As such, it is full of stories about real persons. The Bible provides basic principles and guidelines for ethical decision making. But it does more than that. It "puts flesh and bones" on those principles through the personalities of the Old and New Testaments. It gives us models to live by, including the premier model of Jesus Christ.

As R. E. O. White noted, "The essence of biblical morality is not a legal system, a written code, an abstract moral philosophy, but a spirit and a loyalty, a vision and faith, incarnate in the inexhaustibly rich and varied personality of Jesus."[12] The Scriptures repeatedly invite us to imitate Christ, to pattern our lives after His. For every Christian of every age, the question, "What would Jesus do?" is an everlastingly relevant question.

Finally, in addition to the need for models, Christian ethics must work diligently at keeping a face on the issues. Christian ethics is inherently personal and naturally human; for whatever else ethics involves, it deals with human problems, human choices, and human consequences. Pervasive problems like hunger, poverty, and the threat of nuclear holocaust are massive and global, but ultimately they are also personal and individual. Even as it challenges systemic evil and presses for structural change, the clear focus of ethics should always be on persons. Certainly that was the consistent focus of Jesus during His ministry.

Ethics with a Brain

The wheels of Christian ethics will never turn if the brain is disengaged. Ethics unapologetically involves the mind. Indeed, Christian ethics has no room for intellectual laziness. Today's awesome advances in technology, information, science, medicine, and other fields pose equally awesome challenges which demand the very best thinking from every Christian, including the ethicists.

The process of ethical decision making requires mental exercise as well as spiritual discernment. Lewis B. Smedes reminded us of the "elementary rule" that "we cannot tell right from wrong unless we know the facts in the case."[13] Every Christian who confronts an ethical decision or a moral issue is obligated to do his or her homework. Christians should read, study, listen, and discuss. We should gather the relevant information and analyze the available data. We should learn to sort fact from fiction. Ideally, all the evidence should be in before a decision is made.

Christians should develop what William M. Tillman and Timothy D. Gilbert called "a spirit of inquiry."[14] This spirit of inquiry, said the authors, should address three main questions: "What are the facts? (looking objectively at all perspectives); What do the facts mean? (by analyzing the facts and interpreting them); and What ought we to do about the facts? (applying what you know gives credibility to your research)."[15]

Of course, "facts are never mere facts."[16] They are filtered through the lenses of each individual's personality, belief system, and life experiences. They are interpreted and evaluated. Yet, without attention to the facts as they can be generally understood, ethical decisions become arbitrary and irrelevant.

One word of caution is that ethics' steadfast pursuit of all the facts should be undertaken with genuine humility. While Christian ethics should never waffle on the truth, neither should it pretend to have all the answers. Ethics, of all disciplines, should recognize that there are no easy answers to life's complexities and ambiguities. (It should also be noted that the Christian community should never expect the ethicists to be its professional decision makers in the face of complex issues. The world is already overcrowded with people who are all too willing to think for others and to dish out easy answers.)

Finally, it should be emphasized that a necessary part of the ethics homework for every Christian is to discover what the Bible has to say. Unfortunately, this crucial step within Christian ethics has often been only a half-hearted effort—a problem that will be addressed later. The Bible does not address every moral issue confronting contemporary society, but it does speak directly to some concerns. Where it does not speak or teach specifically, the Bible provides guidelines and moral principles which, under the leadership of the Holy Spirit, can be applied to particular situations.

Ethics with a Heart

While Christian ethics relies on the brain for input and direction, its life pulse comes from the heart. Without this dimension, ethics can be overly objective and narrowly analytical. Intellectual rigor is important, but "it is not necessary to pay for an expansion of the mind with a contraction of the heart."[17]

In the parlance of left brain/right brain philosophy, Christian ethics, both as an academic discipline and a discipline of faith, has characteristically been left-brain oriented at the expense of right brain development. While scientific research in this field is still relatively new, growing information about the two hemispheres of the human brain indicates broadly that the left hemisphere specializes in temporal relations and controls processes which are analytical, logical, abstract, sequential, and so forth, while the right hemisphere deals with spatial relations and controls thinking processes which are synthetic, imaginative, holistic, intuitive, and mataphorical. The challenge is to integrate the two parts of the brain to take full advantage of the wholeness God has intended.

As with other disciplines, ethics needs to be freed from what Walter Wink called "the tyranny of omni-analytical thinking."[18] While logic is important, so is intuition. While rational judgment may be required, other circumstances may call for an empathetic, gut-level decision. While objectivity can be a critical asset in some cases, it can be a hindrance to decisive action in others.

Ethical decision making is more than gathering the evidence, analyzing the data, weighing the facts, and measuring the consequences. For years, Albert McClellan, former associate executive secretary of the Southern Baptist Convention's Executive Committee, had on his desk a small, two-sided sign which he had designed. On one side were the words: "What are all the facts?" On the other side was written: "What is the spirit of the matter?"[19] In its quest for the facts, Christian ethics should never sacrifice the spirit of the matter.

Likewise, ethical decision making is more than the issue of being right or wrong. How one does the right is important. "The supreme treason," says Thomas a Becket in T. S. Eliot's play,

Murder in the Cathedral, "is to do the right thing for the wrong reason."

Without a heart, Christian ethics easily falls into the trap of legalism. The Pharisees in Jesus' day, measured by the letter of the law, were extremely ethical. They were "squeaky clean." Yet their preoccupation with legalism blinded them to the radical implications of the highest ethic of loving God and neighbor as self. In the Sermon on the Mount, Jesus reminded His followers that "unless your righteousness exceeds that of the scribes and Pharisees, you will never enter the kingdom of heaven" (Matt. 5:20, RSV).

Without a heart, prophetic ethics can become caustic, angry, and insensitive. Prophecy should never be unacquainted with compassion. It should never be a stranger to emphathy. The quest to be prophetic, particularly in the context of the local church, can run roughshod over the personal feelings of others, leaving hurt and bitterness along the way. Christian ethics should remember with the apostle Paul that even "if I have prophetic powers, . . . but have not love, I am nothing" (1 Cor. 13:2, RSV).

Without a heart, Christian ethics tends to take itself too seriously. Too often, the ethicist is so serious-minded that he forgets how to laugh. The tragic result is a dry and humorless disposition that turns others off rather than engages and persuades. The issues are critical, yes; the problems are overwhelming, indeed. Hope in Christ, however, brings an abundance of reasons to smile. Indeed, when the costs are high and the issues at stake are enormously important, humor may be a key to survival and endurance. A bumper sticker I noticed while sitting impatiently in rush hour traffic made the point well. It read: "She who laughs LASTS."

Ethics with Hands and Feet

Christian ethics enables the follower of Christ to put feet to her prayers and hands to her intentions. Christian ethics is a reminder that the Christian faith is a summons to action, a call to involvement. The call of Christ was an invitation to costly discipleship. It was a call to commitment, for Jesus made it clear that "he who does not take his cross and follow me is not worthy of me" (Matt. 10:38, RSV).

Christian ethics is applied Christianity. It is that point where word becomes deed. It is the call both to believe and behave, since "faith by itself, if it has no works, is dead" (Jas. 2:17, RSV) and all Christians are called to "be doers of the word, and not hearers only" (Jas. 1:22, RSV).

In an era when much of American Protestantism seems to be preoccupied with orthodoxy, Christian ethics rightly calls the Christian community to orthopraxy as well. It reminds us that "the word without deed is a foreign language without a translator."[20]

Here again, the conservative Protestant community in particular has suffered the consequences of a truncated gospel that has stressed faith at the expense of the biblical emphasis on works. Foy Valentine noted:

> The tragic separation of faith and works keeps manifesting itself, generation after generation, like a defective gene. . . God's gracefull incoming to believers in salvation and our compassionate outgoing to others in good works are a vital unity, one organic whole, two sides of a single coin, a single continum of Christian experience. Faith and works are not rivals but partners. . . . They are inextricably linked together. Faith without works is a road to nowhere.[21]

Christian ethics, by its very nature, is action oriented. It is doing the Word. Ethicist Paul Lehmann defined Christian ethics as "the reflection upon the question, and its answer: What am I, as a believer in Jesus Christ and as a member of his church, to *do*?"[22] Also by definition, Christian ethics is forever dynamic. The Christian faith is always in need of renewed interpretation, translation, and application as new issues and new moral challenges arise with every new generation. Christian ethics should be at the forefront of this critical process.

Christian ethics is a call to an "agenda of incarnational involvement"[23] that seeks to effect social change through the transforming power of Christ and the faithful obedience of Christ's followers.

Foy Valentine was right: The question of which is more important —personal ethics or social ethics—is an "abominable and foolish question. Both are important. We ought to do the one but not to leave the other undone."[24] Martin Luther King, Jr., said it as well, "Any religion that professes to be concerned with the souls of men and is not concerned with the slums that damn them, the economic conditions that strangle them and the social conditions that cripple them is a dry-as-dust religion."[25] Regretfully and shamefully, however, the question of personal ethics versus social ethics and social action continues to be debated in one form or another in Sunday School classes across America.

In its appeal for social action in the name of Christ, Christian ethics must give attention to providing the resources, the strategies, the tools for such action. The church and individual Christians need practical suggestions; they need some "handles" for applying biblical truths to concrete situations. Christian ethics must do more than convict and challenge; it must do some equipping for the battle as well.

Ethics with a Soul

God is Spirit. We have been created in God's image as spiritual beings. Even so, Christian ethics is spiritual ethics. For the Christian, moral decision making is at root a spiritual process because it deals with the practicalities of living the Christian life.

Christian ethics finds its direction in a spiritual book. The old adage that the Christian ought to face life with the Bible in one hand and the newspaper in the other rightly expresses the continual need to address the Christian faith to the contemporary situation. However, Christian ethics must resist the temptation to put the Bible down too quickly before picking up the newspaper. The ethicist must not rush to the application step before first doing his or her biblical homework. The fact is that Christian ethics can never get too much Bible. The sad truth is that too much so-called biblical ethics is long on application and short on exegesis. An ethical position should never be based on shoddy exegesis and shaky interpretation. Christian ethics should be firmly grounded and rooted in Scripture. Without this objective source of reference, ethics is easily dashed to pieces on the rocks of relativism.

On the other hand, Christian ethics is larger than biblical ethics. It includes biblical ethics, but it is more than biblical ethics. Jesus Christ stands as the norm for every moral decisions and ethical issue. He is the ultimate standard by which we measure our values and our actions.

The spiritual nature of Christian ethics is also incomplete without the participation of the Holy Spirit. The Holy Spirit offers guidance in moral decision making, helps us interpret the Scriptures, and energizes us for appropriate application of biblical truths in our daily lives.

Furthermore, Christian ethics as a spiritual process is tied closely to the fellowship of the local church. In the church, Christian values are preached, taught, and modeled. In the context of *koinonia*, Christian ethics is immersed in worship, fellowship, Bible study, and discipleship training. In the community of faith, Christian social action finds direction, affirmation, and accountability.

For these reasons, Christian ethics should embrace the spiritual. Unfortunately, the built-in orientation toward action many times effectively bypasses spiritual formation. The misperception is that the spiritual disciplines are both passive and optional, and holiness is caricatured as otherwordly piety.

This point may be overly polemical, but I am convinced that neglect in this critical area is a perennial problem for every generation of Christian ethics. The Christian life, as Mary Cosby wrote two decades ago, is both a journey inward and a journey outward. Christian ethics deals primarily with the latter, but it ignores the former at its own peril for the mature Christian recognizes that "inner attentiveness to Christ and outward acts of holiness are inseparable."[26]

While church history offers numerous examples of Christians who were both pious and prophetic, two persons in American history who lived two centuries apart serve to illustrate the point. In the eighteenth century, the American Quaker John Woolman stood years beyond the majority of religious leaders in his day through his ardent and effective opposition to slavery, mistreatment of native Americans, and the defilement of God's gift of nature. His words, always carefully chosen and adroitly timed, were authenticated by his own personal life-style. In his journal, Woolman revealed the secret to his quiet, yet prophetic, actions: "I . . . was early convinced in my mind that true religion consisted in an inward life, wherein the heart doth love and reverence God the Creator, and learns to exercise true justice and goodness."[27]

Two centuries later, a Baptist preacher of the South named Martin Luther King, Jr., led a movement of nonviolent resistance to the American social system of racial segregation. While interpreters of his life and thought have developed various theories about the key influences upon and the driving forces behind his brief life, King attested to the truth that Christian social action with lasting power comes from those who "give priority to the search for God."[28] Without that priority, "all our efforts turn to ashes and our sunrises to darkest night."[29]

Consistent attention to the spiritual disciplines and to the continual deepening of the inner life keeps Christian ethics on course. It provides the reservoir of spiritual resources necessary for effective social action. It offers discernment for moral decision making. It acts as a conduit for God's transforming love and enabling energy. It undergirds activism with the proper motivation and gives staying power to deal with the plague of burnout. It injects an eternal quality into earthly deeds.

Conclusion

This description of the body of Christian ethics has been an effort to stimulate your own thinking about what Christian ethics ought to be and to do. Although I am a layman, I have heard enough Baptist sermons to cause me to close with an appeal.

Let us forever accept the challenge of ethics as a way of life. While avoiding the extremes of piecemeal ethics or ethics in isolation, let us celebrate Christian ethics as an integral part of the whole gospel of Jesus Christ and its vital role within the church as the body of Christ. In so doing, let us work faithfully to see that the various dimensions of Christian ethics work together through a comprehensive and holistic approach.

Finally, let us through God's grace be Christian in word and deed, seeking always to love God with all our heart, soul, strength, and mind, and our neighbor as ourselves (Luke 10:27). That, after all, is what Christian ethics is all about.

Notes

1. T. B. Maston, Why Live the Christian Life? (Nashville: Thomas Nelson, Inc., 1974), p. XI.

2. Cardinal Joseph Bernadin, "A Consistent Ethic of Life: Continuing the Dialogue," a speech delivered 11 March 1984 at Saint Louis University, published in "The Seamless Garment," National Catholic Reporter Publishing Company, Kansas City, Mo. See also, "A Consistent Ethic of Life: An American-Catholic Dialogue," a speech delivered December 6, 1983, at Fordham University, published in the same booklet. For an excellent discussion of the implications of this viewpoint within Southern Baptist life, see Robert Parham, "Piecing Together a Pro-Life Ethic," LIGHT, (Nov./Dec. 1986), pp. 4-6.

3. Parham, ibid., p. 6.

4. David Wilkinson, "The Porn Problem in Larger Context," LIGHT, (Feb. 1987), p. 5.

5. Ibid., pp. 5-6.

6. Maston, p. 8.

7. Ezra Bowen, "Looking to Its Roots," Time (25 May 1987), p. 26.

8. Ibid.

9. Foy Valentine, "One Piece of Cloth," LIGHT (Sept. 1986), p. 2.

10. G. K. Chesterton, quoted by James Flamming, "On Making the Obvious a Little Less Obscure," 1984 Christian Life Commission Seminar Proceedings, p. 73.

11. R. E. O. White, Biblical Ethics (Atlanta: John Knox Press, 1979), p. 231.

12. Ibid., p. 11.

13. Lewis B. Smedes, Choices: Making Right Decisions in a Complex World (San Francisco: Harper & Row, Publishers, 1986), p. 41.

14. William M. Tillman with Timothy D. Gilbert, Christian Ethics: A Primer (Nashville: Broadman Press, 1986), pp. 54-55.

15. Ibid., p. 55.

16. Smedes, p. 41.

17. Foy Valentine, *What Do You Say After You Say Amen?* (Waco: Word Books, 1980), p. 35.

18. Walter Wink, *Transforming Bible Study* (Nashville: Abingdon, 1980), p. 31.

19. Leonard Hill, "Point of Personal Privilege," *Baptist Program* (Oct. 1980), p. 4.

20. Valentine, *What Do You Do?* p. 35.

21. Foy Valentine, "Good Works," *LIGHT* (June 1986), p. 2.

22. Paul Lehmann, *Ethics in a Christian Context* (New York: Harper & Row, Publishers, 1963), p. 25, emphasis mine.

23. Valentine, *What Do You Do?*, p. 103.

24. Valentine, "One Piece of Cloth," p. 2.

25. Martin Luther King, Jr., *Strength to Love* (New York: Harper & Row, 1963); Martin Luther King, Jr., *Words of Martin Luther King, Jr.* (New York: Newmarket Press, 1983), p. 66.

26. Loyd Allen, "Reconciling Mary and Martha," *LIGHT* (Feb. 1986), p. 6.

27. John Woolman, *Journal of John Woolman and a Plea for the Poor* (Secaucus, N.J.: The Citadel Press, 1961), p. 8.

28. King, *Strength to Love,* p. 92, as quoted by Allen, p. 6.

29. Ibid., p. 7

CPSIA information can be obtained at www.ICGtesting.com
Printed in the USA
LVOW06s0459130815

449753LV00021B/275/P